HAPPY AND GLORIOUS!

HAPPY
AND GLORIOUS!

An Anthology of Royalty

Edited by
Peter Vansittart

COLLINS
8 Grafton Street London W1
1988

William Collins Sons & Co. Ltd
London · Glasgow · Sydney · Auckland
Toronto · Johannesburg

BRITISH LIBRARY CATALOGUING IN PUBLICATION DATA

Happy and glorious: an anthology of
British royalty
1. Great Britain—Kings and rulers
I. Vansittart, Peter
941′009′92 DA28.1

ISBN 0-00-217763-3

First published 1988
Introduction and compilation © Peter Vansittart 1988

ISBN 0 00217763 3

Phototypeset in Linotron Sabon by
Ace Filmsetting Ltd, Frome, Somerset
Made and printed in Great Britain by
Wm. Collins Sons & Co. Ltd, Glasgow

There is but one lot for rich and poor: both become prey for death and corruption. Do not, therefore, O sons of men, place your trust in princes who deceive.

ORDERICUS VITALIS

A king is always a king – and a woman always a woman: his authority and her sex ever stand between them and rational converse.

MARY WOLLSTONECRAFT

Charles II was always very merry and was therefore not so much a king as a Monarch.

W. C. SELLAR and R. J. YEATMAN

*To Stanley and Alix Pigott, after
many years of friendship and hospitality*

AUTHOR'S NOTE

After some hesitation I have modernized spelling where I thought the reader might welcome it. I obviously owe much to the living authors who have permitted me to quote from them; to the generosity of my old friend and mentor, Wilfrid Blunt; to the hospitality and libraries of Paul and Diana Tory, Louis and Colette Littman, Theodore Wilden and Cecile Brinkley, George and Brenda Rothery. I am extremely grateful to Douglas Matthews for providing such an excellent index. Above all I must acknowledge the help and guidance, stern, but unfailingly expert, of my original editor, Dan Franklin, from whom I have profited over many years and whose suggestion originated this project – a process continued with art and tact by Ariane Goodman with the assistance of Inigo Thomas. But for their diplomacy, this project would indeed have extended into some twenty volumes!

CONTENTS

INTRODUCTION

Imagination craves inter-relations. A child gazes at the glistening, richly moulded ceiling, and imagines an iced cake, very tempting, always out of reach. Symbol and allegory breed fast, become mistaken for facts. People believe whatever they wish to believe, with impressive detail. A seventeenth-century tailor asserted that God was five feet high, a medieval thinker pronounced that the Virgin Mary spoke only four times in her life, a New Hebrides community holds as a god the Duke of Edinburgh. King Alfred was reckoned fiftieth in descent from Adam. By similar ingenious calculations, the Rev. Augustus Toplady, author of *Rock of Ages*, realized in 1776 that, at thirty, everyone has committed 630,720,000 sins. Alphonse de Spina held that of the primal angels, one-third had degenerated to devils who, by 1429, numbered 133,306,668. A hallowed belief endured that the Creation occurred on Sunday 23 October, at 10.30 a.m., 4004 BC. This somewhat modifies the line, 'a rose-red city half as old as Time'.

Monarchy is notably susceptible to this compulsion to embroider and idealize. The historical, morally dubious Saxon, Wild Edric, gets enlarged to the Wild Huntsman, akin to Woden and with elfin wife, then sinks to a spectre haunting Shropshire hills and lead-mines. Cassivellaunus, King of the Cattevellauni, Caesar's opponent, emerges centuries later as 'Son of Beli', a Celtic Hercules triumphant over Rome, then ending as the supernatural Caswallow. Hereward is entangled with magical exploits and overcomes a fairy bear. Helena, mother of Constantine the Great, once perhaps a Balkan brothel-keeper, evolves into a Celtic goddess, Elen of the Hosts, otherwise Elen of the Crossroads, thence to the Christian discoverer of the True Cross, with a Feast Day, 18 August. Sometimes she is also the wife of the majestic Celtic Charlemagne, Macsen Wledig, historically a fourth-century Spanish general, Magnus Maximus, who usurped the Western Empire in AD 383.

13

Such resonant untruths are seldom deliberately fraudulent, but advance unconsciously from hearsay, misunderstandings, mistranslation, the dynamic faultiness of oral traditions, and psychic cravings for heroes and monsters, which neatly simplify experience. Robin Hood, Ulysses, Arthur are different from a Horst Wessel, a minor pimp, deliberately manufactured by the Nazis into a latter-day, martyred Siegfried, with a cheap tune.

Outside Dunsinane the credulous can admire 'Macbeth's Grave', that of a giant. The real MacBeth, a practical and relatively successful ruler, was refashioned by Shakespeare into a poet-criminal, a fate shared with Richard III. Likewise, silver-handed Llyr and his daughter Creiddylad, Celtic divinities associated with wind, sky, sea and underworld, are now Lear and Cordelia, embalmed in world tragedy. Welsh legend depicts Arthur crushing an imaginary Roman Emperor Lucius: Welsh bards hailed the thirteenth-century Llewelyn of North Wales as 'Ruling the Earth'. For monarchs, notably amongst illiterates for whom words imply thrilling depths, to affect modesty was unwise. The Sultan was 'The Shadow of God', the Pope rather more. Pope Boniface VIII pronounced, 'All Kings, Emperors and other Sovereigns, whoever they may be, are subject like all other men to be summoned before the Apostolic Court, for every sort of cause, for We, by permission of God, command the whole Universe.' Of Boniface, Gibbon reflected that he entered like a fox, reigned like a lion, and died like a dog.

The traditional appeal of Monarchy was magical, sacramental, sacerdotal. Kings usually had practical functions, maintaining tribal unity and order, promoting defence – or aggression, but they were also intermediaries between worlds seen and unseen. The Chinese Emperor was 'Son of Heaven', not only safeguarding dykes and frontiers, but sacrificing on behalf of the people and ensuring harvest. G. P. Baker observed (1931), 'King George V descends not merely from a god, but from three gods: Woden, Geat, and Sceaf.'

As supreme representatives of natural order, early rulers could not be permitted to age, and their ritual killings were remembered in tales of resurrection, heroic death, ascension, foreshadowing dramatic Tragedy. In bardic legends, gruesome sacrifice would be softened into the hero vanishing in cloud, earthquake, fiery chariot; perishing from cliff-fall or from treachery. A pre-Celtic custom permitted the king to rule seven years, after which a white goddess 'bore him away to an island'.

A Henry II, an Edward I, would not have relished the position of the legendary Math ap Mathonwy, Lord of Gwynedd, who 'could only exist when his feet were in the lap of a maiden, save when he was saved by the clamour of war'. Some rulers were forbidden to touch ground, their *mana* liable to induce earthquake, so that they had always to be carried, like Popes in ceremonial processions. Being was as important as action, character, appearance, and largely remains so. On Victoria's state visit to Paris, 1855, an observer noted, 'she looked like an untidy cabbage' but her poise and self-assurance outbid the youth, beauty and elegance of the newly-established Empress Eugénie.

Royal life concentrated the elemental powers. A calm and expressionless deportment preserved the harmony of the universe. In *Macbeth*, Duncan's murder disjoints nature, so that horses go mad and eat each other, earth and sky are convulsed. Centuries later, Cathal MacMhuirick lamented four Macdonald chiefs dying in one year. 'Our rivers are denied abundance of fishing, the glen sees no hunting, there is small yield from the field, the sea has gnawed through to the very foot of the mountains.' In 1535, Henry VIII was blamed personally for harvest failure. Pepys, 1662, was doubtless ironic, 'But methought it lessened my esteem of a king that he should not be able to command the rain.' At the coronation of the King of Nepal, 1975, the ruler was smeared with mud from a Himalayan mountain, from a whore's doorstep, from the junction of two rivers, and from an elephant's trunk, all symbols of fertility. Monarchs 'touched for the evil', their *mana* possessing magic. Even Monmouth, royal but illegitimate, in attempts to reinforce his claim on the crown, 'touched' at Crewkerne in 1680, and at Wallasey in 1682. Henry Marten, witty anti-Royalist during Cromwell's republic, gibed that the Great Seal should now replace the royal hand for such cures. Monmouth's buckle, found after his defeat at Sedgemoor, was held capable of cures. Dr Johnson was 'touched' by Queen Anne, Charles X of France still performed the rite until the 1830 revolution. Bonny Prince Charlie's brother, 'Henry IX', was the last British royal to practise it. Evelyn noted in 1684: 'There was so great a concourse of people with their children to be touched for the Evil, that six or seven were crushed to death by pressing at the chirurgeon's door for tickets.' In 1685 he mentions a bishop reporting a blind child being healed by the blood of Charles I.

In death, a Nyabyusan Australian chief would have his orifices blocked, to restrain his spirit which, if it flew away, might remove general fertility. To give lustre and vitality to the land, an early Norwegian king, Halfdan the Black, was, after death, quartered, and buried in four different provinces.

Around the sanctified, anointed, decorated Monarch clustered the oaths and emotions needed for tribal security. Hungary was formally a kingdom until 1945, though in practice only until 1918, when Churchill observed 'a drizzle of empires falling through the air'. All Hungarians were 'members of the Crown', the holy, mystical Crown of St Stephen.

A successful ruler was a semi-supernatural saviour: 'Our sins lay on the King.' In failure he was a scapegoat. After military catastrophe in 1870, Napoleon III wrote: 'A sovereign can utter no excuse, he can plead no extenuating circumstances. It is his highest prerogative to shoulder all the responsibilities incurred by those who have served him – or those who have betrayed him.' The less competent Roman emperors built themselves arches so lofty as to imply the presence of a giant. Hitler and Speer devised similar architecture for a triumphant post-war Reich.

The ancient mystique of Monarchy survives religious, political and technological change, even the actual throne. Dictators have continued monarchical protocol: the boastful uniforms and regalia, ornate titles and music, the language of millennium and apocalypse, the appeal not to reason but to extravagant emotion. Often they too end by fire, weapon, rope, or in exile, though promising some exotic return. Hierarchy, with accompaniments of privilege and snobbery, seems rooted deep in the psyche, virtually immune from legislation and decree. Lenin, embalmed in a glass case, provokes archaic loyalties more powerful than his teachings.

Contemporary regimes, impeccably republican, cherish pageantry, parades, rallies, political mysticism, totemic emblems, personal display. The exchange of a baton for a crown scarcely guarantees moral advance. Republics can countenance arbitrary arrest, torture, slavery, proscriptions, censorship, racialism, sexism, capital punishment, secret police, deification of leaders, on a scale which would have astounded Victoria, Franz Josef or Louis Napoleon.

Simultaneously, foreign nations, not least Third World republicans, do not blanch at a royal invitation, or prefer to visit the homes of miners and left-wing militants rather than Buckingham Palace or Windsor Castle. This may be deplorable, appealing to instincts vulgar and socially divisive, but remains true. Henry Green defined prose as 'a gathering web of insinuations'. This could also relate to the appeal of Monarchy in a republican world.

Walter Bagehot wrote in 1867, 'Royalty will be strong because it appeals to diffused feelings.' Also, 'Its mystery is its life, we must not let in daylight upon the magic.' This can be overdone. In 1923, permission to broadcast the wedding of the Duke and Duchess of York was refused by the Abbey Chapter, because 'disrespectful people might hear it while sitting in public houses with their hats on'.

Monarchy always closely associated itself with religion, its promises, reassurances, warnings. Royal heraldic arms were installed in churches, royal propaganda enlivened sermons; more sensational means could be added. 'The canonization of Edward the Confessor, 1166, was a triumph for the Monarchy and was so regarded by the English kings.' (Frank Barlow) Exploiting the lure of myth and legend, the Plantagenet Monarchy harnessed itself to the Arthurian traditions, so crammed with patriotic glamour in the romances of Geoffrey of Monmouth, rooted deep in antiquity or pretended antiquity. Similarly, the first Poet Laureate, John Skelton, had to produce verse to consolidate the Tudor usurpers.

High-minded zealots, of course, can hate long-established institutions as obstacles to Utopia. They can be as strenuously defended as obstacles to chaos. The British Monarchy has survived with popular support which, in a thousand years, faltered only in the seventeenth century. It thus deserves, not worship, but a certain reasoned respect. For six centuries, British rulers were European figures, for two more they have been world figures. Women had their part. Just discernible is Alfred's daughter, Aethflaed, ruling alone. 'Her military reputation spread across the Irish sea, and before the end of her life she was architect and leader of a great alliance of the kings and rulers of northern Britain, subduer of Welsh princes, Lady of the Vikings at York.' (Pauline Stafford) Earlier, in 722, King Ina's consort, Ethelburgh, had sacked Taunton.

The twelfth-century Geoffrey of Monmouth considered the chief royal duties were to make good laws and maintain them, and to promote fine architecture. Medieval kings included some notable law-givers – Henry I, Henry II, Edward I – and, for architecture, Geoffrey would not have complained of Henry III, Richard II, Henry VII, Henry VIII, George IV. The Monarchy also protected and stimulated trade, built ships, harbours, defensive fortresses. Henry VII ordered the first dry dock, at Portsmouth, in 1496, and its first naval yard. Henry VIII added yards at Deptford and Woolwich. The Crown induced national land surveys, new castle towns, and English expansion – unwisely in Ireland, successfully in Wales, and failing in Scotland. It dealt with foreign governments and the Pope, and debarred the Inquisition from England, and though it connived at executions for heresy, there were relatively few compared with Continental persecutions and crusades.

A medieval Frenchman observed: 'The English will never love or honour their king, unless he be victorious and a lover of arms and war against their neighbours and especially against such as are greater and richer than themselves. Their land is more fulfilled of riches and all manner of goods when they are at war than in times of peace. They take delight and solace in battles and slaughter: covetous and envious are they, above measure, of other men's wealth.' But the Crown could not rely wholly on military prowess abroad. The English, virtually unpoliced, and accustomed to bear arms, were a grumbling, violent people, ill-disposed to hard work, often disrespectful to authority, but not revolutionary, and accepting the intricate feudal pattern of loyalties, custom, leadership. The Crown could be a popular defence against baronial anarchy and pillage.

Kings were never dictators; four were deposed, not by mass hatred but from discontent and faction within the ruling class.

The medieval jurist, Henry de Bracton, asserted: 'The King is under God and the law; for the law makes the King and without the law there is no King.' This was a conception already more English than European. Froissart exaggerates, though with a core of truth: 'The King of England must needs obey his people and do all their will', though an anonymous thirteenth-century chronicler is more persuasive: 'Just as a ship cannot be saved from the peril of the sea without the guidance of the oarsmen, so neither can any king govern his realm prosperously nor defend it from its enemies without the help of his own subjects.' As early as William II and Henry I, this was understood.

Solvency, not glory, was the medieval Crown's ultimate safeguard. George Duby mentions one dimension overlooked by romantics: 'It was notorious that the King of England could draw upon a copious reservoir of husbandless women, many of whom were worth a great deal. Custom constantly fed this reservoir, authorizing the sovereign to marry off the widows and orphans of his deceased vassals, to distribute them judiciously among the bachelors attached to him, as the wages of their good service. Indeed, this was how he ruled, how he controlled more closely than by any other artifice, the nobles of his realm and the lesser men as well.' The Tudor monopoly of artillery was to be a useful if prosaic asset in the movement towards centralization.

Political failures, like Edward II, Richard II, Charles I, could yet be effective cultural influences. James VI and I patronized the theatre, notably Shakespeare, favouring the English Players in Scotland, antagonizing the divines. He established the Board of Trade in 1621, and, as H. A. Harris reports, authorized Britain's first known athletic meeting, 'Mr Robert Dover's Olimpic Games', on the Cotswolds, James regarding it as a blow at Puritanism. His grandsons, Charles and James, popularized yacht racing and James loved the new sport of fox-hunting. Charles founded Greenwich Hospital for disabled seamen, perhaps with some prodding from Monmouth, Captain General of the Royal Forces, with whom he was always sympathetic and easy. The office of Gold Stick alone survives from Monmouth's administration, though he initiated important army reforms, in discipline, training, payment. Charles II was first President of the Royal Society, more active than many honorary presidents. He was a strenuous player of Royal Tennis, for which the Venetian ambassador alleged, surely erroneously, 1,800 courts existed in Britain. His distant successor, Edward VII, as Prince of Wales, once batted for the I Zingari, though failing to score, and, I suspect, to field.

Reputations fluctuate. James I's ill-fated heir, Henry (1594–1612), long remembered chiefly for his intellectual relationship with Ralegh, whom he never met, is now presented by Dr Roy Strong as a principal in an aborted English artistic renaissance uniting traditional native art and design with the latest of Continental sophistication. His three years as Prince of Wales were of achievement outweighed by frustration, his revolutionary policies dogged by lack of money, yet moving towards enthralling fruition. 'The result was a potentially brilliant *mise-en-scene* with far wider intellectual and aesthetic implications than were ever to be inherited by his brother Charles' and, 'unlike his father, Henry emerges as the Prince *par excellence* of Renaissance hermetic science in England'. His premature death ensured that 'the alliance of art, science and the Monarchy snapped in 1612, not to be re-established until after the Restoration, with the foundation of the Royal Society' (Strong).

Charles I, nevertheless, was an early connoisseur of miniatures, supporter of Van Dyke, an assiduous and discriminating collector of Rubens and employer of Inigo Jones. More surprising was the much derided George III, 'who valued paintings as an aid to morality', the received wisdom not only of Wilhelm II, Stalin, Khrushchev, Hitler, but, transferred to the theatre, also of Bernard Shaw. But, in founding the Royal Academy, George fulfilled a serious function of Monarchy which should increase as its political role dwindles. He was a most active patron of the great astronomer William Herschel, discoverer of Uranus, financing several of his telescopes, the one at Windsor costing £4,000. He began the foundations of a National Library which, in 1823, passed to the British Museum. He was also generous enough to award the last Stuart pretender, 'Henry IX', a pension of £40,000, when beggared by Napoleon. George IV, most maligned of all British rulers save Richard III, assembled a great collection of Dutch and Flemish masters – Rembrandt, Ruisdael, de Hooch, Steen – and was patron of Gainsborough and Stubbs. Prince Albert pioneered the appreciation of Italian Primitives. J. H. Plumb adds that Elizabeth II's additions to the Royal Collection are the finest since Prince Albert.

From the seventeenth century the Crown was losing direct political power and many sacramental bonds, though primitive, sometimes irrational allegiances still linger. Yet, well into the eighteenth century 'the King exercised personal control over the use of the Army, and in 1765, 1768, and 1780, directed what were virtually military campaigns against rioters in London' (Brooke). For two further reigns, the Monarch was active head of the armed forces, scrutinizing appointments with rigorous partiality and outbursts of decisive prejudice. General Canrobert confessed himself 'quite stupefied' by Queen Victoria's knowledge of the siege of Sebastopol. 'The position of the trenches, the camps and batteries – all were fixed with an admirable precision in her head. She was as familiar with the siege in all its most minute details as I was myself.' Bagehot, 1872, maintained with whatever seriousness that the Queen, on her own, could disband the armed forces, start a war, create peers, issue pardons. She must have welcomed this reminder, and congratulated herself on her own restraint, perhaps recalling Elizabeth I letting the Commons know in 1593 that

> For liberty of speech her Majesty commandeth me to tell you that to say yea or no to bills, God forbid that any man should be restrained or afraid to answer according to his best liking, with some short declaration of his reason therein, and therein to have a free voice, which is the very true liberty of this house; not as some suppose to speak there of all causes as he listeth and to frame a form of religion or a state of government as to their idle brains shall seem meatest. She saith that no king fit for his state will suffer such absurdities.

Victoria, 1885, initiated inter-party meetings about extending the franchise, and consistently, often ineffectively, interfered in foreign and imperial affairs, areas in which monarchs always claimed special prerogatives. Lord Clarendon once complained that the Queen and Prince Consort 'laboured under the curious mistake that they had the right to control, if not direct, the foreign policy of England'. In 1868 Victoria successfully opposed Clarendon's own reappointment to the Foreign Office and, in 1864, had helped prevent Britain from actively supporting Denmark against Prussia. Until 1918, with relatives occupying most European thrones, the British crown could doubtless exercise some unofficial influence.

Prince Albert probably saved Britain from war with America in 1861, was largely responsible for prohibiting duelling amongst army officers, was an enlightened patron of art, science, social reform. Of him, Robert Rhodes James wrote, 1983, 'a man comparable to Thomas Jefferson in the extraordinary variety and depths of his interests, who died so young and who achieved so much'. His remark on the Free Trader, Cobden: 'Richard, Coeur de Cotton', credits him with some humour. His son, Edward VII, vainly warned Conservative leaders against the Lords rejecting the 1909 Liberal Budget. Roger Fulford asserts that 'without the King's support, Haldane could never have carried the War Office with him in his sweeping army reforms'. On his 1903 visit to Ireland, against official misgivings, Edward won personal success, in contrast to neglect of that country by royalty, save John, Richard II and George IV. In 1904 he vetoed the appointment of Sir John French, despite his popularity and success in South Africa, as chief of the General Staff. His attempts towards understanding with France were preceded by visits, initially unknown to Cabinet and Private Secretary, without assent from his Premier, to Portugal and Italy and then, for Sir Frederick Ponsonby, 'the visit to Paris in 1903 always seemed to me to strain the limitations of a constitutional monarch to breaking point. The King went to Paris with no Cabinet Minister to advise him or to act as a liaison between him and the Government, and yet he reversed the whole policy of this country.' In that year, Ponsonby observed Edward arriving in Naples 'incognito', escorted by eight battleships, four cruisers, four destroyers and a despatch vessel.

George V seems to have advised Lloyd George against granting asylum to his cousin, Tsar Nicholas II, in 1917, despite personal affection, and against Lloyd George's proposal to use Hampton Court as prison for Wilhelm II in 1918, when the Premier optimistically envisaged the defeated Kaiser's trial in London as a war criminal. The King feared turmoil during that daily journey from Hampton Court to Westminster Hall. He made many attempts, usually unsuccessful, to gain practical results for his political opinions and prejudices, always trenchant, seldom muddled or absurd. At least twice, over the flamboyant Irish dilemmas, 1911, and the financial crisis, 1931, he pronouncedly intervened, in the latter being attacked by Harold Laski for unconstitutional and anti-socialist bias, though he did later concede that the King and his family 'were identified with a concern, albeit superficial, for the problems of social and industrial welfare'. Churchill considered that he 'used his influence, now become so great, to bring about the formation of a national, or so-called national administration, to save the country from unnecessary collapse, and unwarrantable bankruptcy'. Churchill himself was omitted from this coalition.

Henry Fairlie, 1961, considered

> George V had a strict and unerring understanding of the important conventions of the constitution: this proved to be of untold value during the crisis of January 1924, when he resisted the most powerful pressures which were put upon him to keep the Labour Party out of office. To his instinctive behaviour on that occasion we can, in part, attribute the development of the Labour Party within the Parliamentary system, instead of outside it, at a time when left-wing movements throughout Europe became émigré groups within their own countries. Holding the ring – for this is what such conduct is – is not confined to strict constitutional questions. In Sir Harold Nicolson's biography there are many examples of George V's anxiety that the dominant party or even interest should not, *so far as it was within his power to influence decisions,* ride roughshod over the rights of any of his people. Twice during the

General Strike, for example, he spontaneously and effectively intervened to prevent the more extreme elements in the Conservative Government from unjustly or cruelly treating the strikers. Interventions of this kind cannot be ignored and neither can their importance. It is no small thing, in an age of strong party government, to have excesses of party spirit rebuked by one to whom Ministers are constitutionally bound to listen. . . .

It is apt to make people uncomfortable today to talk of duty, especially of duty in high places. But no one can read the biographies of George V and George VI, which are not sycophantic, without realizing that it was a simple, almost naive conception of their duty to their subjects, for it affected even George V's attitude to the Indian question, which inspired most of their actions, and certainly their actions at all critical moments.

This is confirmed by Kenneth Rose's 1983 biography of George V. Edward VIII had some influence on the 1936 Anglo-Argentine Treaty and, as Prince of Wales, had actively propagated British commercial and cultural exchanges, as Patron of the British Council, the Travel Association, and the Ibero-American Institute of Great Britain, and by incessant foreign journeys. The extent and effect of his alleged pro-Nazi sentiments remain controversial. His successor, George VI, seems to have queried the proposed appointment of Hugh Dalton as Foreign Secretary, 1945. Harold Macmillan's diary notes that Elizabeth II had demurred at appointing R. A. Butler as deputy premier. 'The Queen has in the past rightly pointed out that there is no such official post. I must not be accused of trying to appoint my successor, and thus injure the prerogative.'

The Monarchy remains a hinge of state, not powerful but imprecisely influential, maintaining its rights, as defined by Bagehot, to be consulted, to advise, to warn.

Royal courts concentrated and distorted human excesses; weakness, absurdity, pride, ambition: courtiers' imaginations strained into the fantasies of tourney and masque, pageant and charade, feast, intrigue, practical joke, sophistication swiftly lapsing into dangerous boredom. As drama, they were stylized yet preyed upon by the involuntary and accidental; by the last sight of Edward V in the Tower, or of Edward VI: 'a white despairing face was seen looking through the window of the Palace – a face with no hair'. Monarchs would possess flair for language. As death approached, Elizabeth uttered, 'I saw one night my body exceeding lean and fearful in a light of fire.' *A light of fire*; so much stronger than 'in firelight'. They might have self-mocking humour. 'A crown', Frederick the Great reflected, 'is only a hat that lets in water.' Their gravest failing was less their disregard for their neighbours' rights than in their unfailing thoughtlessness, which toadies trained like a climbing plant. This can be more unforgivable than political tyranny. Reputedly, Frederick showed gratitude only once in his life – to the horse on which he fled after defeat in battle. William Bray, editing Evelyn's *Diary*, 1818, recalled of Peter the Great:

> When the Czar of Muscovy came to England in 1698, proposing to instruct himself in the art of ship-building, he was desirous of having the use of Sayes Court [Evelyn's home], in consequence of its vicinity to the King's dock-yard at Deptford. This was conceded; but during his stay he did so much damage that Mr Evelyn had an allowance of £150 for it. He especially regrets the mischief done to his famous holly-hedge, which might have been thought beyond the reach of damage. But one of the Czar's favourite recreations had been to demolish the hedges by riding through them in a wheel-barrow.

Courtiers may have been more pleasant to read about than to have known. I enjoy recalling the opera devotee Count Skavronski forcing his servants to communicate in recitative; Madame de Puysieux at Versailles, in one year chewing through 100,000 crowns' worth of Genoese lace; a royal doctor, M. de l'Orme, preparing for the day in a Morocco robe, a mask, six pairs of stockings, several fur hats, a clove of garlic in his mouth, incense in his ears, a stick of rue in his nostrils; sleeping in a brick oven surrounded by hot water bottles; living on sheeps' tongues and

syrup of greengage, and, at eighty-seven, marrying a girl of nine-
teen. Thomas Hinde, in his book on them, depicts a notable gallery
of British courtiers. Lord Melcome bowing to George II's Queen
Caroline, at which 'his breeches broke their moorings in a very
indecorous manner'; Lord Hervey, whose wife was gazetted a
military cornet at birth, calling his mother 'Mount Vesuvius'
because her mouth emitted fire and rubbish; Joan de Neville offering King John 200 chickens for permission to spend a night with her
husband.

Royalty too could be picturesque. Lord Redesdale had audience
with a nineteenth-century Japanese Emperor, 'a tall youth in a
white coat with long padded trousers of crimson silk trailing like a
lady's court train. His eyebrows were shaved off and painted high
up on the forehead; his cheeks were rouged and his lips painted
with red and gold. His teeth were blackened.' Christopher Cope
refers to the wealthy Margaret of Male, described as ugly and badly
dressed, vulgar in habit and taste, and fond of whistling and sitting
on the grass. She was also enormously rich, and married Philip the
Bold.

Carlyle once pronounced that 'the problem is to burn away the
immense dung heap of the eighteenth century with its ghastly cant,
foul black sensualities, cruelties and inanity now fully petrified'.
Petrification, however, can survive fire. Much delicacy and nuance
have vanished; one would not recognize in the occasional modern
snuff-addict what Kenneth Blackmore observes (1977) of the
eighteenth-century manner: 'A little ballet of the fingers . . . beginning as a flourish as the box was produced. The fingers were tapped
on the exquisite little lid, as though to gain admittance. This
knocked the tobacco away from the box opening. Then there was
the taking of a pinch of powder and the carrying of it to the nostrils,
the delicate sniff itself, and finally there was the pirouette with the
handkerchief to wipe away any offending grains.'

Plenty of cant, cruelty and inanity survives in all systems.
Michael De-la-Noy is instructive about honours (1985):

> A romantic and improbable range of foreign orders is
> available. From Albania one might receive the Order of the
> Partisan Star, from Bulgaria the Order of 9 September

1944, China has on offer the Air Force Order of the Ancient Symbols, while friends of Japan may sport the Supreme Order of the Chrysanthemum. Liberia keeps its options open with the Order of Knighthood of Pioneers of the Republic. It seems unlikely that the present fad for small families will result in any subject of Her Britannic Majesty receiving the Russian Order of the Glory of Motherhood, though a lady responsible for the fostering of 350 children, Mrs June Gaunt, was made MBE in 1979. More glamorous perhaps would be a letter from King Bhumibol Adulyadej of Thailand offering the Order of the White Elephant.

All regimes, however exotically disguised, are devices, organic or arbitrary, to force us to do what few of us wish to do. None escapes the ludicrous. A Chinese journal, *Outlook Weekly*, joyously hailed October 1964 as 'The spiritual flavour in full blossom of the Chinese nation'. Leftist CND enthusiasts may have been uneasy when realizing that this encomium referred to China's first nuclear explosion. The momentous decision to make Britain an atomic power was ordained by a socialist Prime Minister without reference to Parliament or people.

Mine is the sort of book which many may enjoy, yet feeling that they themselves could have done it better. Some will find it insufficiently anecdotal, others the reverse. It is not a comprehensive survey of the evolution of the Monarchy, and necessarily reflects my own quirks. I have no governing theme, though I find the past consistently relevant and entertaining. *Quaintiquarianism* – probably my own coinage, and not one to boast of – does not much concern me. Here the momentous and sententious must jostle with the inconsequential. I have an ear for the trivial and enjoy knowing that Richelieu's sister believed herself made of glass, eschewing chairs in order to avoid cracking; that Dr Rutherford of Westminster thought all boys were born knowing the date of the Battle of Leuctra; that, during the Civil War, Charles I in enforced exile at Oxford successfully requested Parliament to permit the despatch of his new tennis suit from anti-royalist London. I would like to have heard Queen Elizabeth II's reply when Robert Graves remarked that they were related through the Prophet Mahomet; William Rufus's utterance when his chaplain confessed that he was pregnant by a man I do not know, but can imagine. I have not forgotten Charles Lamb's remark on Burnet's *History*, 'Full of scandal, which all true history is.'

I am not a shrill Monarchist nor an avid Republican, and present my characters as source of achievements, failures, some tragedy and considerable comedy. If I am ever tempted to sentimentalize, I remember grim incidents, some recorded here, such as Henry VIII's Attorney-General, 1537, at Sir Thomas More's trial, stating: 'Even though we should have no word or deed to charge upon you, yet we have your silence and that is a sign of your evil intention and a sure proof of malice.'

Considerations, not of ignorance or indifference, but of space, make me exclude foreign royalty. This I regret, for in my youth crowned aliens provided much popular entertainment, frequently scandalous:

> King Carol, King Boris, King Zog,
> Went down to the river to bathe;
> Carol and Zog
> Got lost in a bog,
> And Boris begins with B.

Even at their most abject, drunken or demented, our own Monarchs usually contrived some lingering dignity. George IV alone might perhaps be compared to King Carol II of Rumania, of whom Hannah Pakula wrote, 1985:

> Although it took extraordinary imagination to cast himself in the role of saint – particularly when his martyrdom consisted of defecting to Paris with his mistress – Carol made a bold stab at it. To commemorate his suffering in exile, he instituted a new medal, the Order of Suffering, a white enamel medallion with two interlocking Cs under a

royal crown encircled by a wreath of thorns. . . . The King issued new stamps and coins portraying himself under a crown of thorns. 'I wish that every time anyone uses a coin or stamps he shall be reminded of my suffering during the years of my Calvary.'

Few of our rulers have been plagued by what Ben Jonson called 'an itching leprosy of wit', and to have confined this collection to royal observations would have made a volume brief and derogatory, though I hope it contains a few surprises, and I have attempted to readjust several reputations. Above all, I have tried to convey some flavour of the antiquity which always underlies a present however technologically advanced and which Elizabeth Jenkins, one of my many contemporaries whom I have pillaged, understands so well. Of the approach of the Spanish Armada, those haughty, floating fortresses unprecedented in magnitude, and the lighting of beacons to alert all England, she writes:

> While the light flew northwards, summoning the militia to their posts, and Lord Howard of Effingham directed that the sixty ships riding in Plymouth Harbour should put to sea, a defence of immemorial antiquity was brought into action. Above the cliffs of Padstow and Minehead, animals with a head like a horse and a long body composed of a train of men, covered by a fringe of streamers, invoked the might of strange powers to drive away the approaching evil from English shores.

The reader will notice much wickedness but little fanaticism or evil. Fanaticism cannot promote even elementary efficiency over any but a brief period, though personal immorality tends to induce better government than high-minded virtue. Jeremy Potter cites Robert of Normandy, attractive friend, political failure, whose rule in England would surely have been disastrous, 'for it was said of him that if a weeping man was brought to him for justice he would weep with him and set him free'. In general, looking back on some thousand years of rule and attempted rule, I turn with some sympathy to Siegfried Sassoon's evocation of the Wittelsbach dynasty:

Fountains upheave pale plumes against the sky,
Murmuring, *'their Majesties came sauntering by –*
Was it but yesterday?' . . . Proud fountains sigh
Towards the long glades in golden foliage clad,
'Kurfursts could do no wrong? . . .' And the woods reply,
'Take them for what they were, they weren't so bad!'

THE ANTHOLOGY

ABDICATION

I greatly lament that I have so utterly failed my people, but I could not be other than I am; I am pleased that my son who has been thus accepted by all the people should succeed me on the throne.

KING EDWARD II, 1327

Richard told me of his annoyance with the Queen, the silly old frump, for failing to abdicate and thereby condemning the Prince of Wales to an absurd existence; in earlier times, he said, sons became their mothers' guardians when they came of age.

COSIMA WAGNER. Diary, 1880

I have found it impossible to carry the heavy burden of responsibility and to discharge my duties as King as I would wish to do without the help and support of the woman I love ... and I lay down my burden.
KING EDWARD VIII, 1936

I don't think that you have ever realized the shock which the attitude you took up caused your family and the whole Nation. It seemed inconceivable to those who had made such sacrifices during the war, you, as their King, refused a lesser sacrifice. ...

My feelings for you as your mother remain the same, and our being parted and the cause of it, grieved me beyond words; after all, all my life, I have put my country before everything else, and I simply cannot change now.

QUEEN MARY, to Edward, Duke of Windsor, 1938

What better woman is qualified to be Queen of England who has already been through the mill three times?

GEORGE BERNARD SHAW, on Wallis, Duchess of Windsor, 1936

Dickie, this is absolutely terrible . . . I am quite unprepared for it. I've never even seen a state paper. I'm only a naval officer, it's the only thing I know about.

KING GEORGE VI, to Lord Mountbatten, after the abdication of King Edward VIII, 1936

I played fair in 1936, but I was bloody shabbily treated.

EDWARD, DUKE OF WINDSOR, to James Pope-Hennessy

ABRAHAM

The Queen was at Osborne, and she went for her customary drive with Lady Errol, who was then in waiting. These dear, elderly ladies, swathed in crepe, drove in an open carriage, called a sociable. The Queen was very silent, and Leila (Lady Errol) thought it time to make a little conversation. So she said, 'Oh, Your Majesty, think of when we shall see our dear ones again in Heaven!'

'Yes,' said the Queen.

'We will all meet in Abraham's bosom,' said Leila.

'I will *not* meet Abraham,' said the Queen.

PRINCESS MARIE LOUISE, 1956, on Queen Victoria, following the death of her son-in-law, Prince Henry of Battenberg, 1896

ACCESSION

This day our slavery ends,
It is our fountain head of liberty,
End of gloom, beginning of joy . . .
Henry is the King
To cleanse all eyes of tears
And exchange long laments for praise.

SIR THOMAS MORE
on the accession of King Henry VIII

I returned and took horse between nine and ten o'clock; and that
night rode [from London] to Doncaster. The Friday night I came to
my own house at Witherington and presently took order with my
deputies to see the Borders kept in quiet; which they had much to
do: and gave order, the next morning, the King of Scotland should
be proclaimed King of England, and at Morpeth and Alnwick. Very
early, on Saturday, I took horse for Edinburgh, and came to
Norham about twelve at noon, so that I might well have been with
the King at supper time. But I got a great fall by the way; and my
horse, with one of his heels, gave me a great blow on the head, that
made me shed much blood. It made me so weak, that I was forced
to ride a soft pace after: so that the King was newly gone to bed by
the time I knocked at the gate. I was quickly let in; and carried up to
the King's Chamber. I kneeled by him, and saluted him by his title
of 'England, Scotland, France and Ireland'. He gave me his hand to
kiss, and bade me welcome. After he had long discoursed of the
manner of the Queen's sickness, and of her death, he asked what
letters I had from the Council. I told him none: and acquainted him
how narrowly I escaped from them. And yet I brought him a blue
ring from a fair lady, that I hoped would give him assurance of the
truth that I had reported. He took it, and looked upon it, and said,
'It is enough. I know by this that you are a true messenger.' Then he
committed me to the charge of my Lord Hume, and gave straight
command that I should want nothing. He sent for his chirurgeons

to attend me; and when I kissed his hand, at my departure, he said to me these gracious words: 'I know you have lost a near kinswoman and a loving Mistress; but take here my hand, I will be as good a Master to you, and will requite you this service with honour and reward.'   Sir Robert Carey, on King James VI and I. *Memoirs, c.* 1625

I saw the *new Queen* and *King* proclaimed the very next day after her coming to Whitehall, Wednesday, 13th February, with great acclamation and general good reception. Bonfires, bells, guns, etc. It was believed that both, especially the Princess, would have showed some (seeming) reluctance at least, of assuming her father's Crown, and made some apology, testifying by her regret that he should by his mismanagement necessitate the Nation to so extraordinary a proceeding, which would have showed very handsomely to the world, and according to the character given of her piety; consonant also to her husband's first declaration, that there was no intention of deposing the King, but of succouring the Nation; but nothing of all this appeared; she came into Whitehall laughing and jolly, as to a wedding, so as to seem quite transported.

John Evelyn, on Queen Mary II and King William III.
Diary, 1689

'I am Sir Robert Walpole,' said the messenger. The awakened sleeper hated Sir Robert Walpole. 'I have the honour to announce to your Majesty that your royal father, King George I, died at Osnaburg, on Saturday last, the 10th inst.'

'That is one big lie!' roared out his sacred Majesty King George II: but Sir Robert Walpole stated the fact, and from that day until three-and-thirty years after, George, the second of that name, ruled over England.   W. M. Thackeray. *The Four Georges,* 1860

Hail, mighty Monarch! Whom desert alone
Would, without birthright, raise up to the throne;
Thy virtues shine particularly nice,
Ungloomed with a confinity to vice.

LAURENCE EUSDEN, Poet Laureate, to King George II, 1727

I cannot resist telling you that our dear little Queen in every respect is *perfection*. I learnt first of all from the Duke of Argyll that, all the Privy Councillors being assembled round the Council table, the Dukes of Cumberland and Sussex went into an adjoining room, and conducted the Queen in. She took her chair at the head of the table and read her declaration in the most perfect manner possible, and with a most powerful and charming voice. I have since had all the particulars from Tavistock, who had them from Melbourne himself. She sent for him at once, and begged him to draw up the declaration she ought to make; which of course he did, and everybody says it is admirable. She then put herself entirely in his hands in the best possible manner. ... Poor dear King William's last act was *signing pardons*.   THOMAS CREEVEY, on Queen Victoria, 1837

The Marquess of Tavistock was later the seventh Duke of Bedford; William Lamb, Lord Melbourne, was Queen Victoria's first Premier.

Full recognition has been given to . . . the range and diversity of the new King's training. For, admirably lacking in routine, it has effectively multiplied his contacts with almost every drab activity that goes to make up the common round of England. He has heard engineers talk shop, listened to experts planning assaults on foreign markets, and watched the slow alleviation of maladjustments in the workers' lives. The higher salesmanship, group migration, and the mysterious processes by which frozen credits may be thawed have all passed before him; and few men have been vouchsafed a more commanding survey of the whole roaring, creaking, smoky rattle-trap of affairs and industry which goes by the name of England. If it is the business of a modern king to hear and know about such things as that, there is not a more modern king in Europe.

But, happily or not, England is not the only place of which he has to be king; and in the wider field he has rare advantages, since he has been a persevering traveller. If it is an advantage to have seen the world as very few have seen it, he enjoys it to the full. A sight (and he has had more than one) of North and South America, Africa, India, and the Dominions is a generous education in quite a number of things that we are not customarily taught at home, and he has had the chance to learn them all. That is another means by which his years have been augmented in the same process which enabled him to serve his country overseas in foreign markets and the Dominions. PHILIP GUEDALLA, on King Edward VIII, 1936

AN ACCIDENT

This deplorable accident.

Official explanation by QUEEN ELIZABETH I to King James VI of Scotland, 1587, of the execution of his mother, Queen Mary.

ACCUSATION

That whereas Queen Anne has been the wife of Henry the Eighth for three years and more, she, despising her marriage and entertaining malice against the King, and following daily her frail and carnal lust, did falsely and treacherously procure by means of base conversations, touchings, gifts, and other infamous incitations, divers of the King's daily and familiar servants to be her adulterers and concubines, so that several of the King's servants yielded to her vile provocations. ...

Furthermore, that the Queen and other of the said traitors, jointly and severally confessed and imagined the King's death; and that the Queen had frequently promised to marry some one of the traitors, whenever the King should depart this life, affirming she would never love the King in her heart. ...

> At the trial of Queen Anne Boleyn, at the Tower of London, 1536,
> for treason – as adulteress, poisoner, committer of incest

ADVICE

Choose yourself a wife who you will always and only love.

> JOHN SKELTON, first Poet Laureate, to his pupil Prince Henry,
> later King Henry VIII. *Speculum Principis*, c. 1499

... Never repose so much upon any man's single counsel, fidelity, and discretion, in managing affairs of the first magnitude (that is, matters of religion and justice), as to create in yourself or others a diffidence of your own judgement, which is likely to be always more constant and impartial to the interests of your crown and kingdom than any man's. Next beware of exasperating any factions by the crossness and asperity of some men's passions, humours, or private opinions employed by you, grounded only upon the differences in lesser matters, which are but the skirts and suburbs of religion.

Take heed that outward circumstances and formalities of religion devour not at all, or the best encouragements of learning, industry, and piety; but with an equal eye and impartial hand distribute favours and rewards to all men, as you find them for their real goodness both in abilities and fidelity worthy and capable of them. . . .

When these mountains of congealed faction shall, by the sunshine of God's mercy and the splendour of your virtues, be thawed and dissipated, and the abused vulgar shall have learned that none are greater oppressors of their estates, liberties, and consciences than those men that entitle themselves the patrons and vindications of them, only to usurp power over them; let, then, no passion betray you to any study of revenge upon those whose own sin and folly will sufficiently punish them in due time. But as soon as the forked arrow of factious emulations is drawn out, use all princely arts and clemency to heal the wounds that the smart of the cure may not equal the anguish of the hurt.

KING CHARLES I, from his last letter to Charles, Prince of Wales,
later King Charles II, 1649

SIR FREDERICK PONSONBY: 'The Monarchy must always retain an element of mystery. A Prince should not show himself too much. . . . The Monarchy must remain on a pedestal. If you bring it down to the people, it will lose its mystery and influence.'

EDWARD, PRINCE OF WALES, later King Edward VIII: 'I do not agree. Times are changing.'   1919

ALE

The ale drunk in that place is vile to the taste and disgusting to the sight.   PETER DE BLOIS, on the hospitality of King Henry II. *Letters*, 1174

ALFRED THE GREAT

From his cradle he was filled with a love of wisdom above all things.

ASSER

Alfred the king of the Anglo-Saxons, the son of the most pious King Ethelwulf the famous, the warlike, the victorious; the careful provider for the widow, the helpless, the orphan and the poor, the most skilled of the Saxon poets, most dear to his own nation, courteous to all, most liberal, endowed with prudence, fortitude, justice and temperance; most patient in the infirmity from which he continually suffered; the most discerning investigator in executing justice, most watchful and devout in the service of God.

FLORENCE OF WORCESTER. *Chronicon ex Chronicis, c.* 1200

Under the Great Alfred, all the best points of the English-Saxon were first encouraged and in him first shown. It has been the greatest character among the nations of the earth. Wherever the descendants of the Saxon race have gone, have sailed, or otherwise made their way, even to the remotest regions of the world, they have been patient, persevering, never to be broken in spirit, never to be turned aside from enterprises on which they have resolved. In Europe, Asia, Africa, America, the whole world over; in the desert, in the forest, on the sea; scorched by a burning sun, or frozen by ice that never melts; the Saxon blood remains unchanged. Wheresoever that race goes, there, law and industry, and safety for life and property, and all the great results of steady perseverance, are certain to arise.

I pause to think with admiration of the noble king who, in his single person, possessed all the Saxon virtues. Whom misfortune could not subdue, whom prosperity could not spoil, whose perseverance nothing could shake. Who was hopeful in defeat, and generous in success. Who loved justice, freedom, truth, and knowledge. Who, in his care to instruct his people, probably did more to preserve the beautiful old Saxon language, than I can imagine. Without whom, the English tongue . . . might have wanted half its meaning. As it is said that his spirit still inspires some of our best English laws, so, let you and I pray that it may animate our English hearts, at least to this – to resolve, when we see any of our fellow-creatures left in ignorance, that we will do our best, while life is in us, to have them taught; and to tell those rulers whose duty it is to teach them, and who neglect their duty, that they have profited very little by all the years that have rolled away since the year nine hundred and one, and that they are far behind the bright example of King Alfred the Great.   CHARLES DICKENS, 1853

ALIENS

I may be uninspiring but I'm damned if I'm an alien.

KING GEORGE V, 1917, on H. G. Wells' letter to *The Times*
advising the nation to imitate the Russian revolutionaries
and dismantle the Monarchy and 'an alien and uninspiring Court'

AMERICA

The die is now cast, the colonies must either submit or triumph. I do not wish to come to severer measures, but we must not retreat; by coolness and an unremitted pursuit of the measures that have been adopted I trust they will come to submit.   KING GEORGE III, 1774

The history of the present King of Great Britain is a history of repeated injuries and usurpations, all having in direct object the establishment of an absolute tyranny over these states. To prove this, let facts be submitted to a candid world.

He has refused his assent to laws the most wholesome and necessary for the public good.

He has forbidden his governors to pass laws of immediate and pressing importance, unless suspended in their operation till his

assent should be obtained; and when so suspended, he has utterly
neglected to attend to them.

He has refused to pass other laws for the accommodation of
large districts of people, unless those people would relinquish the
right of representation in the legislature – a right inestimable to
them, and formidable to tyrants only. . . .

He is at this time transporting large armies of foreign mercenaries to complete the works of death, desolation and tyranny,
already begun with circumstances of cruelty and perfidy scarcely
paralleled in the most barbarous ages, and totally unworthy the
head of a civilized nation. . . .

He has excited domestic insurrection among us, and has
endeavoured to bring on the inhabitants of our frontiers the merci-
less Indian savages, whose known rule of warfare is an undisting-
uished destruction of all ages, sexes, and conditions. . . .

> From the *American Declaration of Independence*,
> on King George III, 1776

'I wish you, Sir, to believe that it may be understood in America,
that I have done nothing in the late contest but what I thought
myself indispensably bound to do by the duty which I owed my
people. I will be very frank with you. I was the last to consent to the
separation, but the separation having then made and having
become inevitable, I have always said, as I say now, that I would be
the first to meet the friendship of the United States as an independent power.'

> KING GEORGE III, on receiving John Adams,
> first American Minister to Great Britain, 1785

In 1811, America's last king went irrevocably mad. For nine years
he roamed his palace, a pathetic figure in his purple dressing-gown,
with wild white hair and beard, blind, deaf, a Lear-like figure,
playing to himself on his harpsichord and talking, talking, talking
of men and women long since dead.

Yet, the last twenty years had changed the nation's view of its king – half sane or mad though he might be. The people realized that he had tried within the narrow limits of his capacity to discharge the duties and obligations of kingship; that his faults, which were grievous, sprang from the best of intentions. He had succeeded to wide dominions, which he held to be a sacred trust. In his simple-minded way he could not believe that any provocation could excuse the terrible treason of the Americans who tried to break up what God had so obviously joined together and put under his rule.

As it had been with America, so with Wilkes, so with Ireland, so with his children. His motives were honourable; he gave all his pitifully small abilities to the defence of what he thought to be the vital interests and essential rights of the British nation. Had he been as wise as Solomon, Britain and America would have gone their separate ways. The forces that crushed him would have crushed greater men. As it is, he remained a pathetic figure of tragicomedy; and, as the years passed, he acquired even a certain grandeur. There had been many worse kings to exercise rule over America and Britain. If he is to be blamed, it must not be for what he did but for what he was – an unbalanced man of low intelligence. And if he is to be praised, it is because he attempted to discharge honourably tasks that were beyond his powers.

J. H. PLUMB, on King George III, 1963

You suspect the American manners to be very vicious. Alas, where is vice not to be found? I am so little acquainted with it in general that I cannot much enter upon that subject.

QUEEN CHARLOTTE, to Prince William, later King William IV, 1786

It has always been a matter of serious regret to me that I had not been born a free, independent American, so much do I respect that Nation, which has given birth to Washington, the greatest man that ever lived.   KING WILLIAM IV, at a banquet for the American Minister

The Trent Affair

The last political act of the Prince Consort meant the maintenance of peace between England and the United States, where, ever since the spring of 1861, the Civil War between North and South had been raging. On 8th November a Federal warship had stopped the British Mail steamer *Trent* and taken prisoner two Confederate agents. The British Cabinet resolved to demand satisfaction for the insult offered to the British flag and the breach in International Law. The garrison in Canada was reinforced, and the British press adopted a tone of menace. It was due to the Prince Consort that a Note, based on the draft prepared by him and written in a far milder tone than that originally intended, was despatched by Lord John Russell to Washington. The sentence inserted by his advice was that it was impossible to believe that the American captain had acted by the orders of his government, or had properly understood their directions, and the captured Confederates were released.

DR KURT JAGOW, 1938

Lord Palmerston cannot but look on this peaceful issue of the American quarrel as greatly owing to her Beloved Prince, who wrote the observations upon the Draft to Lord Lyons, in which Lord Palmerston so entirely concurred. It was the last of the kind that he ever wrote.

QUEEN VICTORIA, to the Prime Minister, Lord Palmerston, 1862

There can be no doubt that, as Your Majesty observes, the alterations made in the Despatch to Lord Lyons contributed essentially to the satisfactory settlement of the dispute. But these alterations were only one of innumerable instances of the tact and judgment, and the power of nice discrimination which excited Lord Palmerston's constant and unbounded admiration.

LORD PALMERSTON, to Queen Victoria, 1862

The nearest I ever got to the United States was when I walked half across Niagara, took off my hat and walked back again.

KING GEORGE V; a favourite remark

ANIMALS

King Edmund of the East Angles was shot by arrows, then beheaded at Bures near Hoxne, Suffolk, by the pagan Danes, in 870. The head was thrown into Eglesdede woods.

Then the Saxons all went together into the woods, looking everywhere among bushes and brambles to see if they could find the head. And, wonder of wonders, God in His wisdom sent a wolf to guard the head, and protect it against other savage animals day and night. The men went about searching, and always calling out to each other like all woodsmen, 'Where are you now, friend?' And the head answered them, 'Here, here, here.' Whenever they called the head responded. There lay the grey wolf watching over the head, with it clasped between his two forepaws. He was greedy and hungry, yet in fear of God he dared not gnaw up the head but preserved it from the other creatures. At this the men were amazed at the wolf's stewardship, and took the sacred head away with them, thanking the Almighty for the Miracle. And the wolf followed them as they bore away the head, until they reached the town, just as if he were tame, and then returned to the woods.

Chronicle, 10th century

He took delight to have a number of little spaniels to follow him, and lie in his bed-chamber, where often times he suffered the bitches to puppy and give suck, which rendered it very offensive, and indeede made the whole Court nasty and stinking.

JOHN EVELYN, on King Charles II

Charles II, Mary's great-grandson, was prepared to undergo public humiliation for the sake of his dogs. When one of his pets was stolen he was forced to insert a distinctly peevish advertisement in a contemporary newspaper to plead for its return: 'Will they never leave off robbing his Majesty? Must he not keep a dog? This dog's place, though better than some imagine, is the only place which nobody offers to beg.'   JAMES SERPELL, 1986

God save your Majesty, but God damn your dogs!

A courtier, to King Charles II

ANNE

Queen Anne had a person and appearance not at all ungraceful, till she grew exceeding gross and corpulent. There was something of Majesty in her look, but mixed with a sullen and constant frown that plainly displayed a gloominess of soul and a cloudyness of disposition within.   SARAH, DUCHESS OF MARLBOROUGH

I had occasion to observe the calamities which attend human nature even in the greatest dignities of life. Her Majesty was labouring under a fit of the gout and in extreme pain and agony, and on this occasion everything about her was much in the same disorder as about the meanest of her subjects. Her face, which was red and spotted, was rendered somewhat frightful by her negligent dress, and the foot affected was tied up with a poultice and some nasty bandages. . . .

What are you, poor mean-like mortal, thought I, who talks in the style of a sovereign? Nature seems to be inverted when a poor infirm woman becomes one of the rulers of the world; but as

47

Tacitus observes, it is not the first time that women have governed in Britain, and indeed they have sometimes done this to better purpose than the men.   SIR JOHN CLERK, 1706

One of the smallest people ever set in a great place.

                                                        WALTER BAGEHOT

APPREHENSION

When, therefore, the people of England read one year, in the journals, of their future King appearing prominently in the Divorce Court, and in another of his being the centre of attention at a German gaming-table, or public hall, it is not at all surprising that rumours concerning the Queen's health have occasioned in many quarters much anxiety and apprehension.

Reynolds' News, 1871, on Albert Edward,
Prince of Wales, later King Edward VII

THE ARMY

What caused the Duke to resign in 1809 was the fact that his mistress had a habit of making pocket money by selling commissions in the army of which her royal lover happened to be Commander in Chief. Otherwise, the Duke was somewhat of a stickler for honesty in the Service.

CHARLES GREVILLE, on Frederick Augustus, 'the Grand Old Duke of York',
second son of King George III. *Diary*, 1827

ART

Richard II was the patron of Chaucer, of Gower, of Froissart, and we have Froissart's word that he was a charming conversationalist in perfect French. He was the employer of Henry Yevole, the greatest of English medieval architects; his reign is the golden age of the brass-engraver, the mural painter and the sculpture of effigies in the round. . . .

Richard was the first King of England to sign his own letters. He was probably the inventor of the handkerchief, and the first English cookery book was especially compiled for him. But the finest testimonies to Richard's love of the arts are still at Westminster. In the Abbey is the superb tomb he ordered for himself and his first wife, and across the way is the great roof of his Westminster Hall.

HAROLD F. HUTCHISON, 1961

Velasquez did not care for Raphael. William the Fourth did not care for Turner: 'Give me Huggins' he cried. W the 4th was not an artist, but, being a sailor, he could probably draw ships, and found Huggins a better sailor than Turner.

JOHN MASEFIELD, to Audrey Napier-Smith, 1953

Masefield too was, briefly, a sailor, though a bad one, and found much to criticize about the nautical observation of Turner, Ruskin, Breughel, and Robert Louis Stevenson. William Huggins (1781–1845), Marine Painter to William IV, has paintings on the Battle of Trafalgar in Hampton Court, information which I owe to Mr William Buchan.

You have got to be careful of artists. You don't know where they have been.

QUEEN VICTORIA

49

Queen Victoria had far too much character and individuality to have good taste. Apart from the creators of art, the majority of human beings acquire by degrees good taste by sinking their own individual likes and dislikes and adopting the suggestions thrust upon them by experts. Now although the Queen had every desire to encourage art generally, she invariably refused to be influenced in any way by other people's opinions, and having very fixed ideas of her own she clung to what she liked.

In portraiture she considered the likeness to be of paramount importance and the artistic merit of the picture itself to be quite a secondary matter. Therefore she admired Angeli, while artists like Watts were unintelligible to her, and the impressionist school she treated as a joke.   SIR FREDERICK PONSONBY, 1951

Male beauty had been an obsession with the young Victoria, and life with Albert, however satisfying physically, had not changed that. Her eye still caught striking examples, in life and in art, and she would continue their cultivation. At a time when nudity in pictures was denounced, from some pulpits, as morally corrupt, when the virile Thackeray thought that William Etty's nudes should be hidden by a 'great, large curtain of fig-leaves', and the prudish, pontifical Ruskin judged William Mulready's nude drawings 'degraded and bestial', Victoria bought nudes. A century later, when the novelist Compton Mackenzie trod the corridors of Buckingham Palace en route to being knighted, he passed an 'almost nude' canvas of Diana, and asked himself what Victoria would have thought of it. Then he read the inscription – that it was one of the young Queen's wedding presents to Albert. She even bought a black and red Mulready drawing for her husband, in which a muscular young man is seen at full length wearing nothing but a beard and an anxious expression. It was apparently a birthday present for Albert in August 1854. Three years later, Victoria's birthday gift to Albert, designed by Emile Jeannest, was a gilded silver statuette of a nude Lady Godiva, side-saddle on her horse.

STANLEY WEINTRAUB, 1987

He enjoyed *La Vie Parisienne* and seaside postcards as much as the next man; he was even once heard singing 'Yes, We Have No Bananas' to shock a particularly staid nember of the Household.

CHRISTOPHER HIBBERT, 1964
on King George V

Here's something to make you laugh, May.

KING GEORGE V, to Queen Mary, on the Impressionists at the Tate Gallery

I tell you what, Turner was mad. My grandmother always said so.

KING GEORGE V, to the Director of the National Gallery

KING GEORGE V: 'Why won't you come and work for me?' [as Surveyor of the King's Pictures]

SIR KENNETH CLARK: 'Because I wouldn't have time to do the job properly.'

KING GEORGE V: 'What is there to do?'

SIR KENNETH CLARK: 'Well, Sir, the pictures need looking after.'

KING GEORGE V: 'There's nothing wrong with them.'

SIR KENNETH CLARK: 'And people write letters asking for information.'

KING GEORGE V: 'Don't answer 'em. *I want you to take the job.*'

KENNETH ROSE, 1983

Perhaps predictably, Sir Kenneth obliged.

The restoration of Brighton Pavilion and the completion of Holyroodhouse showed Queen Mary's and George V's passionate interest in the royal inheritance and their dedication to its preservation. At both Brighton and Holyroodhouse the highest standards both of scholarship and preservation were maintained; both King George and Queen Mary regarded themselves (as, indeed, had many of their ancestors, particularly George IV and Prince Albert) as guardians rather then owners of national treasures. During Queen Mary's lifetime, there was scarcely a major exhibition at the Royal Academy or elsewhere, to which the royal collection did not make an important contribution; and no exhibition of any magnitude went without a visit from the Queen. She was a pillar of strength to the directors of London's museums and particularly the Victoria and Albert Museum, in which she took a special interest. She learned a great deal about conservation, about the need for careful cataloguing, and for proper scholarly research into so vast a collection as she and her husband possessed. During this reign, the royal collections were placed in the hands of distinguished scholars in the world of art – a process which has continued and expanded until the present day.   J. H. PLUMB, 1977

My *The Art of Botanical Illustration*, published (at a guinea) in 1950, was awarded the Veitch Memorial Gold Medal by the Royal Horticultural Society. At the same time I organized an exhibition of Flower Books for the National Book League in London. Queen Mary, then in her eighty-fourth year, honoured it with a visit, and my mother greeted her arrival with a bouquet of gentians, unluckily kicking a fire-bucket in the hall as she entered. (Badinage about 'kicking the bucket' etc. broke the ice.) At the same time, being aware of Her Majesty's amiable tendency to cadge, I presented her with a copy of my book, hoping thereby to forestall any raids on exhibits from my own collection. But she was in an acquisitive mood. 'And to whom do these two pretty paintings of heather [by Franz Bauer] belong?' 'To me, Ma'am.' 'They're very pretty.' 'Yes, Ma'am.' 'Very pretty *indeed* . . . ?' I did not yield, but seemingly she bore me no grudge, for in due course she sent me the signed photograph . . . as well as a Christmas card. . . .

WILFRID BLUNT, 1986

KING ARTHUR

Presently the Saxon pride was checked for awhile by the mighty Arthur, King of the Britons. They were largely repulsed from the island and conquered. But when this very Arthur, following many triumphs which he gloriously achieved in Britain and Gaul, was finally summoned from human activity, the way was clear for the Saxons to return to the island, greatly oppressing the Britons, destroying churches, persecuting saints. This continued through the rule of many kings, Saxon and Briton struggling hither and yon. . . .

In that time, many holy men surrendered to martyrdom; others, obeying the Gospel, left the Greater Britain, now Saxondom, and sailed over to Lesser Britain. . . .

WILLIAM, *The Legend of Saint Goeznovius, c.* 1019

The fundamental riddle of Arthur now solves itself. The *Goeznovius* passage is the only piece of straight, largely verifiable history bringing him in, and we already know, or should know, who its author is talking about. We have already encountered a 'King of the Britons' in the right decade. Both 'William' and, in his fashion, Geoffrey [of Monmouth] take us back to a man for whom we have factual, early, even contemporary witness. He is Riothamus, that Briton whose style in the continental texts, meaning 'Supreme King' or 'High King', looks like a title. . . .

Riothamus was called 'King of the Britons', and there is surely no room for two Britons so called in the same brief span of time. Riothamus led a British army through Gaul in the late 460s. Riothamus very probably fought against the Saxons along the Loire. In late 469, or 470, Riothamus 'was summoned from human activity', departing from his last fatal battlefield to the neighbouring country of the Burgundians, with no recorded death. . . .

The original Arthur-figure is Riothamus the 'High King', who is attested by firm evidence, including a letter to him, the one written by Sidonius. The association of the name with this man is either historically factual or very early. As the point of origin of the Arthurian legend he explains a whole series of its features – the British kingship, the warfare in Gaul during [Emperor] Leo's reign, the Burgundian finale to this, the disaster through a deputy's treason, the departure with no recorded death, the name of Avalon, and even, perhaps, Geoffrey's bizarre date for the Passing. At the very least he is the only documented person who does Arthurian things, the only documented person who can be regarded as under-lying the Legend.   GEOFFREY ASHE, 1982

Over recent decades, Arthurian scholars have arrived at pretty much of a consensus that Arthur was neither a glorified king on the one hand nor a mere myth on the other, but probably a somewhat Romanized Celt or Welsh tribal chieftain sufficiently superior to his contemporaries that his name was preserved and attached to myths that already formed a rich oral tradition, even in his lifetime.

Dr C. Scott Littleton of Occidental College has been labouring in his own vineyard, cultural anthropology, and studying the work of the great French authority in his field, George Dumezil.

Littleton found that Dumezil long ago struck up a friendship with a band of Soviet-Turkish peoples called the Ossetes in the northern Caucasus. These people, surviving in only a handful, are descendants of an ancient warrior people called the Sarmatians, known to Roman historians and first cousins of the violent Scythians of what is now Russia.

The modern Ossetes, Dumezil found, have preserved not only a Sarmatian dialect but also a rich oral epic tradition that reaches back to the pre-Christian era. Dumezil collected the entire cycle of oral epics, which deals with a band of heroes called the Nants, led by Batradz.

Littleton says that he noted with interest – but not particular astonishment – that the death of Batradz was remarkably similar to that of another hero of oral folk epic, Arthur.

Mortally wounded, Batradz is taken to the shore of a sea or lake by his two faithful companions, as was Arthur, where he commands them to throw his sword into the water. Twice a companion deceives Batradz, but he knows the deception, and the third time the sword is thrown in, whereupon the water turns red and becomes turbulent. Batradz then dies. . . .

Littleton found in the Roman historian Dio Cassius that the Sarmatians had, around AD 150, banded together with the pre-Germanic tribes, the Marcomanni and the Quadi, against the local Roman garrisons of Marcus Aurelius in Pannonia, in modern Hungary.

The coalition was defeated and one Roman commander, Lucius Artorius Castus, was later assigned to Britain, to defend the northern frontier along Hadrian's Wall against the Picts.

Castus, mindful of the Sarmatians' ability on the battlefield, asked that Rome give him 5,500 of the 8,000 Sarmatians demanded as tribute from the defeated coalition. These armed cavalry men were called Cataphracti, and were greatly impressive to the Roman foot-soldiers. The Sarmatians themselves, essentially paid mercenaries in their alliance with the Marcomanni and Quadi, easily switched their affections to the Roman conquerors and went off to Britain, settling in the area round modern Ribchester. . . . After a hundred years or so, the Sarmatians were fairly well intermarried with the Celts. And as the Roman era came to a close, slight vestiges of imperial trappings remained behind in the local memory and got woven into the evolving folk tales.

DAVE SMITH. *Spokesman Review*, 1976

King Cradlemas sits by Thames: a mask o'er gilded
covers his wrinkled face, all but one eye.

Cold and small he settles his rump in the cushions.
　　Through the emerald of Nero one short-sighted eye
　　peers at the pedlars of wealth that stand plausibly by.
The bleak mask is gilded with a maiden's motionless smile . . .

Arthur ran; the people marched; in the snow
　　King Cradlemas died in his litter; a screaming few
　　fled; Merlin came; Camelot grew.
In Logres the King's friend landed, Lancelot of Gaul.

CHARLES WILLIAMS, 1938

AUTHORSHIP

I know no person so perfectly disagreeable and even dangerous as an author. KING WILLIAM IV

It has given a great deal of trouble for one who had so carefully to exclude even the slightest observation which might hurt anyone's feelings. But it has been an interest and an occupation – for no-one can conceive the trouble of printing a book and the mistakes which are endless.

QUEEN VICTORIA, 1867, to her daughter, Crown Princess Victoria of Prussia, on her book, *Leaves from the Journal of Our Life in the Highlands*

It is a dreadful and really scandalous book . . . I cannot say how *horrified* and indignant I am at Mr Greville's indiscretion, indelicacy, ingratitude towards friends, betrayal of confidence towards his Soveriegn. . . . QUEEN VICTORIA, 1877, on Charles Greville's memoirs

In my opinion it is *very important* that the book should be severely censured and discredited. . . . The tone in which he speaks of royalty is unlike anything one sees in history even, and is most reprehensible . . . such an abominable book.

QUEEN VICTORIA, to Disraeli, on the Greville memoirs

King George V's approach to literature was respectful without being reverent. He had scarcely reigned one month when Asquith's private secretary telephoned the palace on Thomas Hardy's seventieth birthday to suggest that a telegram to 'old Hardy' might be appreciated.

'It shall be done,' came the reply; and Mr Hardy of Alnwick, who made the King's fishing rods, was astonished to receive royal congratulations on attaining an age he had not attained, on a day which was the anniversary of nothing. KENNETH ROSE, 1983

People who write books ought to be shut up.

KING GEORGE V, on Margot Asquith's memoirs

AUTUMN

All the Highlanders are so amusing, and really pleasant and instructive to talk to — women as well as men — and the latter so gentleman-like. Albert's shots were heard close by whilst we were at luncheon; and there was a general rush of all the people. Albert joined us soon after; he had had a great deal of trouble in stalking his stag, which he had been after several days, but had killed him at one shot. He was brought for us to see: a very light-coloured one, with fine straight horns, of extraordinary thickness. After this we walked on for a beat quite round *Carrop*; and the view was glorious! A little shower of snow had fallen, but was succeeded by brilliant sunshine. The hills covered with snow, the golden birch-trees on the lower brown hills, and the bright afternoon sky, were indescribably beautiful. The following lines (Arthur Hugh Clough) admirably portray what I then saw:

> . . . the gorgeous bright October,
> Then when brackens are changed, and heather blooms are faded,
> And amid russet of heather and fern, green trees are bonnie;
> Alders are green, and oaks; the rowan scarlet and yellow;
> One great glory of broad gold pieces appears the aspen,
> And the jewels of gold that were hung in the hair of the birch-tree,
> Pendulous, here and there, her coronet, necklace, and earrings,
> Cover her now, o'er and o'er; she is weary and scatters them from
> her.

Oh! how I gazed and gazed on God's glorious works with a sad heart, from its being for the last time, and tried to carry the scene away, well implanted and fixed in my mind, for this effect with the snow we shall not often see again. We saw it like this in 1852; but we have not seen it so since, though we have often had snow-storms and showers with a little snow lying on the highest hills.

QUEEN VICTORIA. From her Highland Journal, 1858

BABIES

I think, dearest Uncle, you cannot *really* wish me to be the 'Mamma d'une *nombreuse* famille', for I think you will see with me the great inconvenience a *large* family would be to us all, and particularly to the country, independent of the hardship and inconvenience to myself; men never think, at least seldom think, what a hard task it is for us women to go through this *very often*. God's Will be done.

QUEEN VICTORIA, 1840, to Leopold, King of the Belgians,
following the birth of her eldest child, Victoria

God's Will ordained the birth of nine children to the Queen, a process halted not by God but by her doctors.

BATTLE

Here gat King Athelstan
And eke his brother
Eadmund Atheling
Life long glory
At sword's edge
Round Brunanburgh
Shield-wall they cleft
War-lindens hewed
Sithen sun up
Till the bright being
Sank to his settle.

ANON. Battle of Brunanburgh against the Danes, 937

The Battle of Hastings

At the fiercest point of the battle, the men of Kent and Essex fought magnificently, turning the Normans again and again. . . . Then about a thousand armoured men, led by the Duke, rushed with closed ranks upon the English. The weight of the horses and the blows of the knights now broke the enemy pack, scattering a crowd before them. Many pursued while many fled; many were the Englishmen who fell around and were trampled under the horses, crawling on the earth, unable to rise. Many of the richest and noblest men fell in that rout, but the English still rallied . . . smiting those who came within reach, continuing to fight as best they could, beating down men and killing horses. One Englishman kept his eyes on the Duke, intending to kill him. He would have struck with his spear, but he was too late, for the Duke struck first, and felled him. . . . Loud now was the clamour and great the slaughter; many a soul then quitted the body. The living marched over the heaps of dead, and each side was weary from striking. He who could still charge, did so; he who could raise an arm no longer, still pushed forward. The strong struggled with the strong, some failing, others triumphing; cowards fell back, the brave pressed on; and sad was his fate who fell in the midst, for he had little chance of rising again. In truth, many fell and were crushed beneath the throng.

ROBERT DE WACE. *Roman de Rou, c.* 1160

THE BEGGARS OF BIARRITZ

King Edward VII was, as usual, the central figure around which the local universe revolved. High and low took their cue from him and set their watches by him, often literally.

Among the lowly examples of this was a pair of blind beggars who posted themselves soon after noon every day on the road from the Hotel du Palais to the beach where they would be sure to catch the King on his regular stroll. Caesar (a terrier), who, of course, went on these walks as well, developed a particular dislike for these tattered creatures and would start barking as soon as he spotted them. For them, however, this was a most convenient signal to warn them of the King's approach and, at the dog's first bark, they would put on their most pitiful look and extend their bowls for money. The King never failed to drop a handsome contribution into each bowl and to give them what must have been a most warming greeting: 'A demain.' One day, only one of the beggars turned up. The King's concern that one of his faithful sentinels might be unwell turned to curiosity when the missing man appeared as usual the following morning. Had he been ill? he asked the beggar. No, sire. Late then? This second question threw the poor man into great embarrassment. Finally he blurted out: 'Pardon, Monsieur Le Roi, it was not me who was late but you who were early!'

The King roared with laughter and offered profuse apologies together with his normal contribution.

GORDON BROOK-SHEPHERD, 1975

BERTIE

On Albert Edward, 'Bertie', Prince of Wales and future King Edward VII.

Handsome I cannot think him, with that painfully small and narrow head, those immense features and total want of chin.

QUEEN VICTORIA, to her daughter, Victoria,
Princess Royal. *Letters 1858-61*

She will be able to give before a greedy Multitude disgusting details of your profligacy for the sake of convincing the Jury, yourself cross-examined by a railing indecent attorney and hooted and yelled at by a Lawless Mob! Oh horrible prospect, which this person has in her power, any day to realize! and to break your parents' hearts! ALBERT, PRINCE CONSORT, 1861, to Albert Edward, on the possibility of the latter receiving a paternity suit from the actress, Nellie Clifden

What Fritz [Crown Prince Frederick of Prussia, the Queen's son-in-law] told me of B was no surprise. When papa wrote to me in his last letter of 27th of November: 'I have one deep heart-sore about which do not ask me, please', I knew directly what it was, as more than one rumour has reached me. My grief then was great. . . .

THE CROWN PRINCESS VICTORIA OF PRUSSIA, to her mother, Queen Victoria, December 1861

Thank dear Fritz (who was a great comfort) for his dear letter and all he did and said to poor, unhappy Bertie. Tell him that Bertie (oh! that boy – much as I pity I never can or shall look at him without a shudder as you may imagine) does not know that I know all (beloved papa told him that I should not be told 'the disgusting details'), that I try and employ him and use him – but I am not hopeful. QUEEN VICTORIA, to Crown Princess Victoria

I have so often longed to talk with you about eternity, about our souls and about death – these subjects are so continually occupying me – and I find the more one thinks on them and the deeper one tries to penetrate their nature the more comforted and relieved and calm and courageous one feels!

Poor Bertie, how I pity him! – but what sorrow he does cause. Perhaps you do not even know how much I grieve over his 'fall'. It was the first step to sin and whether it will be the last no-one knows. I fear not. . . .

The educating of sons is an awful responsibility and a great anxiety and it is bitter indeed if they do not repay one for one's care and trouble – it makes me tremble when I think of my little William and the future.

CROWN PRINCESS VICTORIA, mother of the future Emperor Wilhelm II, 'The Kaiser', to Queen Victoria

A thorough and cunning lazybones.

ALBERT, PRINCE CONSORT, on his son, Albert Edward

A little fat man in red.

The *Pall Mall Gazette*

BIRTHDAYS

After luncheon the children played.
1) Arthur and Alice a little duet.
2) Louise a little piece alone, fairly, but not in time.
3) Alice and Lenchen (Helena) a duet beautifully.
4) Alice and Alfie on the violin a little composition of his own –
   very pretty and of which he is not a little proud.
5) Alice a long, beautiful and very difficult sonata by Beethoven.
   Arthur recited a German poem, and Lenchen and Louise have
   something to say – which however has not yet been said.

QUEEN VICTORIA, on her birthday celebrations,
to Crown Princess Victoria of Prussia, 1858

Birthdays were important events in the family calendar. While we
naturally looked forward to our own with eager anticipation, those
of our parents and grandparents invariably confronted us with an
agonizing problem, for the reason that we were expected according
to family custom to render happy birthday greetings with a poem
we had each committed to memory. Even in English this obligation
was difficult enough at best. Under Mr Hansell we had to memorize
and practise reciting excerpts from Shakespeare or Tennyson until
word perfect. But, as we progressed in French and German, more
was expected of us. And with a view to displaying our newly
acquired virtuosity our foreign tutors were ambitious enough to
have us attempt similar performances in their languages. I

remember the labour of memorizing some of La Fontaine's fables – 'La Cigale et la Fourmi', 'Le Courbeau et le Renard', 'La Laitière et le Pot au Lait' – and later the complicated verses of Uhland's 'Das Schwert', and Goethe's stirring ballads 'Der Sänger' and 'Der Erl König'.

Not only were we required to memorize such pieces but we were further obliged to copy them out with painful care on long sheets of white paper, which were then tied together with bright-coloured ribbons. Directly after breakfast on these birthdays we would bear the compositions to the person celebrating. Mary, Bertie and I would advance in turn, each nervously recite his or her poem, and then, with a bow, present the copy. If it was the birthday of my father or my mother, these prodigies of memory were mercifully performed in private. But at Sandringham my grandparents liked to invite their guests to listen. My grandfather always applauded indulgently, but no more so than my grandmother, who was very deaf; hence I was never quite sure how much pleasure either derived from these performances. In any case, for us children the whole business was a nightmare.

EDWARD, DUKE OF WINDSOR, 1951

The King [George VI], it was announced, had decided to abolish the ancient custom whereby the Home Secretary of the day attended and verified each royal birth. . . . In 1948 Mr James Chuter-Ede was thus spared the embarrassment of one of his predecessors, Sir James Graham, who in 1841 had waited uneasily at the end of a huge Palace bedchamber while at the other end Queen Victoria gave birth to the future King Edward VII. After satisfying himself that all was in order, he approached the bed and intoned: 'I congratulate your Majesty most warmly. A very fine boy, if I may say so.' From behind the heavy curtains of the four-poster an indignant voice replied: 'A very fine *Prince*, Sir James.'

ANTHONY HOLDEN, 1979, on the birth of Charles, Prince of Wales

I suppose I'll now be known as Charley's Aunt.

PRINCESS MARGARET, 1948

BISHOPS

With desire I have desired to see your face and to speak with you; greatly for my sake but more for yours. For my sake, that when you see my face you may recall to memory the services which, when I was under your obedience I gave loyally and zealously to the best of my conscience. . . .

For your sake for three causes: because you are my lord, because you are my king, and because you are my spiritual son. According as you are my lord I owe and offer you my counsel and service, such as a bishop owes his superior in the way of God's honour and the honour of Holy Church. And according as you are my king I am bound to you in reverence and respect. And according as you are my son I am bound by reason of my office to chasten and correct you. . . .

It is certain that kings receive their power from the Church. . . .

THOMAS BECKET, Archbishop of Canterbury, to King Henry II, 1166

What miserable drones and traitors have I nourished and promoted in my household, who let their lord be presented with such shameful contempt by a low-born clerk!

KING HENRY II, on Thomas Becket, 1170

The sword hath been plunged into the very pupil of Christ's eye.

KING LOUIS VII OF FRANCE, on the murder of Becket, 1170

When the Papal legate had seated himself on a raised throne in the middle, and Richard, Archbishop of Canterbury, by right of pri-

65

macy, had sat down on his right, then Roger, Archbishop of York, swollen with his own peculiar arrogance, rejected the other throne on the left that was marked as his own and strove with slight reverence to force himself between the legate and His Grace of Canterbury, thrusting with the less sightly quarters of his body so that he sat down upon his own Primate's lap! Yet hardly had he struck my Lord of Canterbury with the elbow with which he usually fought, than he was humiliatingly grabbed by certain bishops, clerics and laymen, and wrenched from the Archbishop's lap, and thrown upon the ground. But, with staves and fists now being wielded by both factions, the Archbishop of Canterbury leapt up and returned good for evil, snatching away from this disastrous struggle his own rival and his see's unyielding foe. Finally, the contumacious Archbishop of York, rising from the floor with his cape in ignominious tatters from the brawl, fell at the King's feet and spewed out lying slanders against the Archbishop of Canterbury.

GERVASE OF CANTERBURY, on a church conference
held before King Henry II, 1176.
Gesta Pontificum, 12th century

I dined with sixteen bishops the other day and humbugged them gloriously, to their very hearts' content. It was delightful to see how they swallowed it.

WILLIAM, DUKE OF CLARENCE, later King William IV, 1827

A Bishop ought to abstain *completely* from mixing himself up with the politics of the day, and beyond giving a general support to the *Queen's Government*, and occasionally voting for it, should take no part in the discussion of State affairs (for instance, Corn Laws, Game Laws, Trade or Financial questions, etc. etc.); but he should come forward whenever the interests of Humanity are at stake, and give boldly and manfully his advice to the House and the Country (I mean questions like Negro Emancipation, Education of the people, improvement of the health of towns, measures for the recreation of the poor, against cruelty to animals, for regulating factory labour, etc. etc.). . . .

He should likewise boldly admonish the public even against its predominant feeling, if this be contrary to the purest standard of morality (reproving, for instance, the recklessness and the wickedness of the Projectors of Railway schemes, who, having no funds themselves, acquire riches at the expense of others, their dupes). Here the nation is in the greatest danger, as every individual gets corrupted, and every sense of shame is lost.

ALBERT, PRINCE CONSORT, to Dr Wilberforce,
Dean of Westminster, 1845

I do not like Bishops.

QUEEN VICTORIA

I had to tell him to get off it pretty sharply.

KING GEORGE V, on a bishop who stood on
the royal robe during the coronation

THE BLOCKHEAD

It is intolerable that it should be in the power of one blockhead to do so much mischief. CHARLES JAMES FOX, on King George III, 1781

BLOOD

On the childhood in France of Mary Stuart, later Queen of Scots

CATHERINE DE' MEDICI, Queen of France: 'Do you perceive any catastrophe menacing that fair head?'
DR MICHEL DE NOSTRADAMUS: 'Madam, I see blood.'

ANNE BOLEYN

Anne Boleyn's Song

'After the terrible rain, the Annunciation' –
The bird-blood in the veins that has changed to emeralds
Answered the bird-call. . . .
In the neoteric Spring the winter coldness
Will be forgotten
As I forget the coldness of my last lover,

The great grey King
Who lies upon my breast
And rules the bird-blood in my veins that shrieked with laughter
– A sound like fear –
When my step light and high
Spurned my sun down from the sky
In my heedless headless dance –
O many a year ago, my dear,
My living lass!

In the nights of Spring, the bird, the Angel of the Annunciation
Broods over his heaven of wings and of green wild-fire
That each in its own world, each in its egg
Like Fate is lying.

He sang to my blood, as Henry, my first King,
My terrible sun
Came like the Ethos of Spring, the first green streak,
And to me cried,
'Your veins are the branches where the first blossom begins
After the winter rains –
Your eyes are black and deep
As the prenatal sleep
And your arms and your breasts are my Rivers of Life
While a new world grows in your side.'

Men said I was the primal Fall,
That I gave him the world of spring and of youth like an apple
And the orchards' emerald lore –
And sin lay at the core.

But Henry thought me winter-cold
When to keep his love I turned from him as the world
Turns from the sun . . . and then the world grew old –

But I who grew in the heart as the bird-song
Grows in the heart of Spring . . . I, terrible Angel
Of the emeralds in the blood of man and tree,
How could I know how cold the nights of Spring would be

When my grey glittering King –
Old amorous Death grew acclimatized to my coldness:
His age sleeps on my breast,
My veins, like branches where the first peach-blossom
Trembles, bring the Spring's warmth to his greyness.

EDITH SITWELL, 1944

SIR THOMAS MORE: 'How fares the Queen?'
MARGARET, his daughter: 'Never better. There is nothing in the
Court but dancing and sporting.'
SIR THOMAS MORE: 'Alas, it pitieth me to think into what misery she
will shortly come. Those dances of hers will spurn off our
heads like footballs, but it will not be long ere she will dance
headless.'
The Tower of London, 1535

'Master Kingston, I hear say that I shall not die afore noon, and I
am very sorry therefore, for I thought to be dead by this time and
past my pain . . . I heard say the executioner was very good, and it is
so little a neck.'
QUEEN ANNE BOLEYN, to Sir William Kingston,
Governor of the Tower, 1536

That poor ghost, with her gay light dancing movements, went to her nameless grave in the Tower. And her daughter would never, in all her long life, speak her name. The fact that it had once been part of a living reality must be kept in silence for ever, like some appalling obscene secret. Yet through all the life of that child, until she was an old woman, the unnamed ghost, the phantom of her mother's supposed sin, would rise from the grave and come, in the warmth of the sun and the fire of the full moon, bringing the chill of its death and the real or imagined fever of lust that not even death could assuage, to stand between Elizabeth and happiness, or to add its own horror to a later horror, its blood to blood that was still wet. . . .

After the execution of Mary Queen of Scots, those floods of tears, that refusal to eat and inability to sleep. . . . What did Elizabeth see, as she stared before her? Two heads, not one, lying in the dust – a head with greying hair, and a young head with long black hair and great slanting eyes? EDITH SITWELL, 1963

In Spain and Portugal, an *Ana-Bolena* means an evil, designing woman. In Sicily up at least until the 1850s the heretical queen was believed to be confined beneath Mount Etna as punishment for her sins. MARIE LOUISE BRUCE, 1972

Queen Anne Boleyn, popularly regarded as a witch, inspired legends of being seen in the fields as a hare.

BOUDICCA

Boadicea, 'relished by the learned as Boudicca'.
WINSTON CHURCHILL

She was very tall and her aspect was terrifying, for her eyes flashed with ferocity and her voice was rough. Her red hair tumbled in masses down to her hips, and around her neck was a twisted gold torque: over a multi-coloured tunic she wore a thick mantle fastened by a brooch, her invariable costume. Now she grasped a spear to over-awe all who watched, and then harangued them. . . .

On finishing, she consulted the will of the gods by letting a hare escape from the folds of her robe: it fled in what was reckoned a propitious direction, and the mob uttered a tremendous shout. Boudicca then lifted both hands aloft and cried, 'Andrasta, I give you thanks, and call upon you as one woman to another. . . . I implore you for victory and the preservation of our freedom. Lady, be you our leader.'

DIO CASSIUS, 2nd century AD

Designed though it was to titillate Roman sensation-seekers, this picture has the ring of truth about it. Boudicca's golden torque, her brooched mantle and multicoloured – perhaps tartan – tunic all accord with what we know of aristocratic Celtic dress, and Caesar mentions the hare as an animal especially sacred to the Britons. (Long after Christianization, indeed, British witches were regularly credited with the power to turn themselves into hares, and as recently as 1969 the author was assured in a remote Lincolnshire village that a local woman still did so.) The ritual with the hare, the spear, the flashing eyes and harsh voice all combine to give an overwhelming impression of an almost superhuman figure, a great priestess as much as a great ruler. Whether or not she was precisely a sacred queen, it seems more likely that Boudicca's followers saw her as the direct representative of Andrasta, the goddess she invoked.

One further speculation. Andrasta's name seems to mean 'the Invincible One', but Dio later translated it as 'Victoria' – which was, of course, the meaning of Boudicca's own name.

CHARLES KIGHTLY, 1982

THE CHAIR

On a chair needed to hoist the Queen of Württemberg from her yacht, 1831:

ADMIRAL SIR THOMAS BYAM MARTIN: 'I have just the thing.'

KING WILLIAM IV: 'No such thing. You have no notion of her size.'

ADMIRAL MARTIN: 'Sir, the chair is of dimensions to receive any two women in the Kingdom.'

KING WILLIAM: 'I tell you it won't do; she is larger than any three women, aye, than any four women.'

ADMIRAL MARTIN: 'Sir, what I speak of is more like a sofa than a chair.'

KING WILLIAM: 'I tell you again, it won't do, and I desire you will get a larger.'

CHARLES I

His deportment was very majestic, for he could not let fall his dignity . . . for though he was far from pride, yet he was careful of majesty, and would be approached with respect and reverence. . . .

His way of urging was very civil, for he seldom contradicted another by his authority, but by reason . . . he offered his exception by this civil introduction: 'By your favour, Sir, I think otherwise on this or that ground.'

SIR PHILIP WARWICK. *Memoirs of the Reign of Charles I*, 1701

His kingly virtues had some mixture and alloy, that hindered them from shining in full lustre, and from producing those fruits they should have been attended with. He was not in his nature very bountiful, though he gave very much. This appeared more after the duke of Buckingham's death, after which those showers fell very rarely; and he paused too long in giving, which made those to whom he gave, less sensible of the benefit. He kept state to the full, which made his court very orderly; no man presuming to be seen in a place where he had no pretence to be. He saw and observed men long, before he received them about his person; and did not love strangers; nor very confident men. He was a patient hearer of causes; which he frequently accustomed himself to at the council board; and judged very well, and was dexterous in the medicating part: so that he often put an end to causes by persuasion, which the stubbornness of men's humours made dilatory in courts of justice.

He was very fearless in his person, but not very enterprising. He had an excellent understanding, but was not confident enough of it; which made him oftentimes change his own opinion for a worse, and follow the advice of men that did not judge so well as himself. This made him more irresolute than the conjecture of his affairs would admit: if he had been of a rougher and more imperious nature he would have found more respect and duty. And his not applying some severe cures to approaching evils proceeded from the levity of his nature, and the tenderness of his conscience, which, in all cases of blood, made him choose the softer way, and not hearken to severe counsels, how reasonably soever urged.

EDWARD HYDE, EARL OF CLARENDON.
History of the Rebellion, 1702–4

On one occasion when the King and Queen were dining in public, and the King's chaplain began to say an Anglican grace, the Queen's confessor began a Latin one. At this the chaplain gave the confessor 'a zealous push', but he moved to the Queen's side and continued in Latin. The King stopped the competition by setting the carvers to work, but at the end of the meal chaplain and confessor began again, each trying to shout the other down.

Eventually the King decided to expel [the Queen's] French [440 courtiers], first ordering them from Whitehall to Somerset House, then to leave the country. When he told the Queen she was so angry that she pulled the hair from her head and ran her hands through a window, severely cutting them. And for a month the courtiers refused to leave. Eventually the King was forced to send 'the captain of the guard, attended with a competent number of his yeomen, as likewise with heralds, messengers, and trumpeters' to Somerset House with orders to turn them out 'by head and shoulders', and shut the gate after them. At this 'their courage came down and they yielded'. Nevertheless it took four days for them to leave and forty carts to transport them to Dover. And they took with them all the Queen's clothes except for a gown and two smocks. At Dover, as Madam St George, the Queen's Mistress of the Wardrobe, stepped into the boat, one of the crowd threw a stone at her 'strange headdress', at which a gentleman escort ran the man through with his sword, killing him. From France the expelled courtiers sent the Queen a bill for £19,000 in unpaid debts.

THOMAS HINDE, 1986, on the problems of King Charles I
and his Roman Catholic French Queen, Henrietta Maria

CHARLES II

A tall dark young man above two yards high.

From the Rump Parliament's appeal for the capture
of the defeated Charles II after the Battle of Worcester, 1651

Odd's Fish, I am an ugly fellow! 　　　　　　KING CHARLES II

I shall find means to pay the Fleet, and manage economically; it will be difficult and uncomfortable for me, but I will submit to anything rather than endure the Gentlemen of the Commons any longer.

KING CHARLES II

Witty in all sorts of conversation, and telling a story so well that, not out of Flattery, but the Pleasure of hearing it, we seemed ignorant of what he had repeated to us ten times before.

LORD SHEFFIELD, on King Charles II

He was a prince of many virtues, and many great imperfections; debonair, easy of access, not bloody nor cruel; his countenance fierce, his voice great, proper of person, every motion became him; a lover of the sea, and skilful in shipping; not affecting other studies, yet he had a laboratory, and knew of many empirical medicines, and the easier mechanical mathematics; he loved lanting and building, and brought in a politer way of living, which passed to luxury and intolerable expense. He had a particular talent in telling a story, and facetious passages, of which he had innumerable; this made some buffoons and vicious wretches too presumptuous and familiar, not worthy the favour they abused. ... He would doubtless have been an excellent prince, had he been less addicted to women, who made him uneasy, and always in want to supply their unmeasurable profusion, to the detriment of many indigent persons who had signally served both him and his father. He frequently and easily changed favourites to his great prejudice.

JOHN EVELYN

CHILDHOOD

How as a chapman bears his pack,
I bore thy Grace upon my back
And sometimes straddling on my neck
Dancing with many a bend and beck.

SIR DAVID LYNDSAY, on the childhood of
King James V of Scotland

Now as my lady Elizabeth is put from that degree she was in, and what degree she is at now I know not, but by hearsay, I know not how to order her or myself, or her women or grooms. I beg you to be good lord to her and hers, and that she may have raiment, for she has neither gown nor kirtle nor petticoat, nor linen for smocks, nor kerchiefs, sleeves, rails, body stychets, handkerchiefs, mufflers nor legens. . . .

Mr Shelton would have my lady Elizabeth to dine and sup every day at the board of estate. It is not meet for a child of her age to keep such rule. If she do, I dare not take it upon me to keep her Grace in health, for she will see divers meats, fruits, and wine, that it will be hard for me to refrain her from. Ye know, my lord, there is no place of correction there, and she is too young to correct greatly.

> LADY BRYAN, guardian to Princess Elizabeth,
> later Queen Elizabeth I, to Thomas Cromwell, 1536

I will send my pistolles by Master Newton. I will give anie thing I have, both my horses and my books and my pieces and my cross-bowes, or anie thing that you would haive. Good Brother love me and I shall ever loove you.

> CHARLES, DUKE OF YORK, later King Charles I,
> in childhood, to Henry, Prince of Wales

A drawing room yesterday, at which Princess Victoria made her first appearance, a short vulgar-looking child.

> CHARLES GREVILLE. *Diary*, 1831

The most upright child I ever knew and yet arch.

> THE DUCHESS OF NORTHUMBERLAND, state
> governess to Princess, later Queen, Victoria

Thersie was at Church twice to-day. A few days ago she was teaching Florence and asking her who had died for us on the Cross. 'Lord Chesterfield', replied Florence promptly, having heard a good deal lately about his death in connection with the Prince of Wales and Londesborough Lodge. FRANCIS KILVERT. *Diary*, 1871

When I was four years old I went to a Children's Christmas party at the Castle. . . .

When we were all seated at long tables, enjoying a very good meal, the door opened and Queen Victoria entered, accompanied by a Lady-in-Waiting. We were all called to attention and told to stand up and stop eating. The Queen passed slowly along each table, saying a few words to each child. She was told by the Lady-in-Waiting, I suppose, who we all were. Perhaps they had a table plan. I had just greedily grabbed a lot of grapes and piled them on my plate. When the Queen reached me, she said: 'What a lot of grapes you've got.' And I replied, shrilly, but audibly, 'Yes, Queen.' Then she said: 'I expect you'd like me to go away, so that you can eat all those grapes.' And I replied again, 'Yes, Queen.' Whereat she turned to her Lady-in-Waiting and said: 'What a loud voice that child has, just like his father!' For he, of course, had often preached to her, and no one could fall asleep during one of his sermons.

HUGH DALTON, 1953

CLOTHES

Three shillings! You son of a whore, since when has the King worn such a cheap pair of shoes? Go and bring me some for a silver mark.

KING WILLIAM II, to his Chamberlain

A dress of white satin embroidered with leeches, water and rocks, hung with fifteen silver-gilt mussels and fifteen cockles of white

silver, doublet embroidered with gold orange trees on which were
set a hundred silver-gilt oranges.

SACHEVERELL SITWELL, 1969, on the attire of King Richard II

When Henry VI had to don his robes of state for some state
occasion, he atoned for the sin by wearing a hair-shirt underneath.
He was too good for this world; in the end he was put out of it.

A. L. ROWSE, 1966

Robes	19
French Gowns	102
Round Gowns	67
Loose Gowns	100
Kirtles	126
Petticoats	125
Cloaks	96
Bodices	85
Fans	27

From an inventory of Queen Elizabeth I's clothes

Brummell, on establishing himself in London, at once assumed the
position of leader of the *beaux*, and to Chesterfield Street came all
the men of fashion of the day. His pretensions to this high office
were resolutely backed by the Prince of Wales [later King George
IV], who was a constant visitor. His Royal Highness called nearly
every morning, and had long discussions on dress with the young
man, which discussions lasted often until the hour of dinner, when
the Prince would condescend to remain and partake of the meal.

Backed by the Prince, Brummell laid down the law on the vital
questions of attire in no uncertain manner. He ruled his world in a
kindly manner, as may a despot whose sway is unchallenged; but he
would brook no rival near his throne. Many a one tried a lance with
him, only to come wounded out of the fray. Badinage was the
young man's weapon, and a nicely calculated insolence was his

shield; and so skilful was he in the play of wits that but rarely was he overcome. Like Beau Nash at Bath, Brummell was no respecter of persons. It was not the case of his being first among equals; in his kingdom he was monarch, the rest his subjects. More than once he reduced the Heir Apparent to despair by caustic comment on his clothes; and on one occasion, Tom Moore has put it on record, the Prince 'began to blubber when told that Brummell did not like the cut of his coat'.   LEWIS MELVILLE, 1924

Dress is a trifling matter, but it gives also the outward sign from which people in general can and often do judge upon the *inward* state of mind and feeling. . . .

We do not wish to control your tastes and fancies, which, on the contrary, we wish you to indulge and develop, but we do *expect* that you will never wear anything *extravagant* or *slang*, not because we don't like it, but because it would prove a want of self-respect and be an offence against decency, leading – as it has often done in others – to an indifference to what is morally wrong.

QUEEN VICTORIA, 1854 to Albert Edward, Prince of Wales

The Queen must have spun in her grave forty-six years later, in the second year of Edward VII's reign, when the King arrived at Marienbad station wearing a green cap, a pink tie and white gloves, with knee-breeches, grey slippers and a brown overcoat with loud checks.   ANTHONY HOLDEN, 1979

Is it raining in here?

KING GEORGE V, at Buckingham Palace, observing the turned-up trousers of his son, Edward, Prince of Wales, later King Edward VIII.

Lord Stamfordham then spoke at some length about clothes. Will Labour Ministers wear Court dress and frock coats at Privy Councils? The King [George V], it seems, is very touchy about all this. He once refused to take John Burns in his carriage to some function, where Burns was to be Minister in Attendance, because he appeared in a bowler instead of a top hat. When the King wanted to invite J. Ramsay MacDonald, who had recently become Leader of the Opposition, Stamfordham was sent to ask him whether, if invited, he would come and whether he would wear the right clothes. This was the only time Stamfordham had met J.R.M., who had been 'very courteous' and struck him as being 'quite a gentleman'. He had, indeed, made Stamfordham feel very awkward for he had said that, of course, if he was invited to dine at the Palace, he would accept and wear the right clothes. Stamfordham had made a joke about frock coats, saying that he knew that J.R.M.'s colleague, Arthur Henderson, had a beautiful frock coat. J.R.M. had replied: 'Yes, but don't imagine he bought that in order to go to the Palace as a Privy Councillor. He bought it because he is a Methodist preacher. . . .'

J.R.M. of course loved dressing up, so as to show off his good looks. That was human enough! But some others appeared very ridiculous, even in black knee-breeches with evening dress. I remember a devastating photograph of Sidney Webb and Noel Buxton, the dwarf and the stork, side by side in this get-up, crowned with opera hats, outside the Palace. This photograph was circulated in Glasgow, by the I.L.P., over the caption, 'Was this what you voted for?'

HUGH DALTON, on the first Labour Government of 1924

COMPROMISE

Lord Kinross says that the Queen once asked a friend, 'What do you do when your husband wants something badly and you don't want him to have it?'

'Well, Ma'am,' her friend replied, 'I try to reason with him and sometimes we reach a compromise.'

'Oh, that's not my method,' said the Queen. 'I tell Philip he shall have it and then make sure he doesn't get it.'

Time and Tide, 1963, on Elizabeth II

THE COOK

I don't want the Princess to be seen with that cook.

(attrib.) ALBERT EDWARD, Prince of Wales, 1878, on Madame Grévy,
wife of the President of France.

COURTS

The men thrust their toes, the very limits of their bodies, into contraptions resembling snakes curled up like scorpions. Sweeping the dusty floors with vast trains of robe and mantle, they enclose their hands with gloves too broad and lengthy for practical use, and, over-burdened by this useless stuff, find all their limbs degenerating into impotence. Their brows are plucked, like those of criminals, while at the back of their heads they train long tresses, like whores. Such hair is curled with hot irons, and, instead of caps they wear ribbons.

ORDERICUS VITALIS, on the court of King Henry I.
Historia Ecclesia, c. 1141

If the King had promised to remain in a place for that day – and especially if he had announced his intention publicly by the mouth of a herald – he is sure to upset all the arrangements by departing early in the morning. As a result, you see men dashing around as if they were mad, beating their packhorses, running their carts into one another – in short, giving a lively imitation of Hell. If, on the other hand, the King orders an early start, he is certain to change his mind, and you can take it for granted that he will sleep until midday. Then you will see the packhorses loaded and waiting, the carts prepared, the courtiers dozing, traders fretting and everyone grumbling. . . . When our courtiers had gone ahead almost the whole day's ride, the King would turn aside to some other place where he had, it might be, just a single house with accommodation for himself and no one else. I hardly dare say it, but I believe that in truth he took a delight in seeing what a fix he put us in. After wandering some three or four miles in an unknown wood, and often in the dark, we thought ourselves lucky if we stumbled upon some filthy little hovel. There was often a sharp and bitter argument about a mere hut, and swords were drawn for possession of a lodging which pigs would have shunned.

PETER DE BLOIS, a royal chaplain, on King Henry II's court on the move

The court would descend upon an estate, strip it of current produce, and move on to the next. The Monarch, too, had the habit of descending upon some powerful subject, ostensibly to do him honour, but not infrequently with the deliberate intent to impoverish him and so weaken a possible centre of disaffection. Elizabeth I was particularly fond of these raiding expeditions, conducted under the guise of a 'Progress', though her popularity took the sting out of them.

RUSSELL CHAMBERLAIN, 1986

Her Majesty's so often coming and not going so distempers all things with me as upon every change of coming I do nothing but give orders into the country for new provisions: most of the old thrown away by reason of the heat.

SIR THOMAS CECIL, to William Cecil, Lord Burghley, on Queen Elizabeth I

Marjorie Reeves, 1956, mentions provisions provided by Lord North, on a three days' sojourn with him at Kirtling by Queen Elizabeth I:

67 sheep, 34 pigs, 4 stags and 16 bucks used for 176 pastries, 1,200 chickens, 363 capons, 33 geese, 6 turkeys, 237 dozen pigeons, a great many pheasants and partridges, cartloads of oysters and fish, 2,500 eggs and 430 lbs of butter.

Hear now what pains have courtiers in sleeping.
They oftentimes sleep full wretchedly in pain,
And lie all the night in cold wind and rain . . .
Sometimes a leper is signed to thy bed,
Or with other sore one grievously bested.
Sometime thy bedfellow is colder than ice,
To him he draweth thy clothes in a trice.
But if he be hot, by fevers then shall he
Cast all thy clothes and coverlets on thee.
Either is thy fellow alway to thee grievous,
Or else to him art thou alway tedious.
And sometimes these courtiers them more to encumber,
Sleep all in one chamber near twenty in number,
Then it is great sorrow for to abide their shout,
Some fart, some flingeth, and others snort and rout.
Some boke, some babble, some cometh drunk to bed,
Some brawl and some jangle when they be beastly fed.
Some laugh, and some cry, each man will have his will,
Some spew, and some piss, and not one of them is still.

ALEXANDER BARCLAY (d. 1552). From *Eclogue III*

The face of the court was much changed, for King Charles I was temperate, chaste, and serious, so that the fools and bawds, mimics and catamites of the former court grew out of fashion; and the nobility and courtiers, who did not quite abandon their debaucheries, had yet that reverence to the king to retire into corners to practise them.

LUCY HUTCHINSON (b. 1620).
From *Memoirs of the Life of Colonel Hutchinson*, 1806

This evening, according to custom, his Majesty opened the revels of that night by throwing the dice himself in the privy-chamber, where there was a table set on purpose, and lost his 100L. (The year before he won 1500L.) The ladies also played very deep. I came away when the Duke of Ormond had won about 1000L, and left them still at passage, cards, etc. At other tables, both there and at the Groom-porter's, observing the wicked folly and monstrous excess of passion amongst some losers; sorry am I that such a wretched custom as play to that excess should be countenanced in a Court, which ought to be an example of virtue to the rest of the Kingdom.

JOHN EVELYN

This day comes news from Harwich that the Dutch fleet are all in sight, near 100 sail great and small, they think, coming towards them; where, they think, they shall be able to oppose them; but do cry out of the falling back of the seamen, few standing by them, and those with much faintness. The like they write from Portsmouth, and their letters this post are worth reading. Sir H. Cholmley came to me this day, and tells me the Court is as mad as ever; and that the night the Dutch burned our ships the King did sup with my Lady Castlemaine, at the Duchess of Monmouth's, and there were all mad in hunting of a poor moth.

SAMUEL PEPYS, on the court of King Charles II, 1667

Anxious letters passed between Ottawa and London on whether the Governor General of Canada should emboss a royal crown on his stationery, the device of Buckingham Palace, instead of the gubernatorial blue. A Lady of the Bedchamber was allowed a two-horse carriage from the Royal Mews to take her to and from her duties at the palace; a woman of the Bedchamber warranted only a one-horse brougham. An equerry was reproved for addressing an envelope 'His Majesty the King'; the correct style was simply 'the King', although Queen Mary was to be addressed as 'Her Majesty the Queen'. The twin daughters of Major-General Lord Ruthven were denied admission to the royal enclosure at Ascot because they were actresses; their father showed his resentment by refusing the KCVO traditionally conferred on the General Officer commanding London District. Lady Astor, invited to a state banquet at Buckingham Palace [1923] for the King and Queen of Rumania, created scarcely less of a scandal by going up to the dais after dinner and sitting in one of the four royal chairs for a gossip with the visiting Queen.

And always there were disputes about precedence. The Lord Chamberlain, the Lord Steward and the Master of the Horse argued interminably about their places at court. Staying at Windsor, Winifred, Duchess of Portland, insisted on going ahead of the Duchess of Roxburghe, whose rightful place it was, claiming that a former Mistress of the Robes took precedence of all other Duchesses for the rest of her life. When the Allied Prime Ministers came to London in 1918, should the Duke of Connaught go in front of Lloyd George or Orlando behind Clemenceau? 'The German war', Hankey wrote, 'was a trifle compared to this.'

KENNETH ROSE, 1983, on the court of King George V

COURTSHIP

It is more than probable that the passion which Matilda cherished for the fair-haired English envoy, was the most formidable of all the obstacles with which her cousin, William of Normandy, had to contend during the tedious period of his courtship.

A less determined character would have given up the pursuit as hopeless; but William, having once fixed his mind upon this marriage, was not to be deterred by difficulties or discouragements. It was in vain that his foes and jealous kinsmen intrigued against him in the Flemish court; that the parents of the lady objected to his illegitimate birth and doubtful character to the Duchy of Normandy; that the Church of Rome interdicted the marriage between parties within the forbidden degrees of consanguinity; and, worse than all, the lady herself treated him with coldness and hauteur. After seven years' delay, William appears to have become desperate; and if we may trust the evidence of the chronicle of Inger, he, in the year 1047, waylaid Matilda in the streets of Bruges as she was returning from Mass, seized her, rolled her in the dirt, spoiled her rich array, and, not content with these outrages, struck her repeatedly, and rode off at full speed. This Teutonic method of courtship, according to our author, brought the affair to a crisis, for Matilda, either convinced of the strength of William's passion by the violence of his behaviour, or afraid of encountering a second beating, consented to become his wife.

AGNES STRICKLAND, 1840, on Duke William of Normandy,
later King William I of England, and Matilda of Flanders

William proved a devoted husband, and the marriage had a success rare in a turbulent and masculine era. Of Matilda Jeremy Potter writes (1986): 'She stood no more than four feet two inches high, but that proved sufficient for the production of twelve children healthy enough to reach adulthood.' Miss Strickland mentions that an examination of William's body, 1542, showed it 'exceeding in stature the tallest man then known'.

THE COWARD

I thank God there is but one of my children who wants courage — and I will not name him, because he is to succeed me.

KING GEORGE III, on George, Prince of Wales, later King George IV

THE CRYSTAL PALACE

Mathematicians have calculated that the Crystal Palace will blow down in the first strong gale; Engineers that the galleries would crash in and destroy the visitors; Political Economists have prophesied a scarcity of food in London owing to the vast concourse of people; Doctors that owing to so many races coming into contact with each other the Black Death of the Middle Ages would make its appearance as it did after the Crusades; Moralists that England would be infected by all the scourges of the civilized and uncivilized world; Theologians that this second Tower of Babel would draw upon it the vengeance of an offended God.

I can give no guarantee against these perils, nor am I in a position to assume responsibility for the possibly menaced lives of your Royal relatives.

ALBERT, PRINCE CONSORT, to Wilhelm I, King of Prussia

THE CURE

The symptoms of Henry's disease first appeared in August 1612, and his condition grew rapidly worse. The preposterous treatment to which he was subjected, which included the application to his body of the flesh of newly killed cocks and pigeons, did not help, and by November his condition was desperate. The final treatment, a medicine concocted by Sir Walter Raleigh, consisting of pearl, musk, hartshorn, bezoarstone, mint, borage, gentian, mace, sugar, aloes and spirits of wine, administered on his mother's orders, together with a violent purge prescribed by the physician, was enough to kill him on 12 November 1612. He had probably been suffering from typhoid.

D. R. WATSON, 1972, on Henry, Prince of Wales, elder son of King James I

THE DANCER

The world had fallen into winter, and the strawberry paths of the Palace gardens were white with frost as they had been in spring, with the dew. And the cold, almost like that of death, had invaded the heart and veins of the Queen. The deaths of ladies about the Queen (the Countess of Nottingham – the daughter of Lord Hunsdon – Lady Peyton of the Tower, Lady Skolt, and Lady Heyward) seemed like leaves falling, and added to the Queen's melancholy.

Once Lord Semphill, looking through a window of a room in the Palace, saw the old Queen dancing to the sound of a pipe and tabor, leaping into the air like a tall thin flame with, as sole companion apart from the musicians, Lady Warwick, who for forty years as girl, wife, and widow, had been her faithful servant.

EDITH SITWELL, 1963, on Queen Elizabeth I

I am agreeable to see that the Queen dances like a pot.

A Danish aristocrat at the court of Queen Victoria, 1879

DANGER

Pooh! don't talk to me that stuff!

KING GEORGE II, 1745, hearing that Prince Charles Edward's
rebel army had reached Derby

While the guards and his own people now surrounded the King, the assassin was seized by the populace . . . when the King, the only calm and moderate person then present, called aloud to the mob, 'The poor creature is mad! Do not hurt her! She has not hurt me!'

Then he came forward, and showed himself to all the people, declaring he was perfectly safe and unhurt; and then gave positive orders that the woman should be taken care of, and went into the palace, and had his levée.

FANNY BURNEY, on the attempted stabbing of King George III
by Margaret Nicholson. *Diary,* 1786

Never shall I forget His Majesty's coolness. The whole audience was in an uproar. The King on hearing the report of the pistol retired a pace or two, stopped, and stood firmly for an instant, then came forward to the front of the box, put his opera glass to his eye, and looked round the house without the slightest appearance of alarm or discomposure.

MICHAEL KELLY, on the attempted shooting of King George III
by James Hadfield at Drury Lane Theatre. *Memoirs,* 1800

On Wednesday afternoon, as the Queen and Prince Albert were driving in a low carriage up Constitution Hill, about four or five in the afternoon, they were shot at by a lad of eighteen years old, who fired two pistols at them successively, neither shots taking effect. He was in the Green Park without the rails, and as he was only a few yards from the carriage, and, moreover, very cool and collected, it is marvellous that he should have missed his aim. In a few moments the young man was seized, without any attempt on his part to escape or to deny the deed, and was carried off to prison. The Queen, who appeared perfectly cool, and not the least alarmed, instantly drove to the Duchess of Kent's, to anticipate any report that might reach her mother, and, having done so, she continued her drive and went to the Park. By this time the attempt upon her life had become generally known, and she was received with the utmost enthusiasm by the immense crowd that was congregated in carriages, on horseback, and on foot. All the equestrians formed themselves into an escort, and attended her back to the Palace, cheering vehemently. . . . (1840)

This young Queen, who is an object of interest, and has made no enemies, has twice had attempts made on her life within two years. George III, a very popular King, was exposed to similar attempts, but in his case the perpetrators were really insane; while George IV, a man neither beloved nor respected, and at different times very odious and unpopular, was never attacked by anyone. (1842)

CHARLES GREVILLE, Diary

Danger lies not in the power given to the Lower Orders, who are becoming more well-informed and more intelligent, and who will *deservedly* work themselves to the top by their own merits, labour and good conduct, but in the conduct of the *Higher Classes* and of the *Aristocracy*.   QUEEN VICTORIA

DEATH

Cynddylan's hall is dark tonight,
There burns no fire, no bed is made,
I weep awhile, and then am quiet.

Cynddylan's hall is dark tonight,
No fire is lit, no candle burns,
God will keep my wits straight.

Cynddylan's hall. It stabs me
To see it without roof or fire.
My lord is dead, and I remain.

Cynddylan's hall is desolate tonight
Where once I sat in honour.
Men who held it are gone, gone are women.

> Cynddylan's hall. Black the roof
> Since the English slaughtered
> Cynddylan, also Elvan of Powys. . .
>
> ANON. From a lament for a seventh-century Welsh leader,
> ally of King Penda of Mercia

The nobles mounted their steeds and fled with all speed to secure their possessions. But the menials, seeing their lords vanishing, laid hands on the armour, plate, robes, linen, and all the royal furniture, and, leaving the corpse almost naked on the floor, hurried off.

Behold, this mighty prince, who was lately humbly obeyed by more than a hundred thousand armed men, and at a nod from whom entire nations trembled, was thus stripped by his own flunkeys in a house not his own, and left for naught on the bare ground.

> ORDERICUS VITALIS, on the death of King William I at Rouen, 1087

God rot him who cares a damn for that.

> KING WILLIAM II, Rufus, on the death of a pope

The earl [William Marshall, Earl of Pembroke] had not forgotten him. Many a time, he told among his people what he preserved in his memory. With his own eyes, he had seen the sovereign gradually devoured by that disease which had taken him by the heel, risen along his thighs, invaded his whole body, burning him everywhere. He had seen the king drag himself about like an animal, moaning with pain, and knowing that Richard, his eldest son, his heir, his enemy, furious to see him so long in dying, went sneering among the courtiers of the king of France: 'The old man is acting out his farce.' He had seen him turn red, then black. He was not present when death cracked the king's heart, when the clotted blood ran from his nose to his mouth, but he was told that the dying man lay quite alone. All his friends had fled, tugging here, tugging there, taking with them what they could, abandoning the body to the household riffraff. And he told, too, before dying himself, that the 'snatchers' had snatched indeed: Henry had nothing left but his underclothes and his breeches. A few men of great loyalty, and William was among them, hurried to him then, ashamed of what they saw, and flung their cloaks over the corpse. Which was buried then, and properly of course. But the next day the legions of poor men were waiting at the bridge of Chinon, sure of one thing: they would eat. And there was nothing in the king's house, not even a crust of bread. The earl asked whether there were any moneys: no trace of such a thing. And on the bridge, they could hear the poor men's anger swelling, shouting against the scandal, and threatening to destroy everything. The poor had reason to protest. Shame to the dead king who did not feed his people.

GEORGES DUBY, 1986, on King Henry II

I kissed her hand and told her it was my chiefest happiness to see her in safety, and in health, which I wished might long continue. She took me by the hand, and said, 'No, Robin, I am not well,' and then discoursed with me of her indisposition, and that her heart had been sad and heavy for ten or twelve days, and in her discourse she fetched not so few as forty or fifty great sighs. I was grieved at the first to see her in this plight; for in all my lifetime before, I never knew her fetch a sigh, but when the Queen of Scots was beheaded.

ROBERT CAREY, on the last days of Queen Elizabeth I

There was nothing I could learn apart from what my warder chose to tell me. But this I did witness. During those few days in which she lay dying beyond all hope of recovery, a strange silence descended on the whole city, as if it were under interdict and divine worship suspended. Not a bell rang out – though ordinarily they were often heard. WILLIAM WESTON, Jesuit, imprisoned in the Tower, on the death of Queen Elizabeth I, 1603

She would allow no doctors to come near her; she ate and drank very little, lying for hours in a low chair. At last it was seen that some strange crisis was approaching. She struggled to rise, and failing, summoned her attendants to pull her to her feet. She stood. Refusing further help, she remained immovable, while those around her watched in awe-stricken silence. Too weak to walk, she still had strength to stand; if she returned to her chair, she knew that she would never rise from it; she would continue to stand then; had it not always been her favourite posture? She was fighting Death, and fighting with terrific tenacity. The appalling combat lasted fifteen hours. Then she yielded – though she still declared that she would not go to bed. She sank on to cushions, spread out to receive her; and there she lay for four days and nights, speechless, with her finger in her mouth. Meanwhile an atmosphere of hysterical nightmare had descended on the Court. The air was thick with doom and terror. One of the ladies, looking under a chair, saw, nailed to the bottom of it, a queen of hearts. What did the awful portent mean? Another, leaving the Queen's room for a little rest, went down a gallery, and caught a glimpse of a shadowy form, sweeping away from her in the familiar panoply of Majesty. Distracted by fear, she retraced her steps, and, hurrying back into the royal chamber, looked – and beheld the Queen lying silent on the pillows, with her finger in her mouth, as she had left her.

The great personages about her implored her to obey the physicians and let herself be moved – in vain. At last Cecil said boldly, 'Your Majesty, to content the people, you must go to bed.' 'Little man, little man,' came the answer, 'the word *must* is not used to princes.' She indicated that she wished for music, and the instruments were brought into the room; with delicate melancholy they discoursed to her, and for a little she found relief. The consolations of religion remained; but they were dim formalities to that irretrievably terrestrial nature; a tune on the virginals had always been more to her mind than a prayer. Eventually she was carried to her bed. . . . She continued to sleep until – in the cold dark hours of the early morning of March 24th – there was a change; and the anxious courtiers, as they bent over the bed, perceived, yet once again, that the inexplicable spirit had eluded them. But it was for the last time: a haggard husk was all that was left of Queen Elizabeth.

LYTTON STRACHEY, 1928

I can never forget the inexpressible luxury and profaneness, gaming, and all dissoluteness, and as it were total forgetfulness of God (it being Sunday evening), which this dayse'night I was witness of, the King sitting and toying with his concubines, Portsmouth, Cleveland, and Mazarine, etc., a French boy singing love songs, in that glorious gallery, whilst about twenty of the great courtiers and other dissolute persons were at Basset round a large table, a bank of at least £2,000 in gold before them; upon which two gentlemen who were with me made reflections with astonishment. Six days later, was all in the dust.

JOHN EVELYN, on the last Sunday of King Charles II, 1685

I am sorry, gentlemen, for being an unconscionable time a-dying, I hope you will excuse it.   KING CHARLES II

O Death, where is thy sting?
To take the Queen and leave the King?

Popular song on the death of Queen Caroline,
wife of King George II, 1737

I went over at seven. It was a bright morning, the sun just rising and shining brightly. The room had the sad look of night-watching, the candles burnt down to their sockets, the doctors looking anxious. I went in and never can I forget how beautiful my darling looked, lying there with his face lit up by the rising sun, his eyes unusually bright, gazing as if it were on unseen objects, and not taking notice of me. . . .

Albert folded his arms, and began arranging his hair, just as he used to do when well and he was dressing. These were said to be bad signs. Strange! As though he were preparing for another and greater journey.   QUEEN VICTORIA, 1861, on the dying Prince Consort,
to their daughter, Crown Princess Victoria of Prussia

Bless you for your beautiful letter on Sunday received yesterday! Oh! my poor child, indeed 'Why may the earth not swallow us up?' Why not? How am I alive after witnessing what I have done? Oh! I who prayed daily that we might die together and I never survive him! I who felt, when in those blessed arms clasped and held tight in the sacred hours at night, when the world seemed only to be ourselves, that nothing could part us. I felt so very secure. I always repeated: 'And God will protect us!' though trembling always for his safety when he was a moment out of my sight. I never dreamt of the physical possibility of such a calamity – such an awful catastrophe for me – for all. What is to become of us all? Of the unhappy country, of Europe, of all? For you all, the loss of such a father is totally irreparable! I will do all I can to follow out all his wishes – to live for you all and for my duties. But how I, who leant on him for all and everything – without whom I did nothing, moved not a finger, arranged not a print or photograph, didn't put on a gown or bonnet if he didn't approve it, shall be able to go on, to live, to move, to help myself at difficult moments? How I shall long to ask his advice! Oh! it is too, too weary! The day – the night (above all the night) is too sad and weary. . . .

QUEEN VICTORIA, to Crown Princess Victoria,
following the death of Prince Albert, 14 December 1861

He died from want of what they call pluck.

QUEEN VICTORIA, to Lord Derby

DEFEAT

The fight was a long and hard one, with Boudicca hurling in chariot-charges and the governor countering with auxiliary archers: not until the end of the day did the Romans finally triumph, 'killing many around the wagons and in the woods, and taking many archers alive'.

Boudicca was not among them. Tacitus simply states that 'she ended her life with poison': he does not say where or when, though the context implies that she died some time after the battle rather than actually on the field. According to Dio, however: 'no small number of Britons escaped from the disaster, and were preparing to fight again when Boudicca fell ill and died. The Britons, mourning her greatly, gave her a costly funeral: then, feeling that now at last they really had been defeated, they scattered to their homes.'

In the light of what we know or can surmise of Boudicca, the suicide story seems the more credible. Her victorious career had suffered a shattering and quite unlooked-for reverse, and there was little hope of raising another British army before Suetonius was reinforced, still less of winning a guerrilla war once those reinforcements had arrived. Conditional surrender was unthinkable: even if she herself could consider such a course, the governor would never negotiate with a woman who (according to Tacitus, apparently quoting an official report) had slaughtered some 70,000 Romans and allied Britons, the great majority of them defenceless non-combatants. But most insupportable of all, for a leader who had believed herself the instrument of divine vengeance, were the implications of her defeat: either Andrasta had cruelly deceived her worshippers, or the once-invincible goddess had quailed before the stronger gods of Rome. Perhaps, indeed, Boudicca did not need the poison-cup, but willed herself to sickness and death because she could not bear to live with the knowledge that her goddess had failed. . . .

Though Tacitus describes the site of the battle clearly, he gives us no idea of its whereabouts, and this annoying omission has given rise over the centuries to a variety of more or less incredible suggestions, including sites near Chester, others in Essex or even . . . under Platform 10 at King's Cross station.

CHARLES KIGHTLY, on Boudicca's last battle, 61 AD

Since thou, O God, to crown me with confusion and increase my dishonour, hast basely taken from me this day the city I have loved best in all the world, wherein I was born and bred, and my father is buried . . . I also will surely recompense thee as far as I am able, by withholding from thee that which thou lovest best in me.

KING HENRY II, at the loss of Le Mans, 1189

It was a blow from which he did not recover: he died soon after, bemoaning the disloyalty of his sons, Richard and, in particular, John.

DEMOCRACY

These are trying moments and it seems to me a defect in our much-famed Constitution to have to part with an admirable Govt like Lord Salisbury's for no question of any importance, or any particular reason, merely on account of the number of votes.

QUEEN VICTORIA, 1886

DINNERS

I dined at the great entertainment his Majesty [King James II] gave the Venetian Ambassadors, Signors Zenno and Justiniani, accompanied by ten more noble Venetians of their most illustrious families, Cornaro, Massenigo, etc., who came to congratulate their Majesties coming to the Crown. The dinner was most magnificent and plentiful, at our tables, with music, kettle-drums, and trumpets, which sounded upon a whistle at every health. The banquet [dessert] was twelve vast chargers piled up so high that those who sat one against another could hardly see each other. Of these sweetmeats, which doubtless were some days piling up in that exquisite manner, the Ambassadors touched not, but leaving them to the spectators who came out of curiosity to see the dinner, were exceedingly pleased to see in what a moment of time all that curious work was demolished, the comfitures voided and the tables cleared.

JOHN EVELYN

The question is sometimes discussed whether a popular member of the royal family is a gourmet or only a gourmand. Is he really a judge of good things as Brillat-Savarin was, or is he only a good feeder? I heard an interesting story told at a table where this question was discussed. Some years ago H.R.H. accepted an invitation to dine with an eminent statesman who may be called Mr A. ... Mr A, transcendant in most things, is not particularly happy in his cuisine, and is wholly unconscious of the shortcoming. This was well known to an intimate friend, Lord B, who had been invited, and who, knowing H.R.H.'s liking for a good dinner, looked forward in despair to his probable experiences. Then a happy thought occurred to him.

'My dear A,' he said, 'I want you to do me a great favour. My cook François is a devoted admirer of your guest. It would please him beyond anything to be allowed to cook a dinner for royalty. You have it in your power to make the poor man happy for life. Let him take charge of the whole thing.'

Mr A readily consented. François had carte blanche and produced one of those dinners for which his Master's house is famed. Everything went off splendidly, and Lord B was delighted with the success of his little plot.

As they withdrew from the dining-room, H.R.H. pressed his arm and whispered in his ear, 'My dear B, what garbage we've been eating!'   SIR HENRY LUCY, 1890, on Albert Edward, Prince of Wales

DIPLOMACY

Oh Madam, there is not a creature living who more longs to hear your justification than myself; nor one who would lend more willing ears to any answer which will clear your honour. But I cannot sacrifice my own reputation on your account. To tell you the plain truth, I am already thought to be more willing to defend your cause than to open my eyes to see the things of which your subjects accuse you. Did you but know who the persons are by whom I am warned to be on my guard, you would not think that I could afford to neglect these warnings. And now, seeing that you are pleased to commit yourself to my protection, you may assure yourself that I will take care both of your life and honour, that neither yourself nor your nearest relations could be more concerned for your interests. On the word of a prince, I promise you, that neither your subjects, nor any advice which I may receive from my own councillors, shall move me to ask anything of you which may endanger you or touch your honour.

Does it seem strange to you that you are not allowed to see me? I entreat you to put yourself in my place. When you are acquitted of this crime I will receive you with all honour: till that is done I may not; but afterwards, I swear by God, that I shall never see person with better will, and among all earthly pleasures I will hold this to be the first.   QUEEN ELIZABETH I, to Mary Queen of Scots,
following Mary's flight to England under
accusation of murdering her husband, 1568

Put away from your mind the thought that I came hither to save my life. Neither Scotland nor the world would have refused me a refuge. I came to recover my honour and to obtain help to chastise my false accusers – not to answer these charges against me as if I were their equal, but myself to accuse them in your presence. For the cautions which you say you have received from great persons, God forbid that I should be a reproach to you; but my cause requires haste. Let me try what other princes will do for me, and no blame will then rest with you. Restored to my throne by their hands, I will then come again to you, and defend my honour for my honour's sake, and not for any need to answer my traitor subjects. . .   MARY, QUEEN OF SCOTS, to Queen Elizabeth I, 1568

THE DOCTOR

Get another basket, Eaton, at the same time, and pack up the doctor in it, and send him off at the same time.

KING GEORGE III, to a gardener at Kew, 1789

A DREAM

Normally an early start for hunting would have been made. But on the night of August 1, 1100, the King slept fitfully, disturbed by a dream that he was being bled by a surgeon.

'And that the stream, reaching to heaven, clouded the night and intercepted the day. . . . Shortly after, just as the day began to dawn, a certain foreign monk . . . told him that he had that night dreamed a strange and fearful dream about the king: that he had come into a certain church with menacing and insolent gesture, as was his custom, looking contemptuously on the standers-by: then violently seizing the crucifix he gnawed the arms, and almost tore away the legs . . . the image endured this for a long time, but at length struck the king with his foot in such a manner that he fell backwards; from his mouth as he lay prostrate, issued so copious a flame that the volume of smoke touched the very stars.' (William of Malmesbury, *De Gestis Regum*.)

On having the monk's tale related to him Rufus put up a showy front. 'He is a monk,' he laughed. 'Like all monks he dreamed this to get something. Give him a hundred shillings so he won't be able to say he dreamed in vain.'

RICHARD F. CASSADY, 1986, on the last night of King William II, 1100

Does he take me for an Englishman? Let them put off their journeys and business because some old woman has sneezed or had a dream! Not me!

KING WILLIAM II, on the morning of his mysterious death in the New Forest

DWARFS

Both Charles I and the Queen liked to have dwarfs about them. The Queen had several, including Jeffrey Hudson, the son of a bull-baiter, who was often at Windsor, and Anne Shepherd, who married King Charles's dwarf, Richard Gibson, and bore him nine children – five of whom were of normal stature – before dying at the age of eighty-nine. Both Anne Shepherd and her husband were less than four feet in height – the King himself was only about 5ft 6in – but they were tall compared with Jeffrey Hudson, who was said to have stood no higher than eighteen inches when he jumped out of a pie onto the dining table one day, in his miniature suit of armour, to bow politely to the Queen. He grew a little in the years which followed this youthful performance, but he remained small enough to fit into the pocket of the King's gigantic porter whose pretence of eating him as a tasty morsel between the two halves of a loaf of bread was greatly enjoyed at court masques.

CHRISTOPHER HIBBERT, 1964

ECONOMY

We indeed believed that he would make some great oblation; but he offered nothing save a single silken cloth which his servants had borrowed from our sacrist – and they have not yet paid the price. And yet he received the hospitality of St Edmund at great cost to the Abbey, and when he departed he gave nothing at all to the honour or advantage of the saint save thirteen pence sterling, which he offered at his Mass of the day when he left us.

Chronica Jocelini de Brakelonda, on King John, *c.* 1200

EDUCATION

Once, men came from foreign parts seeking wisdom in this our land; today, if we are to acquire any wisdom, we ourselves must seek it abroad. So great has been the decay of knowledge amongst the English that very few on this side [of the] Humber and, I suspect, very few north of it, can understand the Mass or translate a letter from Latin to English. No indeed, I cannot recall any such man south of Thames, at the time of my accession [871]. It appears, therefore, needful that we should render into the tongue we all share some of the books which all should know, and so bring it about – as certainly we can do if only we are granted respite from our foes – that of all the free youth of England, shall first learn to read English, and then, if they agree to continue their education, and wish to rise to the higher ranks of our royal service, they shall be taught Latin.

KING ALFRED, *Liber Pastoralis*

It is your shame (I speak to you all, you young gentlemen of England), that one maid should go beyond you all, in excellency of learning and knowledge of divers tongues. Point forth six of the best given gentlemen of this court, and all they together shew not so much good will, spend not so much time, bestow not so many hours, daily, orderly and constantly, for the increase of learning and knowledge, as doth the Queen's Majesty herself. Yea I believe that, beside her perfect readiness in Latin, Italian, French and Spanish, she readeth here now at Windsor more Greek every day than some prebendary of this church doth read Latin in a whole week. And that which is most praiseworthy of all, within the walls of her privy chamber she hath obtained that excellence of learning, to understand, speak and write, both wittily with head and fair with hand, as scarce one or two rare wits in both the universities have in many years reached unto. Amongst all the benefits that God hath blessed me withal, next the knowledge of Christ's true religion, I count this the greatest, that it pleased God to call me to be one poor minister in setting forward these excellent gifts of learning in this most excellent Prince. Whose only example if the rest of our nobility would follow, then might England be, for learning and wisdom in nobility, a spectacle to all the world beside.

ROGER ASCHAM, on Queen Elizabeth I. *The Scholemaster*, 1570

Though when at home a Prince, on board the *Prince George* you are only a boy learning the Naval Profession; but the Prince so far accompanies you that what other boys might do, you must not. It must never be out of your thoughts that more obedience is necessary from you to your superiors in the Navy, more politeness to your equals and more good nature to your inferiors, than from those who have not been told that these are essential to a gentleman.
KING GEORGE III, 1779, to his son, Prince William, later the 'Sailor King', William IV

He received instruction in Latin and Greek with ease, learnt to sing and play the cello, and was taught to draw, to paint in watercolours, and to appreciate art. He learned French as easily as Latin and had a good knowledge of German and Italian. He took at once, oddly enough, to military engineering, and the careful precision drawing that went with it. He was exceptionally well grounded in literature and history – with his good looks and exquisite manners, he was almost a paragon. But, as his tutor said of him and his brother Frederick, 'They could never be taught to understand the value of money.'

J. H. PLUMB, 1977, on George, Prince of Wales, later King George IV

The mind of Queen Victoria never ceases to astonish. Far in advance of her aristocratic Court, she held views unknown to those who have pursued her memory with braying laughter. She detested the heartlessness of bureaucracy; she defied the prejudices held by so many of her subjects against humble origins or an unfamiliar creed. Her reaction to Dalton's plea (to allow her grandson, Prince Albert Victor, to join his younger brother George for naval training) was no less startling. Although the very focus and epitome of patriotism, she responded in terms which would have captivated the League of Nations Union half a century later:

'Will a nautical education not engender and encourage national prejudices and make them think that their own Country is superior to any other? With the greatest love for and pride of one's own Country, a Prince, and especially one who is some day to be its Ruler, should not be imbued with the prejudices and peculiarities of his own Country, as George III and William IV were.'

KENNETH ROSE, 1983

And to her daughter, Crown Princess Victoria of Prussia, Queen Victoria wrote, 1861, with the following advice on the upbringing of her son Wilhelm, the future Kaiser:

Bring him up simply, plainly, not with that terrible Prussian pride which grieved dear Papa so much and which he always said would stand in the way of Prussia taking that lead in Germany which he ever wished her to do. Pride and ambition are not only very wrong in themselves but they alienate affection and are in every way unworthy for great Princes – and great nations.

For goodness sake, teach Margaret and Lilibet to write a decent hand, that's all I ask you. None of my children could write properly. They all do it exactly the same way. I like a hand with character in it.
KING GEORGE V, to Marion Crawford,
governess to Princess Margaret and Princess Elizabeth

EDWARD THE CONFESSOR

A golden age shone for his English race,
As after David's wars came Solomon and peace,
Which drowned the grievous moans in Lethe's stream,
And Plenty poured profusely for her king
Abundant riches from a bounteous horn;
How, when this leader, patron, king was there,
The dreadful anger of the foe withdraws;
And how with locks of snowy white he blooms,
The glass of virtue, the beloved of God.

ANON. *Vita Edwardi Regis, c.* 1066

This mellow, autumnal hue is the product of idealization; but to one looking back from Christmas 1066 over Edward's reign, the years 1063–4 may with some justice have appeared as the brightest spot in a golden age.
FRANK BARLOW, 1970

EDWARD I

He was a man of tried prudence in statecraft. In adolescence he was
devoted to the practice of arms which gave him a widespread
renown for chivalry – his reputation was finer than that of any
contemporary prince in all Christendom. His appearance was elegant: his height was commanding, taller than an average man from
the leg upwards. His looks were enhanced ds a beard which in
adolescence changed from silver to gold, became black when he
reached manhood and, in old age, changed from grey to the white-
ness of a swan. He had broad forehead and regular features, save
that his left eyelid drooped, recalling his father's appearance. He
had a lisp, but was nevertheless powerfully eloquent when persuasion was needed. His arms were long in proportion to his trunk,
and none was more proficient in wielding a sword with sinuous
skill. He had a paunch, and his long thighs made it impossible for
him to be thrown by the galloping or jumping of the most fiery
steed. When his fighting days were over, he indulged in hunting and
hawking. In particular, he pursued the stag, on a courser, and when
he caught one, struck it not with a hunting spear but with a sword.

NICHOLAS TREVET. *Annales, c.* 1320

He was so handsome and great, so powerful in arms, that of him
may one speak as long as the world lasts.

PETER OF LANGTOFT. *Chronical,* 13th–14th century

Before God and the swans.   KING EDWARD I, swearing

EDWARD II

King Edward II was a handsome man, of outstanding strength, but his behaviour was a very different matter. For, undervaluing the company of the great lords, he was devoted to choristers, actors, grooms, sailors, and others skilled in like callings. He was prodigal in giving, generous and splendid in living, quick and unpredictable in speech, most unlucky in battle, violent with his household, and passionately devoted to one particular individual, whom he loved above all, showered with gifts and always put him first; he could not bear separation from him and honoured him more than anyone else. As a result, the beloved was loathed, and the lover entangled himself in hatred and disaster. He promoted the unworthy and unqualified to bishops' thrones – and these deserted him in his days of trouble.   RANULF HIGDEN, Monk of Chester. *Polychronicon*, c. 1347

From youth, Edward devoted himself in private to the arts of rowing and driving carts, of digging ditches and thatching houses, as people said, and also with companions by night to various works of ingenuity and skill, and other meaningless and trivial occupations unworthy of a king's son.   ANON

Oh! the insane stupidity of the king of the English, condemned by God and man, who should not love his own infamy and his illicit bed, and should never have put aside his noble consort and her soft, wifely embraces, contemptuous of her noble birth.

ROBERT OF READING, *Flores Historiarum*, c. 1327

EDWARD III

Ah dear God, how can it be
    That all things waste and wear away?
Friendship is but vanity,
    And barely lasts the length of day.
    When put to proof, men go astray.
Averse to loss, to gain inclined:
    So fickle is their faith, I say,
That out of sight is out of mind.

Yes, not without a cause I speak,
    And therefore you should take good heed,
For if my meaning you would seek,
    I shall tell you truth indeed,
    And then for shame your hearts will bleed
If to wisdom you're inclined.
    He who was our utmost speed
Is out of sight and out of mind.

Some time an English ship we had:
    Noble it was, and high of tower,
And held through Christendom in dread.
    It bravely bore its battle hour,
    Most stoutly stood the sea squall's power
And other storms of every kind.
    Yet now that ship, which bore the flower,
Is out of sight and out of mind.

I liken this good ship I saw
    To the chivalry of this land.
Who once gave nothing, not a straw,
    For all of France, I understand.
    They caught and killed them with the hand,
The powers of France, of every kind;

Enslaved the king at their command:
But now all that is out of mind.

The rudder was not oak or elm,
    But Edward the third, noble Knight,
The Prince his son, who manned the helm,
    Was never defeated in the fight.
    The King he rode and sailed aright;
The Prince no fear could ever find:
    But now our thoughts of them are slight,
For out of sight is out of mind.

So may your thoughts, good sirs, be one
    With our doughty king who died when old,
And with Prince Edward too, his son,
    True fountain of the spirit bold.
    I know not when we shall behold
Two lords of such a lofty kind.
    Yet now their fame is hardly told
It's out of sight and out of mind.

ANON, on King Edward III and the Black Prince,
14th century

EDWARD IV

He was of youth greatly given to fleshly wantonness: this fault not greatly grieved the people.

SIR THOMAS MORE. History of Richard III, c. 1518

King Edward 'had three concubines which in divers proportions Diversely excelled, one the merriest, the other the wiliest, the third the holiest in the realm.'
EDWARD HALL. Chronicle, c. 1532

EDWARD VI

This boy filled with the highest expectations every good and learned man, on account of his cleverness and sweetness of manner. When a royal gravity was called for, you would think it was an old man you saw, but he was friendly and companionable as became his years. He played upon the lute, took trouble over public affairs, was liberal of mind, and in these respects emulated his father.... He was well trained in philosophic studies. . . . In his humanity he was a picture of our mortal state, his gravity was that of kingly majesty, his disposition worthy of so great a prince. This boy of so much wit and promise was nearing a comprehension of the sum of things. (I do not here adorn the truth with rhetoric, but speak below the truth.) And there was the mark in his face of death that was to come too soon. Otherwise, he was comely because of his age and of his parents, who had both been handsome.

GIROLAMO CARDANO, on King Edward VI. *Autobiography*, 16th century

I have two masters, Diligence and Moderation.

KING EDWARD VI, to Girolamo Cardano, 1552

You pluck out my feathers as if I were but a tame falcon. The day will come when I shall pluck out yours.

KING EDWARD VI, to the Lords of the Council, 1553

Edward is celebrated by historians for the beauty of his person, the sweetness of his disposition, and the extent of his knowledge. By the time he had attained his sixteenth year, he understood the Greek, Latin, French, Italian, and Spanish languages; he was versed in the sciences of logic, music, natural philosophy, and master of all theological disputes; insomuch that the famous Cardanus, in his return from Scotland, visiting the English court, was astonished at the progress he had made in learning; and afterwards extolled him in his works as a prodigy of nature. Notwithstanding these encomiums, he seems to have had an ingredient of bigotry in his disposition, that would have rendered him very troublesome to those of tender consciences, who might have happened to differ with him in religious principles; nor can we reconcile either to his boasted humanity or penetration, his consenting to the death of his uncle, who had served him faithfully; unless we suppose he wanted resolution to withstand the importunities of his ministers, and was deficient in that vigour of mind which often exists independent of learning and culture. TOBIAS SMOLLETT, 1757

EDWARD VII

To his position King Edward brought solid advantages. These did not rest on his physical appearance, which was not altogether prepossessing. He was short and had grown stout. He had a very long nose – a reminder that through both his parents he inherited many personal characteristics of the house of Coburg. Though he was bald, his head was finely drawn and was to look splendid on coinage and postage stamps. His face was given strength, and its character set off, by a well-shaped beard. He loved dressing in ceremonial clothes, and he looked his best in the uniform of a field-marshal in the British army. In the short tunics of some foreign regiments he looked frightful. Although the king may not have been good-looking – he was at a disadvantage when seen against the sombre good looks of his brother, the Duke of Edinburgh, or the flamboyant appearance of his nephew the Kaiser – he had an extraordinary sense of occasion, so that in any gathering, whether he was in uniform, or in a frock-coat, or in a short coat and wearing the familiar curly-brimmed top hat, he was immediately recognized, immediately conspicuous.

ROGER FULFORD, 1964, on King Edward VII
(in *Edwardian England: 1901–1914*)

King Edward the Sev'nth, son of noble reigns,
Husband of one of the Ancient Danes.   ANON

ELIZABETH I

Considering that this woman has caused the loss of so many
millions of souls to the Faith, it is beyond doubt that whoever may
dispatch her from this world with the pious intention of serving
God, not only will commit no sin, but will acquire merit.

Papal Secretary of State, on Queen Elizabeth I, 1580

She is a great woman; and if she were only a Catholic she would be
wholly unequalled. . . . Regard the excellence by which she rules;
she is but a woman, no more than mistress of half an island, and
nevertheless she inspires fear in Spain, in France, within the
Emperor, amongst everyone.   POPE SIXTUS V, on Queen Elizabeth I, 1588

In the 65th year of her age (as we were told), very majestic; her face
oblong, fair but wrinkled; her eyes small but black and pleasant;
her nose a little hooked, her lips narrow and her teeth black (a
defect the English seem subject to, from their too great use of
sugar); she had in her ears two pearls with very rich drops; her hair
was of an auburn colour, but false; upon her head she had a small
crown, reported to be made of some of the gold of the celebrated
Luneburg table; her bosom was uncovered, as all the English ladies
have it till they marry; and she had on a necklace of exceeding fine
jewels; her hands were slender, her fingers rather long, and her
stature neither tall nor low; her air was stately, her manner of
speaking mild and obliging. That day she was dressed in white silk,
bordered with pearls of the size of beans, and over it a mantle of

black silk shot with silver threads; her train was very long, the end of it borne by a marchioness; instead of a chain she had an oblong collar of gold and jewels.   PAUL HENTZNER, 1598

> Naked the fields are, bloomless are the briars
> Yet we a summer have
> Who, in our clime, kindleth these living fires
> Which bloom can on the briars save –
>
> Winter, though everywhere,
> Hath no abiding here.
> On brooks and briars she doth reign alone,
> The sun which lights our world is Always One.

EDMUND BOLTON, on Queen Elizabeth I, 1600

She is quite disfavoured and unattired, and these troubles waste her much. . . .

She walks much in her Privy Chamber and stamps her feet at ill news, and thrusts her rusty sword into the arras in great rage. My Lord Buckhurst is much with her, and few else since the City business; the dangers are over, and yet she always keeps a sword at her side.

SIR JOHN HARINGTON, on Queen Elizabeth I, after the failure of the Earl of Essex to rouse the City of London in armed rebellion, 1601

Her delight is to sit in the dark, and sometimes with shedding tears to bewail Essex.

A courtier, on the last months of Queen Elizabeth I, 1603

> Great lady of the greatest isle, whose light,
> Like Phoebus' lamp, throughout the world doth shine.

EDMUND SPENSER, *The Faerie Queene*

That disgrace to humanity, that pest of society, Elizabeth.

JANE AUSTEN (aged fifteen). *History of England,* 1790

So unkind to my ancestress the Queen of Scots.

QUEEN VICTORIA

Ruler of England for forty-four years, Elizabeth has attained a posthumous reputation far in excess of her actual achievements. It is plain that her own propaganda, the cult of Gloriana, her sheer longevity, the coincidence of the Shakespearian moment, and the lucky defeat of the Armada have beguiled us into joining a crescendo of adulation that ignores the simple fact that she quietly allowed England to become ungovernable.

JOHN GUY, 1984

ENGLAND

Solomon declares that three things are hard to discover, and a fourth barely to be discovered: the way of an eagle in the air, the way of a ship on the sea, the way of a snake on the ground, and the way of a man in his youth. I can add a fifth, the way of a King in England.

PETER DE BLOIS, Archdeacon of Bath under King Henry II. 12th century

A wonderful land is this, and a fickle; which hath exiled, slain, destroyed or ruined so many kings, rulers and great men, and is ever tainted with strife and variance and envy.

KING RICHARD II, 1399, in the Tower, before abdication

The land we live in, and let those who don't like it, leave it!

A toast, by King William IV, 1830

ENGLISH MOTHERS

Though the general public was much less of a nuisance than at Marienbad, the problem of guarding the King on those Biarritz visits was, if anything, greater. It was mainly those afternoon (and sometimes day-long) excursions into the surrounding countryside that caused the headaches. The sedate tea-picnics were, from the security point of view, fairly harmless, despite the King's occasional preference for a roadside site, where the dust of passing cars and carriages was liable to settle with the paprika on the plovers' eggs. The worst hazards here were those aspiring English mothers, their cars laden with débutante daughters, who would contrive to break down at the precise spot where the King had halted.

GORDON BROOK-SHEPHERD, 1975, on King Edward VII

ENTENTE CORDIALE

The drive from the Bois de Boulogne station, where President Loubet was to meet King Edward, along the Champs Elysées to the British Embassy, showed that the Parisians were not to be swept into enthusiasm by order. There was cheering, but its spontaneity in general rose from the large groups of English tourists who were on their traditional visit to Paris in springtime. Elsewhere were heard strident whistles of disapproval.

In the sumptuously decorated Rue de la Paix, newspaper vendors sold the *Patrie*; its front page flaunted a photograph of King Edward flanked by portraits of Marchand, Paul Kruger and Joan of Arc. A demonstration began outside the British Embassy in the Faubourg St Honoré: a group of young men and women shouting, 'Long live the Boers! Long live Russia! Long live Marchand!' Plain-clothes policemen acted with speed and discretion. Quietly the ring-leaders were removed.

'They don't seem to like us,' a member of the King's retinue remarked.

'Why should they?' replied Edward without resentment.

That evening, the Café de la Paix was framed in red, white and blue electric lights. The Vendôme columns were floodlit. The next day the King, in scarlet uniform, attended a parade at Vincennes, and the races at Longchamp. Edward had the right phrase for everyone who was presented to him: during an evening at the opera, he spent the intervals strolling along the corridors with an ease of manner reminiscent of his Paris years. He greeted old acquaintances, talked with actresses and invited a number of journalists to visit him in London.

On Sunday night, during the Embassy dinner, seated at a table decorated with orchids, azaleas and roses, Edward raised his glass to toast France, and made a speech so warmly human that every newspaper printed it in full.

When the King left Paris on the following Monday, all traces of animosity had vanished. On the contrary, he received a rapturous ovation. His charm had conquered.

A year later, the Entente Cordiale was signed.

P. J. BOUMAN, 1954, on King Edward VII, 1903

EPITAPHS

A mild man, soft and good, and he did no justice.

Anglo-Saxon Chronicle, on King Stephen, 12th century

Here lies Henry's daughter, wife and mother, by birth great, by marriage greater, by motherhood greatest.

Inscribed on the tomb of MATILDA FITZ EMPRESS, 'Lady of the English',
daughter of King Henry I, wife of Emperor Henry V and of
Count Geoffrey of Anjou, mother of Henry II, King of England, Duke of Normandy,
Duke of Aquitaine, Count of Anjou, Lord of Ireland

The Black Prince

Such as thou art, some time was I;
Such as I am, such shalt thou be.
I little thought on the hour of death
So long as I enjoyed breath.

Great riches here I did possess
Whereof I made great nobleness.
I had gold, silver, wardrobes and
Great treasure, horses, houses, land.

But now a caitiff poor am I,
Deep in the ground, lo here I lie.
My beauty great is all quite gone,
My flesh is wasted to the bone.

From French verses on the Prince's tomb in Canterbury Cathedral,
trs. John Weever

While he lived none feared enemy invasion; when he was present no
man was scared of foreign assault, nor was any evil action or
military fault allowed – as men once spoke of Alexander the Great,
he assailed no people without victory, besieged no city in vain.

THOMAS WALSINGHAM, on the Black Prince. *Greater Chronicle, c.* 1380

*Froissart adds: 'The Prince captured Limoges by undermining the
walls, and brutally massacred the inhabitants', 1370.*

I had put up with but too much disrespect to my person, but I
warned him he should not touch my sceptre.

QUEEN ELIZABETH I, on Robert Devereux, Earl of Essex, executed 1601

I am no lover of pompous title, but only desire that my name may be recorded in a line or two, which shall briefly express my name, my virginity, the years of my reign, the reformation of religion under it, and my preservation of peace.

QUEEN ELIZABETH I, to her attendants, on her own epitaph

To tell you that our Rising Sun is set ere scarce he had shone, and that all our glory lies buried, you know and do lament as well as we, and better than some do, and more truly, or else you were not a man, and sensible of this kingdom's loss.

RICHARD SACKVILLE, EARL OF DORSET, on the death of Henry,
Prince of Wales; to Sir Thomas Edmondes, 1612

Here lies poor Fred
Who was alive and is dead:
Had it been his father,
I had much rather;
Had it been his brother,
Still better than another;
Had it been his sister,
No one would have missed her;
Had it been the whole generation,
Still better for the nation;
But since 'tis only Fred
Who was alive and is dead
There's no more to be said.

ANON, on the death of Frederick, Prince of Wales,
son of King George II and Queen Caroline,
and father of King George III, 1751

ETON

The King told me that as he possibly might want to retire when he got to the Provost's House, I had better arrange that the Provost should ask him to come and see some particular picture which would give him the excuse of leaving the room. I therefore explained this to Dr Hornby. When we got to the Provost's drawing-room the Provost said in a rather sheepish way, 'There is a picture I should like to show Your Majesty in the next room', and then blushed all over, having probably never told a lie in his life. But the King didn't want to retire and replied that he would come and see it after tea, whereupon the Provost must have felt like a naughty boy who has been caught telling lies.

SIR FREDERICK PONSONBY, 1951, on King Edward VII

EVIL

At present the democratic and social evils are forcing themselves on the people. The unequal division of property, and the dangers of poverty and envy arising therefrom, is the principal evil. Means must necessarily be found, *not for diminishing riches* (as the communists want), but to make facilities for the poor. But there is the rub. I believe this question will be first solved here, in England.

ALBERT, PRINCE CONSORT, 1849, to Duke Ernst of Saxe-Coburg-Gotha

EXPEDIENCY

My lord, I have been taught to judge between what is right and what is wrong. *Expediency* is a word that I neither wish to hear again nor to understand.

QUEEN VICTORIA, to a minister, discussing the South African war

EXPENDITURE

For flutes in a case £3 10 0

For a lute for my Lady Mary 13 4

To the princess's string minstrels at Westminster 2 0 0

To a woman that singeth with the fiddle 2 0

To the Welsh harper 6 8

To the trumpets that blow when the king comes
over the water 3 4

To the children for singing in the garden 9 4

To a mariner that brought an eagle £0 6 8

To Clement for a nightingale 1 0 0

To a woman for a nest of leverets 3 4

To beer drunken at the farmer's house 1 0

To a poor woman for cherries and strawberries 1 8

To the reapers in the way of reward 0 2

To the smith of Richmond for a little clock 13 4

To one that joculed before the King £0 10 0

To a tumbler upon a rope 3 4

To a fellow for eating coals 6 8

To Ringley Abbot of misrule 5 0 0

To the Scottish boy with the beard 10 0

To the little maiden that danceth 12 0 0

For a lion 2 13 4

For a leopard 13 6 8

For tennis balls 3 0

From the Household Accounts of King Henry VII

*Therein we also find a note of payment to John Cabot, for the
discovery of Newfoundland, 1497:*

To him that found the new isle £10 0 0

Though it be continually alleged that great sums are due, yet why such sums are due, or to whom they are due, and who are paid, and who are not paid, is never certified.

QUEEN ELIZABETH I, complaining of financial mismanagement
of the Earl of Leicester's campaign in the Netherlands
against the Spanish invaders, 1587

I was never any greedy, scraping grasper, nor a strait, fast-holding prince, nor yet a waster. My heart was never set on any worldly goods, but only for my subjects' good. What you bestow on me, I will not hoard it up, but receive it to bestow on you again. Yea, mine own properties I account yours, to be expended for your good; and your eyes shall see the bestowing of it all, for your good.

QUEEN ELIZABETH I, to some members of the Commons, 1601

Jewels	£2294	3	3½
Hoses	524	3	4
Lute strings	74	3	4
Perfumes	68	7	1
Binding of books	1	6	8
Curtains for Privy Chambers	6	8	0
One sackbut for Queen's use	15	9	0
Food for Queen's deer	145	3	8
Payments made to the Queen's silk woman	702	11	0¼
Payments made to David Smith, Embroiderer	203	15	7
Payments made to Peter Trinder, Goldsmith	32	15	0
Payments made to Mrs Taylor, Queen's laundress	4	0	0

Accounts of the Keeper of the Queen's Purse, to Queen Elizabeth I

The collapse in 1720 of the South Sea Company, of which George I was governor, was a financial disaster which affected many people in Britain. The King was overheard to say, 'We had very good luck, for we sold out last week.' JOSEPH SPENCE, 1820

The most important aspect of the Privy Purse is the light it throws on the character of King George. No man is a hypocrite in his pleasures, said Johnson; and no man spends money on things he does not like. A large proportion of the King's income was spent on books, works of art, and music. In 1766 bills to booksellers and bookbinders came to £1,030, in 1767 to £1,713. Three entries (in 1768 . . .) record payments to 'various booksellers' of £356 8s. 4d., £405 14s. 8d., and £103 13s. 9d. The king was a particularly good customer of Tom Davies, who introduced Boswell to Johnson and whose shop in Covent Garden was the scene of their first meeting. . . . He was an assiduous reader of newspapers, the bill for which came to about £40 a year.

The names of some of the great artists of the period appear in the accounts. On 7 December 1763 the King paid Reynolds £210 for a portrait of Bute, and on 3 February 1769 £378 to Allan Ramsay for portraits of himself, the Queen, and their two eldest children. The Royal Academy, which the King founded in 1769, was subsidized out of the Privy Purse and cost £911 during the first year. Alexander Cumming, the great clock maker, received £1,178 0s. 6d. on 14 February 1765 for a barometrical clock (now in Buckingham Palace), and on 5 July 1765 Christopher Pinchbeck was paid £1,042 for another clock. In February 1764 the King bought three harpsichords at a cost of £278 10s. and in April 1767 an organ for the Queen for £241 10s. The annual cost of tuning the harpsichords and organs (the King also had one) came to £45. The King employed two men to copy music for him: Mr Tweed, who copied *The Messiah* in full score in 1766 for seven guineas; and Mr Simpson, whose expenses for copying music in 1767 came to £22 16s. Scientific instrument makers also figure in the accounts (though

Herschel, the greatest of all, was yet to come); and the Queen kept a private zoo in St James's Park, consisting of an elephant and a zebra, which cost the King over £100 a year.

JOHN BROOKE, 1972, on King George III

FAMILY LIFE

He was the kindest of fathers to his legitimate children during their childhood and youth, but as they grew older regarded them with an evil eye, behaving to them worse than a stepfather, and despite possessing sons so distinguished and illustrious, whether due to fear of them prospering too swiftly, or whether they simply did not merit better treatment, he was unable to tolerate the thought of them eventually replacing him. And as mortal prosperity can neither be permanent nor perfect, such was the exquisite nastiness of fortune against this prince, that where he deserved comfort he received opposition; where entitled to security met danger; where he merited peace he was granted disorder; looking for support he received ingratitude; his need for rest and tranquility was rewarded by uproar and alarms.   GIRALDUS CAMBRENSIS, on King Henry II.
Conquest of Richard

Although I do not write more often, you must not think me ungrateful, for just as I seldom put on my best clothes, yet I love them more than the others.

PRINCE EDWARD, later King Edward VI,
to Princess Mary, later Queen Mary I

I've tried him drunk, and I've tried him sober, and there's nothing in him.   KING CHARLES II, on Prince George of Denmark,
later Consort to his niece, Queen Anne

In May 1684 the long series of births and miscarriages begins:

1684 May 12: a still born daughter.

1685 June 2: Mary or Marie (died 8.2.1686).

1686 June 2: Anne Sophia (died 2.2.1687).

1687 Between January 20 and February 4: a miscarriage.

1687 October: a miscarriage (male).

1688 April 16: a miscarriage.

1689 July 24: William Duke of Gloucester (died 30.7.1700).

1690 October 14: Mary (two months premature, lived two hours).

1692 April 17: George (born at Syon, lived a few minutes).

1693 March 23: a miscarriage (female).

1694 January 21: a miscarriage.

1696 February 18: a miscarriage (female).

1696 September 20: a double miscarriage (a son of 7 months' growth, the other of 2 or 3 months).

1697 March 25: a miscarriage.

1697 December: a miscarriage.

1698 September 15: a miscarriage (male).

1700 January 25: a miscarriage (male).

> DAVID GREEN, 1970, on the marriage fortunes of
> Queen Anne and Prince George of Denmark

Mr Green quotes Lady Mary Wortley Montague: 'Queen Anne died sadly worn out with a complication of distemper.'

Nothing will happen which will make me change the final attachment I have for your interests. I should be the most unhappy man in the world if you were not persuaded of it. . . . I shall be to the last breath of my life, yours, with zeal and fidelity.

> WILLIAM, PRINCE OF ORANGE, to his uncle, King James II, 1685, against whom he
> led the successful invasion, 1688, which led to his accession as King William III

I cannot too strongly set before your eyes that if you permit yourself to indulge every foolish idea you must be wretched all your life, for with thirteen children I can but with the greatest care make both ends meet and am not in a situation to be paying their debts if they contract any, and to anyone that has either the sentiments of common honesty or delicacy, without the nicer feelings which every gentleman ought to possess, the situation of not paying what is due is a very unpleasant situation. In you I fear that vanity, which has been too prominent in your character, has occasioned this but I hope for the future you will be wiser.

KING GEORGE III, 1784, to the Prince of Wales, later King George IV

The royal hope proved unjustified.

Into this alliance his Royal Highness entered not for his private desire and gratification, but because it was pressed upon him for the purpose of providing for the succession of the Throne . . . (*loud laughter*).

GEORGE CANNING, to the House of Commons, on begging an increase of allowance to the Duke of Clarence, later King William IV, on his marriage to Princess Adelaide of Saxe-Coburg-Meiningen

Eh! What! Eh! What! Take William away? Take William away? He shan't go! Just arrived from Hanover – want to know how things are going on there. Fine stud! Fine stud.

KING GEORGE III, to the Prince of Wales, later King George IV, when the Prince had invited Prince William to a Carlton House fête, on his brother's first night home from Hanover

I trust in God that my life may be spared for nine months longer, after which period, in the event, no Regency would take place. I should then have the satisfaction of leaving the royal authority to that Young Lady and not in the hands of the person now near to me, who is surrounded by evil advisors and who is herself incompetent to act with propriety in the stations in which she would be placed. I have no hesitation in saying that I have been insulted, grossly and continually insulted, by that person, but I am determined to endure no longer a course of behaviour so disrespectful to me. . . . I would have her know that I am King, and that I am determined to make my authority respected.

KING WILLIAM IV, at a banquet, 1836, on his sister-in-law the Duchess of Kent and her daughter, Princess, later Queen, Victoria

FATHERHOOD

I trust in God for his salvation. He has cost me enough, but I wish he had lived to cost me more.

KING HENRY II, to William Marshal, Earl of Pembroke, on the death of his heir, Henry, 'The Young King', 1183

You baseborn whoreson, do you want to give away lands now, you who never gained any? As the Lord lives, if it was not for fear of breaking up the Kingdom you should never enjoy your inheritance.

KING EDWARD I, in a rage, while pulling out the hair of his son, Edward, Prince of Wales, later King Edward II

The eldest, Henry, is about twelve years old, of a noble wit and great promise. His every action is marked by a gravity most certainly beyond his years. He studies, not with much delight, and chiefly under his father's spur, not of his own desire, and for this he is often admonished and set down. Indeed one day the King, after giving him a lecture, said that if he did not attend more earnestly to his lessons the crown would be left to his brother, the Duke of York, who was far quicker at learning and studied more earnestly. The Prince made no reply, out of respect for his father, but when he went to his room and his tutor continued in the same vein, he said, 'I know what becomes a Prince. It is not necessary for me to be a professor, but a soldier and a man of the world. If my brother is as learned as they say, we'll make him Archbishop of Canterbury.' The King took this answer in no good part; nor is he overpleased to see his son beloved and of such promise that his subjects place all their hopes in him; and it would almost seem, to speak quite frankly, that the King was growing jealous; and so the Prince has great need of a wise counsellor to guide his steps.

NICOLE MOLIN, on King James VI and I and Henry, Prince of Wales.
Relazione, 1607

Good morning, children, am I not a funny-looking old man?

KING EDWARD VII, in coronation robes, 1901

Here a duchess remarked that he was not funny, not old and by no stretch of the imagination could be called a gentleman.

After I am dead, the boy will ruin himself in twelve months.

KING GEORGE V, on Edward, Prince of Wales, later King Edward VIII.
To Stanley Baldwin, Prime Minister, 1935

FAVOURITES

Gaveston

Queen Isabella: Unto the forest, gentle Mortimer,
To live in grief and baleful discontent;
For now my lord the king regards me not,
But dotes upon the love of Gaveston:
He claps his cheeks, and hangs about his neck,
Smiles in his face, and whispers in his ears;
And, when I come, he frowns, as who would say,
'Go whither thou wilt, seeing I have Gaveston.'

King Edward: My Gaveston!
Welcome to Tynmouth! Welcome to thy friend!
Thy absence made me droop and pine away;
For, as the lovers of fair Danae,
When she was lock'd up in a brazen tower,
Desir'd her more, and wax'd outrageous,
So did it sure with me: and now thy sight
Is sweeter far than was thy parting hence
Bitter and irksome to my sobbing heart.

CHRISTOPHER MARLOWE, *Edward II*

He sought his own glory rather than the king's and, as if scorning the English, who came in cloth of gold, rode among the guests in purple silk embroidered with pearls, more splendidly dressed than the king. ANNALES PAULINI, on Piers Gaveston, sweet Brother Piers, at Edward II's Coronation Banquet

The King's wild love for Gaveston was fiercer than that of David for Jonathan, of Achilles for Patroclus. ANON, *Vita Edwardi Secundi*

My God, what a fool he was. I could have told him never to get into Warwick's hands.

KING EDWARD II, on hearing of Gaveston's beheading by a group of noblemen headed by the Earl of Warwick

King Edward: By earth, the common mother of us all,
By heaven, and all the moving orbs thereof,
By this right hand, and by my father's sword,
And all the honours 'longing to my crown,
I will have heads and lives for him as many
As I have manors, castles, towns and towers –
Treacherous Warwick! Traitorous Mortimer!
If I be England's king, in lakes of gore
Your headless trunks, your bodies will I trail,
That you may drink your fill, and quaff in blood,
And stain our royal standard with the same,
That so my bloody colours may suggest
Remembrance of revenge immortally
On your accursed traitorous progeny,
You villains that have slain my Gaveston!

CHRISTOPHER MARLOWE, *Edward II*

John Bushy

Sir John Bushie, a knight of Lincolnshire, accounted to be an exceeding cruel man, ambitious and covetous beyond measure.

Sir John Bushie, in all his talk, when he proposed any matter unto the King, did not attribute to him titles of honour, due and accustomed; but invented unused terms, and such strange names as were rather agreeable to the divine Majesty of God, than to any earthly potentate. The prince, being desirous enough of all honour, and more ambitious than was requisite, seemed to like well of his speech and gave good ear to his talk.

RAPHAEL HOLINSHED, on a favourite of King Richard II.
History of England, 1577

There is a bush that's overgrown,
Crop it close and keep it down
    Or else it will run wild.

The long grass that is so green,
It must be mowed and raked clean;
    It has overrun the field.

That great bag that is so wide,
It shall be trimmed and smaller made,
    The bottom's nearly out;
It is so rotten through and through
That never a stitch will hold thereto
    To patch it with a clout.

ANON, on the favourites of King Richard II:
Sir John Bushy, Sir Henry Green (both
executed 1399) and Sir William Bagot

Robert Dudley, Earl of Leicester

I am insulted both in England and abroad for having shown too much favour to the Lord Robert. I am spoken of as if I were an immodest woman. I ought not to wonder at it: I have favoured him because of his excellent disposition and his many merits, but I am young and he is young and therefore we have both been slandered. God knows they do us grievous wrong, and the time will come when the world will know it also. A thousand eyes see all that I do, and calumny will not fasten on me for ever.

QUEEN ELIZABETH I, to Don Guzman de Silva, Spanish Ambassador, 1564

My lord of Leycester. How contemptuously we conceive ourself to have been used by you, you shall by this bearer understand, whom we have expressly sent unto you to charge you withal. We could never have imagined, had we not seen it fall out in experience, that a man raised up by ourself, and extraordinarily favoured by us above any subject of this land, would have in so contemptible a sort have broken our commandment, in a cause that so greatly toucheth us in honour, whereof, although you have showed yourself to make but little account, in most undutiful a sort, you may not therefore think that we have so little care of the reparation thereof as we mind to pass so great a wrong in silence unredressed: and therefore, our express pleasure and commandment is, all delays and excuses laid apart, you do presently, upon the duty of your allegiance, obey and fulfill whatsoever the bearer hereof shall direct you to do in our name: whereof fail you not, as you will answer the contrary at your uttermost peril.

QUEEN ELIZABETH I, to Robert Dudley, Earl of Leicester, when, without permission from London, he accepted at the Hague the Netherlands Estates-General offer of 'the absolute government of the whole provinces' in their rebellion against Spain

I may fall many ways and have more witnesses thereof than others who perhaps be no saints either.

ROBERT DUDLEY, EARL OF LEICESTER, after admonition from the Puritan, Thomas Wood

Here lies the worthy warrior
That never bloodied sword.
Here lies the loyal courtier
That never kept his word.
Here lies his noble excellence
That ruled all the states.
Here lies the Earl of Leicester
Whom earth and heaven hates.   ANON, 1588

He now is dead and all his glory gone
And all his greatness vapoured to nought,
That as a glass upon the water shone
Which vanished quite as soon as it was sought,
His name is worn already out of thought.

EDMUND SPENSER. 'The Ruins of Time', 1591

He was a major patron of the arts with huge building projects at his
three houses, Leicester House, Wanstead and Kenilworth Castle.
His picture inventories reveal a large collection, and it was he who
was the first major patron of the young Nicholas Hilliard, as well as
being instrumental in bringing to England the Roman Mannerist
painter, Federigo Zuccaro, in 1575. That year Leicester staged the
'Princely Pleasures' at Kenilworth in honour of the Queen, a somewhat crude attempt to imitate the *magnificences* which represented
the cultural apogee of Valois court civilization. To all this we can
add a massive and calculated patronage of literature in the Puritan
interest. And in 1585 it was Leicester who led the flower of English
chivalry to the low countries to fight against Spain.

ROY STRONG, 1986

Oberon's 'mermaid on a dolphin's back' in A Midsummer Night's
Dream *is often held to be a recollection of the elaborate theatricals
presented for the Queen's entertainment at Kenilworth in 1575.*

Robert Devereux, Earl of Essex

Happy were he could he finish forth his fate
In some unhaunted desert, where, obscure
From all society, from love and hate
Of worldly folk, there should he sleep secure;
And wake again, and yield God ever praise;
Content with hip, with haws, and brambleberry;
In contemplation passing still his days
And change of holy thoughts to keep him merry:

Who, when he dies, his tomb shall be the bush
Where harmless Robin resteth with the thrush:
     – Happy were he! ROBERT DEVEREUX, EARL OF ESSEX

Most dear lady, your kind and often sending is able either to preserve a sick man, or rather to raise a man that were more than half dead to life again. Since I was first so happy as to know what love meant, I was never one day, nor one hour, free from hope and jealousy; and as long as you do me right, they are the inseparable companions of my life. If your Majesty do in the sweetness of your own heart nourish the one, and in the justness of love free me from the tyranny of the other, you shall ever make me happy.

        THE EARL OF ESSEX, to Queen Elizabeth I

He hath played long enough on me, and now I mean to play awhile upon him, and stand as much upon my greatness as he hath upon stomach.   QUEEN ELIZABETH I

He prayed for all the Estates of the Realm, and he repeated the Lord's Prayer. The executioner, kneeling before him, asked for his forgiveness, which he granted. The clergymen requested him to rehearse the Creed, and he went through it, repeating it after them clause by clause. He rose and took off his doublet; a scarlet waist-coat, with long scarlet sleeves, was underneath. So – tall, splendid, bare-headed, with his fair hair about his shoulders – he stood before the world for the last time. Then, turning, he bowed low before the block; and, saying that he would be ready when he stretched out his arms, he lay down flat upon the scaffold. 'Lord, be merciful to thy prostrate servant!' he cried out, and put his head sideways upon the low block. 'Lord, into thy hands I recommend my spirit.' There was a pause; and all at once the red arms were seen to be extended. The headsman whirled up the axe, and crashed it downwards; the body made no movement; but twice more the violent action was repeated before the head was severed and the blood poured forth. The man stooped, and, taking the head by the hair, held it up before the onlookers, shouting as he did so, 'God save the Queen!' LYTTON STRACHEY, 1928

The man's soul seemed tossed to and fro like the waves of a troubled sea. SIR JOHN HARINGTON

George Villiers and King James VI and I

Disputes with his Parliaments, and his hunting, and his drinking, and his lying in bed – for he was a great sluggard – occupied his Sowship pretty well. The rest of his time he chiefly passed in hugging and slobbering his favourites. The first of these was Sir Philip Herbert, who had no knowledge whatever, except of dogs, and horses, and hunting, but whom he soon made Earl of Montgomery. The next, but a much more famous one, was Robert Carr . . . who came from the Border country, and whom he soon made Viscount Rochester, and afterwards, Earl of Somerset. The way in which his Sowship doted on this handsome young man is even more odious to think of, than the way in which the really great men of England condescended to bow down before him. The favourite's great friend was a certain Sir Thomas Overbury, who wrote his love-letters for him, and assisted him in the duties of his many high places, which his own ignorance prevented him from discharging. But this same Sir Thomas having just manhood enough to dissuade the favourite from a wicked marriage with the beautiful Countess of Essex, who was to get a divorce from her husband for the purpose, the said Countess, in her rage, got Sir Thomas put into the Tower, and there poisoned him. Then the favourite and this bad woman were publicly married by the King's pet bishop, with as much to-do and rejoicing, as if he had been the best man, and she the best woman, upon the face of the earth.

But, after a longer sunshine than might have been expected – of seven years or so, that is to say – another handsome young man started up and eclipsed the Earl of Somerset. This was George Villiers, the youngest son of a Leicestershire gentleman; who came to Court with all the Paris fashions on him, and could dance as well as the best mountebank that ever was seen. He soon danced himself into the good graces of his Sowship, and danced the other favourite out of favour. Then, it was all at once discovered that the Earl and Countess of Somerset had not deserved all those great promotions and mighty rejoicings, and they were separately tried for the murder of Sir Thomas Overbury, and for other crimes. But, the King was so afraid of his late favourite's publically telling some disgraceful things he knew of him – which he darkly threatened to do – that he was even examined with two men standing, one on either side of him, each with a cloak in his hand, ready to throw it over his head and stop his mouth if he should break out with what he had it in his power to tell. So, a very lame affair was purposely made of the trial, and his punishment was an allowance of four thousand pounds a year in retirement, while the Countess was pardoned, and allowed to pass into retirement too. They hated one another by this time, and lived to revile and torment each other some years. . . .

The new favourite got on fast. He was made a viscount, he was made Duke of Buckingham, he was made a marquis, he was made Master of the Horse, he was made Lord High Admiral – and the Chief Commander of the gallant English forces that had dispersed the Spanish Armada, was displaced to make room for him. He had the whole kingdom at his disposal, and his mother sold all the profits and honours of the State, as if she had kept a shop. He blazed all over with diamonds and other precious stones, from his hatband and his earrings to his shoes. Yet he was an ignorant presumptuous swaggering compound of knave and fool, with nothing but his beauty and his dancing to recommend him. This is the gentleman who called himself his Majesty's doer and slave, and called His Majesty Your Sowship. His Sowship called him Steenie; it is supposed, because St Stephen was generally represented in pictures as a handsome saint.

CHARLES DICKENS, 1853

As an art collector, Buckingham was warmly praised by Peter Paul Rubens.

A few days before the assassination the dead father of the duke appeared to Parker, an old servant (now the duke's servant) telling him to advise Buckingham to change his plans or be murdered. After a second visitation Parker went to the duke but was dismissed as 'an old Doting Fool'. That night the elder Villiers appeared a third time, giving Parker a token which only the duke could understand; the apparition even showed the servant what sort of weapon would be used. Next day Buckingham admitted his belief in the apparition, but his honour was at stake and he could not alter his plans to suit his dead father's shade.   R. C. FINUCANE, 1982

The murderer was John Felton, who escaped, but was detected by his hat which he had left behind in Buckingham's lodgings. 'No villain did it, but an honourable man. I am the man. . . . In your hearts you rejoice at my deed.'

Felton justified his deed with, 'God himself has enacted this law, that whatsoever is for the profit or benefit of the Commonwealth should be accounted lawful.' Before execution, however, he withdrew this, assenting to the counter-proposition, 'The common good could in no way be a pretence to a particular mischief.'

Sarah, Duchess of Marlborough

It is a common observation that differences of taste, understanding and disposition, are no impediments to friendship, and that the closest intimacies often exist between minds each of which supplies what is wanting to the other. Lady Churchill was loved and even worshipped by Anne. The Princess could not live apart from the object of her romantic fondness. She married, and was a faithful and even an affectionate wife. But Prince George, a dull man whose chief pleasures were derived from his dinner and his bottle, acquired over her no influence comparable to that exercised by her female friend, and soon gave himself up with stupid patience to the dominion of that vehement and commanding spirit by which his wife was governed. Children were born to the royal pair: and Anne was by no means without the feelings of a mother. But the tenderness which she felt for her offspring was languid when compared with her devotion to the companion of her early years. At length the Princess became impatient with the restraint which etiquette imposed on her. She could not bear the words Madam and Royal Highness from the lips of one who was more to her than a sister. Such words were indeed necessary in the gallery or the drawing room; but they were disused in the closet. Anne was Mrs Morley; Lady Churchill was Mrs Freeman; and under these childish names was carried on during twenty years a correspondence on which at last the fate of administrations and dynasties depended.

LORD MACAULAY, 1848, on Princess Anne, later Queen Anne, and Sarah Jennings, later Duchess of Marlborough

But what my dear Mrs Freeman said a little before she went from me this evening I cannot help fearing she may have heard some new lie of her poor unfortunate faithful Morley and therefore I beg you to open your dear heart, hide nothing but tell me even the least thing that gives you any hard thoughts of me, that I may justify myself, which I am sure I can do, never having done anything willingly to deserve your displeasure.

I would have made this request when I parted from you, but I found my heart and eyes growing so full I durst not attempt it, being sure if I had I should not have been fit to have seen anybody. For the same reason I desire an answer to this in writing and that for Jesus' sake as soon as it is possible, for I am on the rack and cannot bear living as we do now, being with the same sincere tender passion that I ever was my dear dear Mrs Freeman's and shall be so inviolably to my last moment. QUEEN ANNE, to Sarah, Duchess of Marlborough, 1706

Abigail Hill

A person of plain sound understanding, of great truth and sincerity without the least falsehood or disguise; of an honest boldness and courage superior to her sex, firm and disinterested in her friendship

137

and full of love, duty and veneration for the Queen [Anne] her mistress.   JONATHAN SWIFT, on Abigail Hill (Mrs Masham)

Exceedingly mean and vulgar in her manners, of very unequal temper, childishly exceptious and passionate.

LORD DARTMOUTH

When as Queene Anne of Great Renown
Great Britain's sceptre sway'd
Besides the Church she dearly lov'd
A dirty Chambermaid.

O! Abigail that was her name
She stick'd and starch'd full well
But how she pierc'd this Royal Heart
No Mortal Man can tell.

However, for sweet Service done
And Causes of great Weight
Her Royal Mistress made her O!
A Minister of State.

Her Secretary she was not
Because she could not write
But she had the Conduct and the Care
Of some Dark Deeds at Night.

(attrib.) ARTHUR MAYNWARING, 1708

John Brown

Soon after my arrival in England, at a table where all the company were gentlemen by rank or position, there were constant references to and jokes about 'Mrs Brown'. I lost the point of all the witty sayings, and should have remained in blissful ignorance throughout the dinner had not my host kindly informed me that 'Mrs Brown' was an English synonym for the Queen.

I have been told that the Queen was not allowed to hold a

review in Hyde Park, because Lord Derby and the Duke of Cambridge objected to John Brown's presence; that the Queen was insane, and John Brown her keeper; that the Queen was a spiritualist, and John Brown was her medium – in a word, a hundred stories, each more absurd than the other, and all vouched for by men of considerable station and authority.

Anon (American), on John Brown, Queen Victoria's Highland attendant.
Tinsley's Magazine, 1866

Balmoral. Tuesday.   'Court Circular'

Mr John Brown walked on the slopes.
He subsequently partook of a haggis.
In the evening Mr John Brown was pleased to listen to a bagpipe.
Mr John Brown retired early.   *Punch*, 1866

Lady Reid has stated, 1986, that her husband's grandfather, Sir James Reid, one of Queen Victoria's doctors, mentions in his diary that the dying queen held Brown's portrait and a lock of his hair.

The Queen was hardly cold in her grave before busts of Brown were smashed, photographs of him were burned, and, crowning insult, Brown's apartment at Windsor Castle was converted into a billiard-room, all on Edward VII's orders.   Tom Cullen, 1960

THE FIELD OF THE
CLOTH OF GOLD

The name itself is dazzling. The reality, in that June of 1520, was of a sumptuousness inconceivable. It cannot be said that these amazing spectacles were without a touch of fancy. When Francis and Leonardo da Vinci had met one another at Bologna in 1516, brought together by Pope Leo X, and the spark of mutual recognition had leapt from the old man of superb and curious vision to the gallant and perceptive youth, it could not be forgotten that for many years Leonardo had lent himself to devising the extravagant and soaring ceremonials of the Sforzas of Milan. These were ephemeral, like the gestures and movements of great actors, and the songs of birds. Leonardo was dead in 1519, but the Francis who was joining in this present spectacle had shown by the passionate delight with which he had brought Leonardo to France, and the ardour with which he and the man of genius had conversed, that he was not a mere lover of puppetry. He seduced Leonardo from Italy, but he had bought the Mona Lisa, and honestly paid for it four thousand florins. There was an impulse of crass, yet natural ostentation, of crude yet positive grandeur, of sheer royal magnificence, in these outdoor parties that included thousands of sparkling participants and invited the weather to keep smiling for a month.

Such magnificence, unfortunately, was promoted by Wolsey against every economic principle. Martin du Bellay noted dryly that 'Many carried on their shoulders their mills, their forests and their meadows.' Only by the wars that were adumbrated, only by turning towns into shambles and living men into carrion could this sunburst begin to see knighthood in pocket once again. A hundred Mona Lisas could have been commissioned, a hundred Erasmuses relieved from cadging for half a century, out of one petty morsel of this Cloth of Gold. But no reason except reason of state urged Wolsey to such incredible extravagance. He saw politics theatrically, accustomed to vast, stinking, miserable hordes of common people, who knelt on the tombstones of their forebears and breathed the smell of corpses, while the chant of angelic voices rose through clouds of incense, and light was poured like jewels into uplifted eyes. The Field of the Cloth of Gold was the last throe of churchly ceremonial: and long years after would Manchester shake its salt-and-pepper head over this lamentable orgy, which was indeed lamentable, and which even before it happened made the alarmed Francis inquire if Henry could 'forbear the making of rich tents and pavilions'.

FRANCIS HACKETT, 1929

FLIGHT

And as I was holding my horse's foot, I asked the smith what news. He told me that there was no news that he knew of, since the good news of the beating of the rogues the Scots. I asked him, whether there was none of the English taken; that joined with the Scots? He answered, that he did not hear that the rogue Charles Stuart was taken; but some of the others, he said, were taken, but not Charles Stuart. I told him that if that rogue were taken, he deserved to be hanged, more than all the rest, for bringing in the Scots. Upon which he said that I spoke like an honest man, and so we parted.

KING CHARLES II, on his flight from defeat at Worcester,
disguised as 'Mr Will Jackson', 1651

The truth of Charles's escape from Worcester was, if anything, more remarkable than the many legends. He wandered about England for forty-three days, living mostly on sherry and biscuits. He darkened his face with walnut juice, had his hair cut with a pair of shears, and donned green breeches, a leather doublet and a felt hat. He even imitated a country accent. After the Restoration, he used to bore friends and sycophants alike with tales of his 'miraculous escape'. Numerous pamphlets commemorated every last detail of the odyssey. The anonymous *Extract Narrative and Relation* began: 'Fortune has now twice counterfeited and double-gilt the trophies of rebellion.' Another called his account simply *The Royal Oath*. The third was entitled *England's Triumph*. Each was a best seller, and there were some forty other versions of the story prior to the official account, dictated by Charles himself during a drunken weekend at Newmarket racecourse almost thirty years after the event.

TONY PALMER, 1979

Two hours later a militia man named Henry Parkin whilst searching some fern and brambles found beneath an ash-tree a brown skirt. In a ditch lay the Duke asleep. . . .

It was hardly credible that this man in the rough clothes of a shepherd, with a beard, and ashen face could be Monmouth. Lord Lumley now rode up, and it was agreed that (Sir William) Portman should search him. There was found on his person his watch, a purse, a few raw peas, his pocket book, his diary, and the most useful object to identify him, his 'George'. . . .

There is a tradition that Henry Parkin, the soldier who discovered Monmouth, reproached himself bitterly, and wept when he learnt who his captive was. As for Amy Farrant (whose cottage lay about one hundred yards from the scene of Monmouth's capture), the superstitious people who abounded in the countryside related that a curse now fell on the old woman's cottage. Henceforward her cottage was shunned as a place of ill-omen, and people would shiver at her very name. Among the Secret Service expenses of James II is recorded: 'To Amy Farrant, bounty of £50 for giving notice to the Lord Lumley where the Duke of Monmouth lay concealed, whereby he was apprehended . . .'.

Parkin received £20 and the two troopers who captured Monmouth, 10 guineas each.

BRYAN BEVAN, 1973, on James Scott, Duke of Monmouth, captured in 1685 at Horton, Hampshire, after defeat at Sedgemoor

It was strange that a great king, who had a good army and a strong fleet, should choose rather to abandon all than either try his fate with that part of the army that stood firm to him, or stay and see the issue of Parliament. This was variously imputed to his want of courage, his consciousness of guilt, or the advice of those about him; but so it was that his deserting in this manner, and leaving them to be pillaged by an army that he had ordered to be disbanded without pay, was thought the forfeiture of his right and the expiration of his reign.

BISHOP GILBERT BURNET, on the flight of King James II in 1688 before William, Prince of Orange. *History of His Own Time*, 1724

FOOD

The Duchess of York had the biggest appetite of any woman in the kingdom. Here was a pleasure which she could properly indulge, and what she was deprived of in other ways she made up for at table. It was most instructive to watch the Duchess eat, and while the Duke dissipated his energies in the constant pursuit of new fancies, and grew steadily thinner, his poor wife, who nourished herself most conscientiously, grew quite astonishingly fat.

> ANTHONY HAMILTON, on Anne Hyde and James,
> Duke of York, afterwards King James II.
> *Memoirs of the Life of the Comte de Gramont*, 1713

FORGIVENESS

KING RICHARD I, dying: 'What injury have I done you, for you to have slain me?'

THE ARCHER OF CHALUZ: 'You killed my father and both my brothers. Therefore, revenge yourself on me as you wish, for I will readily suffer the worst torture you can contrive, so long as you yourself die after afflicting the world with evils so many and so great.'

RICHARD: 'I forgive you my death. You may go free.'

The youth was blinded, flayed, torn apart by horses.

I pray God save the King, and send him long to reign over you, for a gentler and more merciful Prince was there never; and to me he was ever a good, a gentle, and sovereign Lord.

> QUEEN ANNE BOLEYN, on the scaffold, 1536

It is all I have now left me, a power to forgive those that have deprived me of all; and I thank God I have a heart to do it, and joy as much in this grace, which God hath given me, as in all my former enjoyments; for this is a greater argument of God's love to me than any prosperity can be. Be confident (as I am) that the most of all sides, who have done amiss, not out of malice, but misinformation, or misapprehension of things.

KING CHARLES I, 1649, from his last letter to his son,
Charles, Prince of Wales, later King Charles II

FUNERALS

The funeral was regal. It reached the expectant capital through Southwark, passing the parks of noblemen, the new mansions of wealthy merchants, the jolly taverns, the bawdy quarter, the little graveyard of nameless women. At London Bridge the Mayor received the funeral, attended by the city companies, and from every arch and hole in London Wall crept curious cut-purses and scallywags, mingling with honest boatmen from gate and wharf, stout carters and their housewives, bronzed and brawny mariners. Away from Thames, toward the great Gothic St Paul's, the proud procession mounted. Everywhere the houses were candle-lit, and through the narrow glowing channel of these dense streets the mourners rumbled and chanted behind the chariot as it rocked over broken ways. Boys' thrush-like voices, clerks' jackdaw voices, rose and fell in a multiple jargon that was mellowed by the vault of heaven. Thousands of soft-shod attendants pattered in rank on rank behind the corpse with its waxen effigy, while the flare and fume of six hundred torches moved with the chariot and cast dancing shadows on the rapt Londoners' gaze.

That generous heart of London had no reproach for the dynast who was going to his grave. Not yet an empire within an empire, but already the aspirant to a soul, London could view its king with equanimity, now he had on him the mantling dignity of death. Eager, sober, illuminated faces peered through the glow of the endless pathos of the common fate. The white-hued messenger, the burly brewer, the cobbler, the pinched tailor, the blacksmith, the tanner, the hooper, the surgeon-barber, the German merchant from the steelyard, the French embroiderer, the Flemish weaver, the stone-cutter from Italy, the thronging Cockney apprentices with their sharp-cut noses and rapid tongues, were welded together, hot and palpitant, into a receptive and wondering throng. Even in death the Monarch held supremacy.

While multitudes poured on the heels of the winding cortège, now ablare of sonorous Latin, now a flare of fuscous red, St Paul's opened its wide arms to receive the body of a king. Gradually the waves of life were gathered to its bosom. Gradually in the distant thoroughfares under Tower Hill and near the Thames the spring twilight resumed its peace and these streets lay pensive in emptiness. A fresh air came from the meadows of Finsbury. The evening light, a dim blue crystal, bathed once again the deserted houses. Blue shadows washed the black-beamed walls. A star rose over a thatched roof. At St Paul's they would be praying. To-morrow at Westminster the great officers of state would break their white wands and cast them into Henry's grave. . . . And when all the kings were buried, the month of May would still come of an evening and whisper eternity in a London street.

FRANCIS HACKETT, 1929, on King Henry VII

King George V was sincerely mourned. The papers appeared with heavy black lines on the day of his death and on that of his funeral. All broadcasting programmes were cancelled and theatres and cinemas closed. On January 23rd, 1936, the body was brought to London, where it lay in state at Westminster Hall, crowds filing past it every day, often at the rate of fifteen thousand an hour. The funeral was to take place on Tuesday the 28th, and on the night before, at midnight, the new King himself and his three brothers mounted guard for half an hour over their father's coffin. A day of

National Mourning followed. The streets of London were sparingly but harmoniously draped in purple. The crowd, a large part of which had waited all night on the pavement, made quite a jolly affair of the funeral with lunch-baskets and camp-stools. 'Where's George?' someone cried gaily in Trafalgar Square; for the cortège from Westminster to Paddington station, where it was to take train for the interment at St George's Chapel, Windsor Castle, had failed to appear on time. The cry was taken up and a great roar of laughter arose. 'Where's George?' was a popular advertising catchword of Lyons' restaurants. Yet there was no disrespect in the laughter. 'He was a good little man and we'll miss him.' The new King, Edward VIII, walked behind the coffin with five other kings, and the representatives of numerous states, including Nazi Germany. According to the *Daily Worker*, General Goering had wished to come himself, but was warned by the Foreign Office that his personal safety could not be guaranteed in view of the hostility of Jewish refugees and others; Baron von Neurath and some generals came instead. The USSR sent Marshal Tukachevsky and his wife. There were seven thousand casualties in the funeral crowds.

ROBERT GRAVES AND ALAN HODGE, 1950

Christ: What's going to happen next?

KING EDWARD VIII, when the Maltese Cross topping the Imperial Crown
fell off during the procession of the royal coffin
from King's Cross to Westminster Hall

THE GAME

One evening we played The Game – a form of charades which is also popular in America. Queen Elizabeth (wife of King George VI) acted as a kind of master of ceremonies and chose the words that the rest of us were called upon to act out in such a way that they could be guessed. She puzzled for some time over various words and occasionally turned to Mr Churchill for assistance, but without success. The former Prime Minister, with a decoration on the bosom of his stiff, white shirt with a cigar in his hand, sat glumly aside and would have nothing to do with The Game which he obviously regarded as inane and a waste of time for adults. Not even the Queen's pleas for advice could move him to take a small part in the activities. He just kept on being glum.

ELEANOR ROOSEVELT, 1959

GARDENS

Proud prelate, remember what you were before I made you what you are. If you do not at once comply with my request, by God, I will unfrock you.

QUEEN ELIZABETH I, on an objection by the Bishop of Ely to her demand that he surrender his gateway and forty-acre garden at Ely Palace, now remembered as Hatton Garden. Reluctantly complying, he received, in return, rent of one rose a year; also, permission periodically to walk in the garden and annually to gather twenty bushels of roses.

Its garden was a picture. Those twenty bushels of roses were never missed. The eye was ravished by the beauty and the number of the roses that remained. There were besides lilies and heartsease and rosemary and cloves, and wide beds of delicious strawberries. Fountains played where they could best be seen. There were fishponds and arbours, and a long row of beehives, and a big blind dovecote with pigeons flying in and out of the roof.

Mrs Norsthworthy, on Ely Palace Garden,
quoted by HELEN G. NUSSEY, 1939

GENEALOGY

We came from the Devil, and to the Devil we will return.

(attrib.) KING RICHARD I, on his family, the Plantagenets

He is the twenty-first English Prince of Wales, but the first in direct descent from both the great Welsh princes, Owen Glendower and Lewelyn-ap-Gruffydd, the last native Prince of all Wales. He is descended from all the British monarchs save his namesake Charles I and his sons, and from every royal house of Europe. His ancestors include Charlemagne and Genghis Khan, El Cid and George Washington, Shakespeare and Count Dracula. He is thirty-ninth from William the Conqueror, fifth from Queen Victoria, and eighth from a London plumber called John Walsh.

ANTHONY HOLDEN, 1979, on Charles Philip Arthur George
Mountbatten-Windsor, Prince of Wales, Earl of Chester, Duke of Rothesay,
Earl of Carrick and Baron Renfrew, Lord of the Isles and Great Steward
of Scotland, Knight of the Most Noble Order of the Garter, Knight of
the Most Ancient and Most Noble Order of the Thistle, Great Master and
Principal Knight Grand Cross of the Most Honourable Order of the Bath

THE GENTLEMAN

A gentleman does not indulge in careless self-indulgent lounging ways such as lolling in armchairs or on sofas, slouching in his gait, or placing himself in unbecoming attitudes with his hands in his pockets. . . .

He will borrow nothing from the fashions of the groom or the gamekeeper, and whilst avoiding the frivolity and foolish vanity of dandyism, will take care that his clothes are of the best quality.

ALBERT, PRINCE CONSORT; memorandum for his son,
Albert Edward, Prince of Wales, 1858

GEORGE I

When the crown did come to George Louis he was in no hurry about putting it on. He waited at home for awhile; took an affecting farewell of his dear Hanover and Herrenhausen; and set out in the most leisurely manner to ascend 'the throne of his ancestors', as he called it in his first speech to Parliament. He brought with him a compact body of Germans, whose society he loved, and whom he kept round the royal person. He had his faithful German chamberlains; his German secretaries; his negroes, captives of his bow and spear in Turkish wars; his two ugly, elderly German favourites, Mesdames of Kielmansegge and Schulenberg, whom he created respectively Countess of Darlington and Duchess of Kendal. The duchess was tall, and lean of stature, and hence was irreverently nicknamed the Maypole. The countess was a large-sized noblewoman, and this elevated personage was denominated the Elephant. Both of these ladies loved Hanover and its delights; clung round the linden-trees of the great Herrenhausen avenue, and at first would not quit the place. Schulenberg, in fact, could not come on account of her debts; but finding the Maypole would not come, the Elephant packed up her trunk and slipped out of Hanover unwieldly as she was. On this the Maypole straightway put herself in motion, and followed her beloved George Louis. One seems to be speaking of Captain Macheath, and Polly, and Lucy. The king we had selected; the courtiers who came in his train; the English nobles who came to welcome him, and on many of whom the shrewd old cynic turned his back – I protest it is a wonderful satirical picture. I am a citizen waiting at Greenwich pier, say, and crying hurrah for King George; and yet I can scarcely keep my countenance, and help laughing at the enormous absurdity of this advent!

Here we are, all on our knees. Here is the Archbishop of Canterbury prostrating himself to the head of his church, with Kielmansegge and Schulenberg with their raddled cheeks grinning behind the defender of the faith. Here is my Lord Duke of Marlborough kneeling too, the greatest warrior of all times; he who betrayed King William – betrayed King James II – betrayed Queen Anne – betrayed England to the French, the Elector to the Pretender, the Pretender to the Elector; and here are my Lords Oxford and Bolingbroke, the latter of whom has just tripped up the heels of the former; and if a month's more time had been allowed him, would have had King James at Westminster. The great Whig gentlemen made their bows and congées with proper decorum and ceremony; but yonder keen old schemer knows the value of their loyalty. 'Loyalty', he must think, 'as applied to me – it is absurd! There are fifty nearer heirs to the throne than I am. I am but an accident, and you fine Whig gentlemen take me for your own sake, not for mine. You Tories hate me; you archbishop, smirking on your knees, and prating about Heaven, you know I don't care a fig for your Thirty-nine Articles, and can't understand a word of your stupid sermons. You, my Lords Bolingbroke and Oxford – you know you were conspiring against me a month ago; and you, my Lord Duke of Marlborough – you would sell me or any man else, if you found your advantage in it. Come, my good Melusina, come, my honest Sophia, let us go into my private room, and have some oysters and some Rhine wine, and some pipes afterwards: let us make the best of our situation; let us take what we can get, and leave these bawling, brawling, lying English to shout, and fight, and cheat, in their own way!'   W. M. THACKERAY, 1860

GEORGE II

Some days afterwards we had in the opera-house at Hanover, a great assembly. The King appeared in a Turkish dress; his turban was ornamented with a magnificent agraffe of diamonds; the Lady Yarmouth was dressed as a Sultana; nobody was more beautiful than the Princess of Hesse. So, while poor Queen Caroline was resting in her coffin, dapper little George, with his red face and his white eyebrows, and goggle-eyes, at sixty years of age, is dancing a pretty dance with Madame Walmoden, and capering about dressed like a Turk!

W. M. THACKERAY, 1860

> You may strut, dapper George, but 'twill all be in vain,
> For we know 'tis Queen Caroline, not you, who reign,
> You govern no more than Don Philip of Spain.
> If you want all your subjects to kneel and adore you,
> Lock up your fat spouse, as your dad did before you.
>
> ANON

GEORGE III

Unfortunately George III was as unlucky in his heredity as in his environment. Neither George II nor his queen, Caroline, was devoid of character or without some gifts above the commonplace. Her intelligence and his memory were unusual in monarchs, and their hatred of their son was tinged with genuine disappointment. Frederick, George III's father, was known to posterity as 'Poor Fred', and the epithet is not unjust. He possessed a small talent for music, a mild interest in games, particularly cricket, and little else. The unsympathetic Lord Shelburne described his life as 'a tissue of

151

childishness and falsehood'; and his friends as well as his enemies despised him. George II married his son to Princess Augusta of Saxe-Gotha simply because there was no one else. The other Protestant princesses of sufficiently high birth had madness in their families, and George II rejected them, for as he said, 'I did not think ingrafting my half-witted coxcomb upon a madwoman would mend the breed.' As it turned out, it could not have made matters much worse, for an astonishing number of Princess Augusta's children and grandchildren turned out to be congenital idiots or subject to fits of insanity, or mentally unbalanced, or blind; the rest were odd or wicked or both. In some ways George III can be described as the best of the bunch. He was very stupid, really stupid. Had he been born in different circumstances it is unlikely that he could have earned a living except as an unskilled manual labourer. He was ten before he could read, and he never mastered grammar or spelling or punctuation. He was lethargic, apathetic, childish, a clod of a boy whom no one could teach. His major response to life was a doting love for his brother Edward. In late adolescence he began to wake up, largely because of a passionate romantic attachment to Lord Bute, the close friend and confidant of his mother. (The public at large thought she was his mistress. Probably she was not. The slander deeply distressed George III and made his attachment to Bute firmer.) Somehow Bute made the young prince conscious not only of his destiny but also of his shortcomings. The Prince promised time and time again to throw off his lethargy so that he could accomplish great things for Bute's sake. Naturally the greatest of things was to get rid of his grandfather's evil ministers and to install Bute in a position of power. The ill-spelt, ungrammatical, childish, heartfelt notes that he sent to Bute make pathetic reading. They are charged with a sense of inadequacy, a feeling of hopelessness before the immensity of the burden which destiny had laid on his shoulders, and with an anxious need for help that is almost neurotic in its intensity.   J. H. PLUMB, 1963

The vulgar view of King George III is quite simply that he was mad and, to make matters worse, that he also succeeded in losing the American colonies. The fact that he had wide and civilized interests, was a great patron of the arts and sciences and devoted a vast quantity of time to affairs of state has been conveniently neglected.

CHARLES, PRINCE OF WALES, reviewing
Queen Victoria was Amused by Alan Hardy, 1976

GEORGE IV

He is a violator of his word, a libertine over head and ears in debt and disgrace, a despiser of domestic ties, the companion of gamblers and demirips, a man who has just closed half a century without one single claim on the gratitude of his country or the result of posterity. LEIGH HUNT, 1811

He spent over £20 a week on cold cream and almond paste, perfumed almond powder and scented bags. CHRISTOPHER HIBBERT

Royalty did not monopolize extravagance. From R. G. Thorne's edition of The History of Parliament *can be learnt that in the 1802 Carmarthenshire election, a defeated candidate bought for his putative constituents 11,000 breakfasts, 40,000 dinners, 25,000 gallons of ale.*

He was, indeed, the most extraordinary compound of talent, wit, buffoonery, obstinacy and good feeling – in short, a medley of the most opposite qualities with a great preponderance of good that I ever saw in any character in my life. THE DUKE OF WELLINGTON, 1830

King George IV was *un roi, grand seigneur*. There are no others left.

TALLEYRAND, 1830

GEORGE VI

Then I saw Mr Attlee and asked him to form a government. He accepted and became my new Prime Minister. I told him he would have to appoint a Foreign Secretary and take him to Berlin. I found he was very surprised his Party had won and had had no time to meet or discuss with his colleagues any of the Offices of State. I asked him whom he would make Foreign Secretary and he suggested Dr Hugh Dalton. I disagreed with him and said that Foreign Affairs was the most important subject at the moment and I hoped he would make Mr Bevin take it. He said he would but he could not return to Berlin till Saturday at the earliest. I told him I could hold a Council on Saturday to swear in the new Secretary of State. I hoped our relations would be cordial and said that I would always be ready to help him.   KING GEORGE VI. *Diary*, 1945

Mr Attlee's personal relationship with King George was at first not easy. Both were essentially shy men and the initiation of conversation did not come easily to either of them. At the outset the Prime Minister's audiences were not infrequently marked by long silences. This, however, quickly wore off. Both persevered – and with success.

The King writes in his diary later of 'long talks with Mr Attlee', in the course of which he was able, apart from conducting the business of the day, to put to the Prime Minister some of the aspects of thought which were current at the time, not infrequently surprising him by the extent, detail and accuracy of his information. 'I told Attlee,' he wrote on one occasion, 'that he must give the people here some confidence that the Government was not going to stifle all private enterprise. Everyone wanted to help in rehabilitating the country but they were not allowed to.'...

On the subject of strikes also the King was emphatic with his Prime Minister. A stoppage of work by gas employees, which had not been accorded official Trade Union recognition, caused considerable inconvenience during the winter of 1945 and Mr Attlee expressed the hope that it would be settled quickly. King George commented that 'the liberty of the subject was at stake if a strike interfered with home life. Essential services such as gas, electricity and water should never be used for those purposes in an unofficial strike. He and I could easily go on strike. He would send me no papers and if he did I would not sign them. But we don't.'

JOHN W. WHEELER BENNETT, on King George VI, 1958

GIFTS

Very often she received purses of money, but sometimes her servants gave her quaint things like:
  a pot of green ginger,
  a figure of St George made in marzipan,
  a white bear of gold and mother of pearl holding a ragged staff
      wherein is a clock,
  6 small tooth-picks of gold,
  a box of nutmegs,
  a model of St Paul's church in marzipan,
  18 larks in a cage.

MARJORIE REEVES, 1956, on Queen Elizabeth I

GOD'S WORK

God's Work, done in God's way.

> Chaplain to the Fifth Monarchist, Colonel Overton, a Cromwellian officer,
> on the execution of King Charles I, 1649

GRIEF

Oak that has grown up on the grounds
Of the woody promontory fronting the contending
    waves of the Severn sea;
Woe! to him who is not old enough to die.

Oak that has grown up in the storms
Amid dins, battles, and death;
Woe! to him that beholds what is not death.

> ROBERT, DUKE OF NORMANDY, imprisoned for twenty-eight years
> by his younger brother, King Henry I, in Cardiff Castle,
> where he died, 1134. Trs. Alan Borg, 1978

The Queen of Scots is lighter of a fair son, but I am but a barren stock.

> Attributed by Sir James Melville to QUEEN ELIZABETH I, on the birth of
> James Stuart, later King James VI and I, 1560

The Queen of Scots coming to my charge will make me soon grey-headed.

> GEORGE TALBOT, EARL OF SHREWSBURY, 1568, on appointment as 'guardian',
> or jailer, of Mary Queen of Scots, refugee from Scotland,
> professed claimant to the English Crown

Circumstances proved him correct.

My lyre is changed into the sound of mourning; and my song into the voices of people weeping.

SIR WALTER RALEGH, on the death of Henry, Prince of Wales, 1612.
History of the World, 1614

To express what the Queen's desolation and utter misery is, is almost impossible; every feeling seems swallowed up in that one of unbounded grief. She feels as if *her life* had ended on *that* dreadful day. . . . She sees the trees budding, the days lengthening, the primroses coming out, but she *thinks* herself still in the month of December.

QUEEN VICTORIA, mourning Prince Albert, to Lord Derby, 1862

GUILT

King Arthur

I was the cause of the disastrous end . . .
I in my early manhood sowed the seed
That made the Kingdom rend.
I begot Modred in my young man's greed.
When the hot blood betrays us, who gives heed?
Morgause and I were lovers for a night,
Not knowing how the fates had made us kin.
So came the sword to smite,
So was the weapon whetted that made bleed:
That young man's loving let the ruin in.

JOHN MASEFIELD, 'Midsummer Night'

In an Arthurian legend, Modred was the result of Arthur's incest with his sister, and ultimately ruined the Brotherhood of the Table by treachery, culminating in his own death and that of his father–uncle.

I have done amiss.

KING JAMES VI AND I, on the betrayal and final arrest of
Sir Walter Ralegh, 1618, with royal connivance

There isn't any power. There can be influence. The influence is in direct ratio to the respect people have for you.

CHARLES, PRINCE OF WALES, 1979

THE HAT

WILLIAM PENN, the Quaker: 'Friend Charles, why dost thou
  remove thy hat?'
KING CHARLES II: 'It is custom in this place for only one person to
  remain covered.'

*This amiable retort compares well with that of his stately cousin,
Louis XIV, who, when a minister arrived for an audience with
absolute punctuality, said severely: 'I was within an ace of being
kept waiting.'*

THE HEART

Her death took place on the 7th of January 1536. And, although it
was a cold winter day, the Keeper of the house decided that she
must be embalmed that same night, and enclosed in lead, far from
the eyes of men. The work was done quickly, as if the fires of the sun
that flare over the dead woman's native Granada were at their
height.

In the early morning following the night they had spent with the
dead queen's body, the embalmers told her devoted Spanish servants that her heart, when it lay exposed to their eyes, was entirely
black, and hideous to the sight. ... They washed the heart,
strongly, in water that they changed three times. But that frightful
blackness did not alter. Then one of the embalmers clove the heart
in two, and they found a black thing clinging to the core, with such

force that it could not be dislodged. That black heart, and the body it had consumed as a fire melts wax, were shut away in a covering of lead before the light of day could witness the fate that had befallen them.

Next day, which was a Sunday, the Court rang with the noise of balls and feasts.

EDITH SITWELL, 1963, on Queen Katharine of Aragon,
wife of King Henry VIII

HENRIETTA MARIA

The king's [Charles I's] affection to the queen was of a very extraordinary alloy; a composition of conscience and love, and generosity and gratitude, and all those noble affections which raise the passion to the greatest height; insomuch as he saw with her eyes, and determined by her judgment; and did not only pay her this adoration, but desired that all men should know that he was swayed by her: which was not good for either of them. The queen was a lady of great beauty, excellent wit and humour, and made him a just return of noblest affections; so that they were the true idea of conjugal affection, in the age in which they lived. When she was admitted to the most secret affairs (from which she had been carefully restrained by the duke of Buckingham whilst he lived), she took delight in examining and discussing them.

She had felt so much pain in knowing nothing, and meddling with nothing, during the time of that great favourite, that now she took pleasure in nothing but knowing all things, and disposing all things; and thought it but just, that she should dispose of all favours and preferments, as he had done; at least, that nothing of that kind might be done without her privity: not considering that the universal prejudice that great man had undergone, was not with reference to his person, but his power; and that the same power would be equally obnoxious to murmur and complaint, if it resided in any other person than the king himself. And she so far concurred with the king's inclination, that she did not more desire to be possessed of this unlimited power, than that all the world should take notice that she was the entire mistress of it: which in truth (what other unhappy circumstance soever concurred in the mischief) was the foundation upon which the first and the utmost prejudices to the king and his government were raised and prosecuted. And it was her Majesty's and the kingdom's misfortune that she had not any person about her, who had either ability or affection, to inform and advise her of the temper of the kingdom, or humour of the people; or who thought either worth the caring for.

When the disturbance grew so rude as to interrupt this harmony, and the queen's fears, and indisposition, which proceeded from those fears, disposed her to leave the kingdom, which the king, to comply with her, consented to; (and if that fear had not been predominant in her, her jealousy and apprehension, that the king would at some time be prevailed with to yield to some unreasonable conditions, would have dissuaded her from that voyage;) to make all things therefore as sure as might be, that her absence should not be attended with any such inconvenience, his Majesty made a solemn promise to her at parting, that he would receive no person into any favour or trust, who had disserved him, without her privity and consent; and that, as she had undergone so many reproaches and calumnies at the entrance into the war, so he would never make any peace, but by her interposition and mediation, that the kingdom might receive that blessing only from her.

EDWARD HYDE, EARL OF CLARENDON

HENRY I

He was of middle height, taller than a short man, shorter than a tall man. His black hair receded from the forehead, his eyes were gentle but shining, he had a brawny chest and fat body.

WILLIAM OF MALMESBURY

A good man he was; and there was great dread of him. No man durst do wrong with another in his time. Peace he made for man and beast. Whoso bare his burthen of gold and silver, durst no man say aught to him but good.   *Anglo-Saxon Chronicle*

One of the most repulsive among the kings who have ruled in England. . . .

His chief vices . . . were lust, avarice and cruelty, and while he shared these with many of his contemporaries, his methods of indulging them were his own. . . .

His cruelty was revolting. Though he cannot with certainty be convicted of fratricide, there is strong evidence that he connived at the murder of one brother (William II) and he kept another (Robert of Normandy) in close confinement for nearly thirty years. He allowed two of his granddaughters to be blinded when they were hostages in his hands, and his punishments of malefactors was [sic] hideously savage. . . .

Henry was of course not isolated in his brutality, but he was perhaps exceptional in the false geniality with which it was cloaked.

DAVID C. DOUGLAS, 1976

It has been left to modern historians to hint that a baronial conspiracy . . . in the interests of Count Henry [Henry I] had contrived William's death. But there is not a shred of good evidence and the theory merely avoids the obvious. Hunting accidents were, after all, not uncommon. The deaths of the king's brother and nephew (in the New Forest) have already been noticed.

FRANK BARLOW, 1983, on the killing of King William II, 1100

HENRY II

Henry II, King of England, had a reddish complexion, somewhat dark, and a head big and rounded. His grey eyes were bloodshot, and in anger they would glitter. His face was fiery, his voice tremulous, and his neck slightly protruded; his chest, however, was broad and his arms muscular. He was well-fleshed with an enormous paunch, due more to nature than to over-eating. . . . When his spirits were untroubled and his mood not enfuriated, he spoke very eloquently, and, remarkable for that time, he was well educated. He was also affable, flexible, and jocular, and, however he concealed his private thoughts, was surpassed by none in courtesy. Altogether, he was so clement a prince, that, when victorious, he was then himself overcome by compassion for his foes. Resolute in warfare, provident in peace, he was so alarmed by the wavering fortunes of battle that, in the words of the comic poet, he tried all courses before resorting to arms. Whoever he lost in combat he mourned with a sorrow more than ordinary in a ruler, feeling more humanity for the dead soldiers than for the living; bewailing them more than rejoicing with those around him. In disturbed times none was more courteous, and, in calm days, none more harsh. He was severe to the disorderly, but kindly to the humble, harsh to his retainers but liberal to outsiders, extravagant abroad but frugal at home, scarcely ever able to love whoever he had once hated, and seldom ceasing to care for those whom he loved. . . . People say that after the grievous quarrels between himself and his sons, brought up by their mother, Queen Eleanor, he had no respect for the obligations of the most solemn treaties. It is true that from a certain inherent inconstancy he often broke promises, preferring rather, when driven to the wall, to forfeit his word than to relinquish his goal. . . . I had almost forgotten to mention that his memory was so good that, despite the crowds always surrounding him, he never failed to recognize anyone he had ever met before, nor did he forget anything of significance once he had heard it. He was also master of almost the entire range of human history, and finely versed in most matters of common experience.

GIRALDUS CAMBRENSIS, *Expugnatio Hibernica c.* 1187

HENRY III

This king was deemed to be as imprudent in secular affairs as he was foremost in piety. For he habitually heard three masses daily and, desirous of hearing even more, he assiduously attended others, sung in private. Indeed it happened that St Louis, the French king, discussing this with him, opined that he should not always pass his day at Mass, but should listen more frequently to sermons. King Henry wittily replied that he preferred to see his Friend more often than to hear Him talk, whatever good things He might utter. Henry was of medium height, compactly built, with one eyelid drooping, so that it hid part of the black pupil; he was physically strong but of rash behaviour.   NICHOLAS TREVET, *Annales, c.* 1320

Henry endowed London with its first public lavatory, an amenity lacking in 1850.

HENRY V

In strength and nimbleness of body from his youth few to him were comparable; for in wrestling, leaping, and running, no man well able to compare. In casting of great iron bars and heavy stones he commonly excelled all men; never shrinking at cold nor slothful from heat; and, when he most laboured, his head was commonly uncovered; for harness wearing no more than a light cloak.

RAPHAEL HOLINSHED. *Chronicles*, 1577

No contemporary ever expatiated on Henry's kindliness, beauty or gaiety, although there is ample evidence that he was very fond of music and wherever he went his minstrels accompanied him. Henry's only other relaxation seems to have been the chase – a passion shared by most of our mediaeval kings – and for reading we are told he loved the histories of chivalry and in particular the life-story of Godfrey of Bouillon . . . Henry himself composed competent music for his Chapel Royal.

HAROLD F. HUTCHISON, 1964

HENRY VI

I would have no Christian man so ill-treated for my sake.

KING HENRY VI, seeing the remains of a traitor
quartered over Cripplegate, London

HENRY VII

His body was slender but well built and strong; his height above the average. His appearance was remarkably attractive and his face was cheerful, especially when speaking; his eyes were small and blue, his teeth few, poor and blackish; his hair was thin and white; his complexion sallow. His spirit was distinguished, wise and prudent; his mind was brave and resolute and never, even at moments of greatest danger, deserted him. . . . In government he was shrewd and prudent, so that no one dared to get the better of him through deceit and guile. . . . He was most fortunate in war, although he was constitutionally more inclined to peace than war. He cherished justice above all things; as a result he vigorously punished violence, manslaughter and every kind of violence. . . . He was the most ardent supporter of our faith and daily participated with great piety in religious services. . . .

POLYDORE VERGIL. *Anglica Historia*, 1531

Towards his Queen he was nothing uxorious, nor scarce indulgent, but companionable and respective and without jealousy.

FRANCIS BACON, on King Henry VII and Queen Elizabeth of York.
History of Henry VII, 1622

HENRY VIII

Bluff King Hal, full of beans,
married half a dozen Queens.

Child's verse

HOMOSEXUALITY

And yet I cannot content myself without sending you this present, praying God that I may have a joyful and comfortable meeting with you and that we may make at this Christmas a new marriage ever to be kept hereafter; for, God so love me, as I desire only to live in this world for your sake, and that I had rather live banished in any part of the earth with you than live a sorrowful widow's life without you. And so God bless you, my sweet child and wife, and grant that ye may ever be a comfort to your dear dad and husband.

KING JAMES VI AND I, to George Villiers,
first Duke of Buckingham, 1627

Homosexual acts between women are not illegal here, due, it is said, to Queen Victoria having refused her assent to a bill which would have made them so, because she would not recognize that such things could occur.   MICHAEL S. HOWARD, 1971

I thought men like that shot themselves.   KING GEORGE V

HONOUR

The Duke and Duchess of Windsor were at Monte Carlo . . . then on the night before the [Kane–Louis] fight, a group of sportswriters was presented to the Duke. One of the things for which he had been criticized was visiting Hitler, so, greatly daring, as I was much the youngest member of the group, I asked the man who had been King if he thought there would be war. His reply was unequivocal: 'As you know, I have met Herr Hitler. He assured me that he had no desire for war. I am certain he is a man of honour. I am sure there will be no war.'

That was 5 August 1939. On 1 September Hitler invaded Poland. Two days later Neville Chamberlain announced that Great Britain was at war.   PETER WILSON, 1977

HONOURS

I know the title of a King is a glorious title; but assure yourself that the shining glory of princely authority hath not so dazzled the eyes of our understanding, but that we well know and remember that we also are to yield an account of our actions before the great judge. To be a King and wear a crown is a thing more glorious to them that see it, than it is pleasant to them that bear it. For myself, I was never so much enticed with the glorious name of a King or royal authority of a Queen, as delighted that God hath made me His instrument to maintain His truth and glory, and to defend this Kingdom (as I said) from peril, dishonour, tyranny and oppression.

QUEEN ELIZABETH I, to the Commons, 1601

Instead of remaining as the fountain of honour, James I became the centre of an honours racket. Between 1605 and 1609 an average of seventy-four knighthoods were sold annually, which may not sound excessive but was in reality a carefully arrived at figure, just about the number that the market would bear if the price was not to fall. The king received £60 for each ceremony, and almost everyone took a rake-off, with sums payable to heralds and sergeants-at-arms and even to the king's jester. One herald claimed to hold himself above the fray, writing in 1604, 'Without all doubt he that buyeth his knighthood loseth the honour of knighthood', and within seven years James himself had come to accept and apologize for the dishonour he had heaped upon the honours system. 'Ye saw I made Knights then by hundreths and Barons in great numbers,' he told Parliament on 21 March 1610, referring to his progress from Scotland to London, adding, 'but I hope you find I doe not so now, nor mind to do so hereafter.' But James was no more capable of relinquishing his love of patronage nor meeting his need for funds through the sale of favours than he was of ceasing to fawn on the necks of beautiful boys or eating and drinking until he was sick.

In 1547 there had been seventy-four peers. By 1625 there were 123, James I having conferred 108 English peerages on sixty-eight individuals, of whom twelve were already peers, while restoring five peerages and confirming the disputed title of a peeress. One of James's new earls was actually a pirate, and the king's affection for the noble seafarer's son may have accounted for this particular quirk. MICHAEL DE-LA-NOY, 1985

The Revolution [1688] completely altered the relations between the Court and the higher classes of society. It was by degrees discovered that the King, in his individual capacity, had very little to give; that coronets and garters, bishoprics and embassies, lordships of the Treasury and tellerships of the Exchequer, nay, even charges in the royal stud and bedchamber, were really bestowed, not by him, but by his advisers. Every ambitious and covetous man perceived that he would consult his own interest far better by acquiring the dominion of a Cornish borough, and by rendering good service to

the ministry during a critical session, than by becoming the companion, or even the minion, of his prince. It was therefore in the
antechambers, not of George the First and of George the Second,
but of Walpole and of Pelham, that the daily crowd of courtiers was
to be found. . . . They had indeed their days of reception for our
nobility and gentry; but the reception was mere matter of form, and
became at last as solemn a ceremony as a funeral.

Not such was the court of Charles the Second. Whitehall, when
he dwelt there, was the focus of political intrigue and of fashionable
gaiety. Half the jobbing and half the flirting of the metropolis went
on under his roof. Whoever could make himself agreeable to the
prince, or could secure the good offices of the mistress, might hope
to rise in the world without rendering any service to the government, without being even known by sight by any minister of state.
This courtier got a frigate, and that a company; a third, the pardon
of a rich offender; a fourth, a lease of crown land on easy terms. If
the King notified his pleasure that a briefless lawyer should be made
a peer, the gravest counsellors, after a little murmuring, submitted.
Interest, therefore, drew a constant press of suitors to the gates of
the palace; and those gates always stood wide. The King kept open
house every day, and all day long, for the good society of London,
the extreme Whigs only excepted.

Hardly any gentleman had any difficulty in making his way to
the royal presence. The levée was exactly what the word imports.
Some men of quality came every morning to stand round their
master, to chat with him while his wig was combed and his cravat
tied, and to accompany him in his early walk through the Park. All
persons who had been properly introduced might, without any
special invitation, go to see him dine, sup, dance, and play at
hazard, and might have the pleasure of hearing him tell stories,
which indeed he told remarkably well, about his flight from Worcester, and about the misery which he had endured when he was a
state prisoner in the hands of the canting, meddling preachers of
Scotland. Bystanders whom His Majesty recognized often came in
for a courteous word. This proved a far more successful kingcraft
than any that his father or grandfather had practised. It was not
easy for the most austere republican of the school of Marvell to

resist the fascination of so much goodhumour and affability: and many a veteran Cavalier, in whose heart the memory of unrequited sacrifices and services had been festering during twenty years, was compensated in one moment for wounds and sequestrations by his sovereign's kind nod, and 'God bless you, my old friend.'

LORD MACAULAY. *History of England*, 1848

Lord North cannot seriously think that a private gentleman like Mr Penton is to stand in the way of the eldest son of an earl. Undoubtedly if that idea holds good it is diametrically opposed to what I have known all my life.

KING GEORGE III, to the Prime Minister, Lord North, 1780

During the reign of George V, racial prejudice entered into the question of honours for Indians. A member of the royal household decided that they were not, if knighted, entitled to the prefix 'Sir', apparently on the grounds that such knighthoods were honorary. As Indians were members of the Empire and subjects of the King their knighthoods could in no way be regarded as honorary, and the King very sensibly reversed the decision. He shared with Queen Victoria an enlightened colour blindness when it came to questions of race or racial prejudice, a liberal tendency out of tune with certain members of his family and household. The Lord Chamberlain, in 1919, spotted Lady Diana Cooper sitting beside the Aga Khan at the Ritz, and delivered himself of the opinion that 'the sight of natives entertaining smart society women was not a pleasant one'. Queen Mary's brother, Prince Francis of Teck, refused to dine with Grand Duke Michael of Russia when he learned that the duke's wife was to be taken into dinner by an Indian prince. When Lord Lee of Fareham gave a garden party his wife recorded in her diary, 'One thing Arthur was firm about was that he would not have any *Indians* asked.' Yet Lee had the audacity to preside over a Royal Commission on the Indian Civil Service, and then pester the government until he was made a Knight Grand Cross of the Star of India.

MICHAEL DE-LA-NOY, 1985

Would you like a Dukedom, or anything like that?

QUEEN ELIZABETH II, to Sir Winston Churchill,
on his retiring from the Premiership, 1955

HUMOUR

William Herbert, Earl of Pembroke, was known to have a horror of frogs and on one occasion James I pushed one down his neck. The king, however, had a horror of pigs and the next time he visited Wilton, Pembroke hid one under the commode in the royal bedchamber. 'His Majesty was extremely annoyed when he made the discovery.'

THOMAS HINDE, 1986

I don't mind praying to the Eternal Father, but I must be the only man in the country afflicted with an eternal mother.

EDWARD ALBERT, Prince of Wales, to the Archbishop of Canterbury,
after Queen Victoria's Diamond Jubilee, 1897

Edward VII was not remarkable for his wit, but there is something endearing in his mild rebuke to a footman who accidentally emptied a jug of cream over him: 'My good man, I'm not a strawberry.'

ARNOLD TOYNBEE, 1967

I said to your predecessor, 'You know what they're all saying, no more coals to Newcastle, no more Hoares to Paris.' The fellow [Sir Samuel Hoare] didn't even laugh.

KING GEORGE V, to Anthony Eden, Foreign Secretary

HYSTERIA

Her passionate weeping, her raging anger, have caused the word hysterical to be applied to her, but the ascription proves much truer than is usually the case in a casual use of medical terms. Modern clinical descriptions of hysteria go very far to explain the effect upon her of her circumstances and to illuminate some of the most debated actions and tendencies of her life. Hysterical subjects, it is said, are almost always found to be suffering from some sort of sexual inadequacy; they have frequently been deprived of affection in early childhood, a condition which has bred in them an insatiable demand for attention; above all, they develop a capacity for preventing the right hand from knowing what the left hand is doing. When she passed beyond the restraints and limitations of childhood, Elizabeth showed all three of these symptoms. Most strongly.   ELIZABETH JENKINS, 1961, on Queen Elizabeth I

ILLEGITIMACY

The heraldic marks used to denote illegitimacy point in the same direction as much of the other evidence concerning high-born bastards in medieval society. In theory, the law penalized them severely; in practice, they were accepted into the aristocracy as the sons and daughters of their fathers, and usually given every opportunity to prosper in much the same way as other nobles. Moreover, the origins of an illegitimate family were soon forgotten. King John did not think it beneath him to marry Isabel of Gloucester, the granddaughter of Henry I's bastard Robert of Gloucester. James I of Scotland was content to marry Joan Beaufort only a quarter of a century after the family's legitimation. Writing in the seventeenth century, Sir George Buck, Master of the King's Revels, made his position on the matter quite clear: 'And let it not be thought any disparagement for a noble family to be descended from a natural issue, considering that there have been and are infinite number of noble and princely families which are derived and propagated from bastards or natural sons.' Aeneas, Romulus, Theseus, Themistocles, Hercules, William the Conqueror, the Stewart kings of Scotland, and the Beauforts are among the examples he gives. . . .

CHRIS GIVEN-WILSON AND ALICE CURTEIS, 1984

Among English monarchs Henry I takes the prize for marital infidelity. The number of his illegitimate children established a record never surpassed, more than twenty being publicly acknowledged.

JEREMY POTTER, 1986

ILLNESS

Across the wires the gloomy message came:
'He is not better; he is much the same.'

ANON, on the illness of Albert Edward, Prince of Wales,
later King Edward VII

INDIA

The future Vice Roy must really shake himself more and more free
from his red-tapist narrow-minded Council and Entourage. He
must be *more independent, must hear for himself* what the *feelings*
of the natives really are, and do what he thinks right and not be
guided by the *snobbish* and vulgar, over-bearing and offensive
behaviour of our Civil and Political Agents, if we are to go on
peaceably and happily in India, and to be liked and beloved by high
and low – as well as respected as we ought to be – and not trying to
trample on the people and continually reminding them and making
them feel that they are a conquered people.

QUEEN VICTORIA, to Lord Salisbury, 1900

INTOXICATION

The lady who did play the queen's part did carry the most precious
gifts to both their Majesties; but, forgetting the steps rising to the
canopy, overset her caskets into his Danish Majesty's lap, and fell at
his feet. His Majesty then got up and would dance with the Queen
of Sheba, but he fell down and humbled himself before her. And

was carried to an inner chamber and laid on a bed of state, which was not a little defiled with the presents of the queen which had been bestowed upon his garments, such as wine, cream, jelly, beverage, cakes, spices and other good matters. The entertainment and show went forward, and most of the presenters went backwards, or fell down, wine did so occupy their upper chambers. Now did appear in rich dress Hope, Faith and Charity. Hope did essay to speak but wine rendered her endeavours so feeble that she withdrew and hoped the King would excuse her brevity. Faith left the court in a staggering condition. . . .

The two royal guests did most lovingly embrace each other at table. I think the Dane hath strangely wrought on our good English nobles, for those now follow the fashion and wallow in beastly delights. The ladies abandon their sobriety and are seen to roll about in intoxication.

Sir John Harington, on a celebration at Theobalds when King James VI
and I entertained King Christian IV of Denmark, and during which
the masque of the Queen of Sheba visiting
King Solomon was performed.

King James was sometimes called, with whatever undertones, the English Solomon.

INVECTIVE

King William II: 'I've got you, sir!'

Count Helias de la Flèche, captive: 'Only by a fluke! And if I can escape I know what I'm going to do.'

King William: 'You do? You clown, you! Do you think I care what you would do? Go away! Get out! Sod off! You can do whatever you like. And by the Face of Lucca, if next time you're the winner, I shan't be asking for something back for this.'

William of Malmesbury, on the meeting of the king and his prisoner,
captured at Le Mans, 1098. Trs. Professor Frank Barlow, 1983

Fool, beast, knave, arrant knave, fool!

KING HENRY VIII, to Secretary Wriothesley

The expression of Essex that the Queen was cankered, and that her mind had become as crooked as her carcase cost him his head, which his insurrection had not cost him but for that speech.

SIR WALTER RALEGH, on Robert Devereux, Earl of Essex, executed 1601

IRELAND

The King of Connacht

'Have you seen Hugh,
The Connacht king, in the field?'
'All that we saw
Was his shadow under his shield.'

ANON. Early medieval,
trs. from Gaelic by Frank O'Connor

Because that in our land of Ireland there are three kinds of people, the Wild Irish our enemies, the Irish Rebels, and the obedient English, it appeared to us and our council that, considering that the Irish Rebels are perhaps so rebellious by reason of the grievances and wrongs done to them on the one part, and that redress hath not been made to them on the other part; and that likewise if they be not wisely managed, and put into good hope of favour, they will probably join our enemies; wherefore, it shall not be any fault of ours that a general pardon be granted them.

KING RICHARD II, 1393

It is not recorded in living memory that a King of England ever undertook an expedition on so large a scale, and with so many men-at-arms and archers, against the Irish. He remained in their country over nine months; the expense involved was considerable, but it was willingly borne by the kingdom at large, for the city merchants and the great towns of England thought it well worth while when they saw the King return home in honour and glory. Only men-at-arms and archers had gone on the expedition, four thousand of the former and thirty thousand of the latter. They were all paid regularly every week, and were consequently well satisfied. I must tell you that Ireland is one of the worst and most unfavourable countries in which to carry on warfare; it abounds in deep forests and in lakes and bogs, and much of it is uninhabitable. It is often impossible to come to grips with the people, for they are quite ready to desert their towns and take refuge in the woods, and live in huts made of branches, or even among the bushes and hedges, like wild beasts. And when they hear of the approach of an invader, they retire into such remote and impenetrable fastnesses that it is impossible to come up with them. It happens quite often, however, that from their minute knowledge of the country they find a favourable opportunity for attacking their enemies; they are very alert on such occasions, and no man-at-arms, however well mounted, can overtake them, so light are they on their feet; they can even leap up onto a horse and drag the rider to the ground, or else pin his arms behind him so that he cannot escape, for their own arms are immensely strong. They have pointed, two-edged knives, with broad blades, and they never regard an enemy as dead until they have cut his throat, like a sheep. They then cut out the heart and carry it off; some people, who are well acquainted with their customs, say that they actually eat the human heart, and regard it as a great delicacy. They never allow prisoners to be ransomed, and when they have the worst of any skirmish, they scatter and hide in hedges or bushes, or underground, and seem to disappear without trace.

FROISSART, on King Richard II's expedition to Ireland, 1394

His first Irish expedition was wholly to his credit. Where Henry II had tried nothing but brute force, where his son John had spoilt good plans by unseemly levity and snobbery, where succeeding Kings had been content with mere instructions to viceroys, Richard II went in person, and, to the satisfaction of all concerned, succeeded by methods of intelligent understanding and chivalrous diplomacy. It was the first and last time that England ever used such methods in Ireland.   HAROLD F. HUTCHISON, 1961

To judge from the articles in *The Times*, *Star*, *Standard* all is *couleur de rose* in Ireland, throughout the length and breadth of that happy land there is a feeling of tumultuous joy, the mere vote has proved a sop for the hungry monster discontent, who now has nothing to do but to crawl about on all fours to catch a ray of sunshine from the luminous body of Royalty.

Irishmen, we are told by special correspondents, are decorating their wretched hovels so that things may look pleasing to royal eyes, are furnishing their rusty harps with strings to prepare a proper accompaniment to the performance on royal light fantastic toes – they are prepared, it is said, ever after the glorious advent of the Queen's son, you know gratitude is one of their chief characteristics, to starve themselves and their pigs for their English masters.

This is the English translation and now listen to the Irish original. The following are the words of the Irish leader John Martin: 'If, he says, the Prince of Wales is authorized to bear to Ireland any reassuring message from her Majesty or the English Cabinet, with an intention to restore our national rights, then let the Irish people receive him not with cold and silent politeness only. . . If the Prince comes authorized to open the prison doors for every Irishman convicted and suspected of political offence, then let the people cheer him heartily . . .'.

Yes, their nationality, an amnesty for their imprisoned countrymen, the Irish are willing to receive at the hands of a Royal or any other 'Jolly Nash' – and that is about the whole extent of their loyalty. Of course I do not mean to deny that great preparations *are* being made for the royal reception. The question is by *whom* are

they made? By official corporations, by the Lord Mayor, by worth-
ies elected to their lucrative offices by the English ... by the servile
scum that floats on all societies?'

JENNY MARX, to Paul Lafargue, 1869

KING GEORGE V: 'Are you going to shoot all the people in Ireland?'
DAVID LLOYD GEORGE, Prime Minister: 'No, Your Majesty.'
KING GEORGE V: 'Well, then, you must come to some agreement
    with them. This thing cannot go on. I cannot have my people
    killed in this manner.'

*This account of the King's dislike, 1921, of the use of the Black and
Tans in Ireland, has been queried and denied, but receives some
support from Kenneth Rose, the King's latest and most substantial
biographer.*

IRONY

The first Nonparell, grown so famous of late,
Renown'd for his wisdom, in matters of state;
In Politicks skilfull, in Judgment so sound,
There's none can excel him search all ye World round.

Broadsheet against King George III, c.1762

JAMES VI AND I

'Our cousin of Scotland' was ugly, awkward, and shuffling both in mind and person. His tongue was much too large for his mouth, his legs were much too weak for his body, and his dull goggle-eyes stared and rolled like an idiot's. He was cunning, covetous, wasteful, idle, drunken, greedy, dirty, cowardly, a great swearer, and the most conceited man on earth. His figure – what is commonly called rickety from his birth – presented a most ridiculous appearance, dressed in thick padded clothes, as a safeguard against being stabbed (of which he lived in continual fear), of a grass-green colour from head to foot, with a hunting-horn dangling at his side instead of a sword, and his hat and feather sticking over one eye, or hanging on the back of his head, as he happened to toss it on. He used to loll on the necks of his favourite courtiers, and slobber their faces, and kiss and pinch their cheeks; and the greatest favourite he ever had, used to sign himself in his letters to his royal master, His Majesty's 'dog and slave', and used to address his majesty as 'his Sowship'. His Majesty was the worst rider ever seen, and thought himself the best. He was one of the most impertinent talkers (in the broadest Scotch) ever heard, and boasted of being unanswerable in all manner of argument. He wrote some of the most wearisome treatises ever read – among others, a book upon witchcraft, in which he was a devout believer – and thought himself a prodigy of authorship. He thought, and wrote, and said, that a king had a right to make and unmake what laws he pleased, and ought to be accountable to nobody on earth. This is the plain true character of the personage whom the greatest men about the court praised and flattered to that degree, that I doubt if there be anything much more shameful in the annals of human nature. CHARLES DICKENS, 1853

The child of Mary Queen of Scots,
A shifty Mother's shiftless son,
Bred up among intrigues and plots,
Learned in all things, wise in none;
Ungainly, babbling, wasteful, weak,
Shrewd, clever, cowardly, pedantic,
The sight of steel would blanch his cheek,
The smell of baccy drive him frantic.
He was the author of his time
He wrote that witches should be burnt
He wrote that monarchs were divine
And left a son who – proved they weren't!

RUDYARD KIPLING

JANE SEYMOUR

My Lord, as upon Friday last the Queen sat abroad as Queen, and was served with her own servants. And they were sworn that same day. And the King and Queen came in his great boat to Greenwich the same day, with his Privy Council and hers, and the ladies in the great barge. I do ensure you, my Lord, she is as gentle a Lady as ever I knew, and as fair a Queen as any in Christendom. The King hath come out of hell into heaven, for the gentleness in this, and the cursedness and the unhappiness in the other. Wherefore, my Lord, me think it were very well done, when you do write to the King again, that you do rejoice that he is so well matched with so gracious a woman as she is, and you hear reported by her; and wherein you shall content his Grace in so doing.

SIR JOHN RUSSELL, 1536, to Lord Lisle, on Queen Jane Seymour,
successor to Queen Anne Boleyn

The surgeon was sent for,
    He came with all speed,
In a gown of black velvet
    From heel to the head.
He gave her rich caudle,
    But the death-sleep slept she,
And her right side was opened,
    And the babe was set free.

The babe it was christened,
    And put out and nursed,
While the royal Queen Jane
    She lay cold in dust.

So black was the mourning
    And white were the wands,
Yellow, yellow the torches
    They bore in their hands.
The bells they were muffled,
    And mournful did play,
While the royal Queen Jane
    She lay cold in the clay.

Six knights and six lords
    Bore her corpse through the grounds;
Six dukes followed after,
    In black mourning gownds,
The Flower of Old England
    Was laid in cold clay,
Whilst the royal King Henrie
    Came weeping away.

ANON. From 'The Death of Queen Jane', 1537

JOHN

Caught in the toils and snared by the temptations of unstable and dissolute youth, he was as wax to receive impressions of evil, but hardened against those who would have warned him of its danger; compliant to the fancy of the moment; more given to luxurious ease than to warlike excesses, to enjoyment than to endurance, to vanity than to virtue.
GIRALDUS CAMBRENSIS. Opera Omnia, c. 1185

SALISBURY: 'The colour of the king doth come and go between his
    purpose and his conscience. Like heralds 'twixt two dreadful
    battles set: his passion is so ripe, it needs must break.'
PEMBROKE: 'And when it breaks, I fear will issue thence the foul
    corruption of a sweet child's death.'
KING JOHN: 'They burn in indignation. I repent: there is no sure
    foundation set on blood, no certain life achieved by others'
    death.'
WILLIAM SHAKESPEARE

JUSTICE

If the new King hangs a man before he is tried, will he then try a man before he has offended?

SIR JOHN HARINGTON, on King James VI and I,
who had a thief executed without trial, 1603

Strafford,

The misfortune that has fallen upon you by the strange mistaking and conjecture of these times, being such that I must lay by the thought of employing you thereafter in my affairs; yet I cannot satisfy myself in honour or conscience without assuring you (now in the midst of your troubles), that upon the word of a king you shall not suffer in life, honour, or fortune. This is but justice, and therefore a very mean reward from a master to so faithful and able a servant as you have showed yourself to be; yet it is as much as I conceive the present times will permit, though none shall hinder me from being   Your constant, faithful friend,

Charles R.

KING CHARLES I, to Thomas Wentworth, Earl of Strafford,
following the Bill of Attainder passed in Parliament, 21 April 1641

(An Act of Attainder was a parliamentary measure declaring the accused's guilt, thus dispensing with the formalities of a trial.)

My Lords,

I did yesterday satisfy the justice of the kingdom, by the passing of the Bill of Attainder against the Earl of Strafford; but mercy being as inherent and inseparable to a king as justice, I desire, at this time, in some measure, to show that likewise, by suffering that unfortunate man to fulfil the natural course of his life in a close imprisonment; yet so that, if ever make the least offer to escape, or offer directly or indirectly to meddle in any sort of public business, especially with me, by either message or letter, it shall cost him his life, without further process. This, if it may be done without a discontentment to my people, would be an unspeakable contentment to me. To which end, as in the first place, I by this letter do earnestly desire your approbation, and, to endeavour it the more, have chosen him to carry it that of all your House is most dear to me; so I desire that, by a conference, you would endeavour to give the House of Commons contentment likewise; assuring you that the exercising of mercy is no more pleasing to me, than to see both Houses of Parliament content, for my sake, that I should moderate the severity of the law in so important a case. I will not say that your complying with me in this my intended mercy shall make me more willing, but certainly it will make me more cheerful, in granting your just grievances. But, if no less than his life can satisfy my people, I must say *Fiat Justitia*. Thus again earnestly recommending the consideration of my intention unto you, I rest,

Your unalterable and affectionate friend,

Charles R.

If he must die, it were a charity to reprieve him until Saturday.

KING CHARLES I, delivered to the House of Lords, 11 May 1641, by Charles, Prince of Wales, later King Charles II

The royal letter was rejected, a vast and dangerous crowd surrounded Whitehall Palace and, fearing for his family, particularly the Catholic Queen, Henrietta Maria, and following a letter from Strafford himself, urging the sacrifice of his own life 'to free the kingdom from the many troubles it apprehended' and to secure the safety of the Royal House, Charles was forced to assent to Strafford's death.

Put not your trust in Princes.

THOMAS WENTWORTH, Earl of Strafford, before execution, 1641

KATHARINE OF ARAGON

The Queen of Castile has a daughter
Who won't come home again
She lies in the grey cathedral
Under the arms of Spain.
O the Queen of Castile has a daughter
Torn out by the roots.
Her lovely breast in a cold stone chest
Under the farmers' boots.

CHARLES CAUSLEY. From 'A Ballad for Katharine of Aragon', 1961

KINGSHIP

. . . I think this country can bear no merchant to have more land than £100, no husbandman nor farmer above £100, or £200, no artificer above 200 marks; no labourer much more than he spendeth.

I speak now generally, but this is sure, this commonwealth may not bear one man to have more than two farms, than one benefice, than 2000 sheep. . . .

The gentleman ought to labour in service in his country. True gentlemen . . . have little or nothing increased their rents . . . yet their house-keeping is dearer, their wages greater; which thing at length, if speedy remedy be not had, will bring that state into utter ruin. . . .

These sores must be cured with these medecines or plasters. 1. Good education. 2. Devising of good laws. 3. Executing the laws justly, without respect of persons. 4. Example of rulers. 5. Punishing of vagabonds and idle persons. 6. Encouraging the good. 7. Ordering well the customers. 8. Engendering friendship in all parts of the commonwealth....

Wherefore I would wish . . . that those noblemen, except a few that should be with me, went to their countries, and there should see the statutes fully and duly executed; and that these men should be put from being Justices of the Peace that be touched or blotted with those vices that be against these new laws to be established; for no man that is in fault himself can punish another for the same offence. And these justices being put out, there is no doubt for execution of the laws.

KING EDWARD VI, aged thirteen.
A Discourse About the Reformation of Many Abuses.

Justice, Temper, Magnanimity, Judgement.

QUEEN ELIZABETH I, on royal values

I am your anointed Queen. I will never be by violence constrained to do anything. I thank God I am endowed with such qualities that if I were turned out of the Realm in my petticoat I were able to live in any place in Christendom. QUEEN ELIZABETH I, to the Commons

Though God hath raised me high, yet this I count the glory of my Crown, that I have reigned with your loves.

QUEEN ELIZABETH I, to the Commons

Have a care to my people. You have my people – do you what I ought to do. Every man oppresseth and spoileth them without mercy. They cannot avenge themselves, nor help themselves. See unto them – see unto them, for they are my charges. I care not for myself, my life is not dear to me. My care is for my people.

QUEEN ELIZABETH I, to the Judges

This I must say for Scotland, and may truly vaunt it. Here I sit and govern it with my pen; I write and it is done; and by a clerk of the council I govern Scotland now – which my ancestors could not do by the sword.   KING JAMES VI, to the English Parliament

Kings are justly called gods, because they exercise a manner of resemblance to Divine power on earth. . . .

They have power to exalt low things and abase high things and to make of their subjects like men at chess.

KING JAMES VI AND I, 1609

For the people, truly I desire their liberty and freedom as much as anybody whatsoever, but I must tell you, their liberty and freedom consists in having government, those laws by which their lives and goods may be most their own. It is not their having a share in the government; that is nothing appertaining to them. A subject and a sovereign are clear different things.

KING CHARLES I, on the scaffold, 1649

Go home. Get you gone. I am King. I will be obeyed.

KING JAMES II, to the Fellows of Magdalene College,
Cambridge, on the election of a new President, 1687

We may be thankful that King George III was not a statesman. It is not desirable that a constitutional king should be a statesman. Statesmanship is the prerogative of ministers not of monarchs. It is better for a nation to be governed by a George III than by a Frederick the Great or a Joseph II. Happy the nation that numbers no great men among its Kings! The ideal constitutional monarch should in the quality of his mind be no greater than the average of his politically conscious subjects: he should share their ideals, their prejudices, perhaps even their follies: and should act as a brake on change rather than as a stimulant. He should appeal to the common of mankind. It was fortunate for Great Britain that King George III did not attempt to find a solution of the American problem independent of the House of Commons. For that he deserved well of his people. Far from reproaching him for having lost the American colonies, subsequent generations should be grateful that he preserved the British constitution with all its possibilities of peaceful change. America was a small price to pay for that blessing.

JOHN BROOKE, 1972

The Monarchy exists in Canada for historical reasons. It exists also because it was thought to be of benefit to the country and the nation. If at any stage people decide that the system is unacceptable to them, then it is up to them to change it.

It is a complete misconception to imagine that the Monarchy exists in the interest of the Monarchy. It does not. It exists in the interest of the people in the sense that we do not come here for our health, so to speak. . . .

We can think of other ways of enjoying ourselves. Judging by some of the programmes we are required to do here and considering how little we get out of it, you can assume that it is done in the interests of the Canadian people and not in our own interest.

If at any time, any stage, people feel that it has no future part to play, then for goodness sake let's end the thing on amicable terms without having a row about it.

PHILIP, DUKE OF EDINBURGH, in Canada, 1969

THE LABYRINTH

One day Queen Eleanor saw the King walking in the pleasance of Woodstock, with the end of a ball of floss silk attached to his spur, and that, coming near him unperceived, she took up the ball, and the King walking onward, the silk unwound, and thus the Queen traced him to a thicket in the labyrinth or maze of the park, where he disappeared. She kept the matter secret, often revolving in her own mind in what company he could meet with balls of silk. Soon after, the King left Woodstock for a distant journey; then Queen Eleanor, bearing this discovery in mind, searched the thicket in the park, and found a low door cunningly concealed; this door she had forced, and found it was the entrance to a winding subterranean path, which led out at a distance to a sylvan lodge in the most lonely part of the adjoining forest.

JOHN BROMPTON OF GERVANIX, on the discovery,
by Queen Eleanor of Aquitaine, of Rosamund Clifford,
mistress of her husband, King Henry II.
Chronicle 588–1199, *c.*1458

Agnes Strickland, 1840, rather surprisingly alludes to Queen Eleanor as 'at that era the greatest naval potentate in the world'. She was certainly powerful enough to contain, though not, as tradition maintained, to destroy Rosamund Clifford.

LAMB

Sir Sidney Lee, the Shakespearean scholar, came to the Prince with a proposal. It was on the eve of the publication of the *Dictionary of*

National Biography. It was Sir Sidney's idea that the Prince ought to give a dinner to those responsible for the completion of this monumental work. The monumental work had escaped the Prince's attention, don't you know, and Sir Sidney had painfully to explain to him what it was. The Prince, you know, was not an omnivorous reader. Sir Sidney managed to obtain his grudging assent. 'How many?' asked the Prince. 'Forty,' said Sir Sidney. The Prince was appalled. 'For-r-ty!' he gasped. 'For-r-ty wr-ri-ters! I can't have for-r-ty wr-ri-ters in Marlborough House! Giff me the list.' Sir Sidney gave it him, and the Prince, with a heavy black pencil, started slashing off names. Sir Sidney's heart sank when he saw that the first name the Prince had slashed was that of Sir Leslie Stephen. He conveyed, as tactfully as he could, that this was a bad cut, since Stephen was the animating genius of the whole enterprise. Reluctantly, the Prince allowed Sir Leslie to come. Eventually, Sir Sidney put over his entire list. The dinner took place. Among the contributors present was Canon Ainger, a distinguished cleric whose passion was Charles Lamb, on whom he was considered a very great authority indeed. He had written the articles on Charles and Mary Lamb for the *Dictionary*. Sir Sidney sat at the Prince's right hand and found it heavy weather, don't you know. The Prince must have found it heavy going also; to be having dinner with forty writers was not his idea of a cultivated way to spend an evening. His eye roamed the table morosely, in self-abjurgation for having let himself in for a thing like this. Finally, his eye settled on Canon Ainger. 'Who's the little person?' he asked Lee. 'Vy is *he* here? He's not a wr-ri-ter!' 'He is a very great authority,' said Lee apologetically, 'on Lamb.' This was too much for the Prince. He put down his knife and fork in stupefaction; a pained outcry of protest heaved from him: 'On lamb!'

Max Beerbohm, recalled by S. N. Behrman, 1960,
on Albert Edward, Prince of Wales, later King Edward VII

LAST WORDS

Shame, shame on a conquered king. HENRY II

Brothers, by the journey upon which I am bound, I have not wronged the King. But it is true that long before the King took me, I loved Culpeper, and I wish to God I had done as he wished me, for at the time the King wanted to take me he urged me to say that I was pledged to him. If I had done as he advised me I should not die this death, nor would he. I would rather have had him for a husband than be mistress of the world, but sin blinded me and greed of grandeur; and since mine is the fault, mine also is the suffering, and my great sorrow is that Culpeper should have to die through me. . . .

Pray hasten with thy office. [To the executioner]

I die a queen, but I would rather die the wife of Culpeper. God have mercy on my soul. Good people, I beg you pray for me. . . .

QUEEN CATHERINE HOWARD, 1541

I am not able to say my long prayer, but I will say my short one: 'Lighten my eyes, O Lord, lest I sleep the sleep of death.'

PRINCESS ANNE, daughter of King Charles I, dying in childhood

Let me alone. I am looking into Hell. KING GEORGE III, 1820

A little later, close to death, he added: 'Tom's a cold.'

Stocky, they have made me drunk.

PRINCESS CHARLOTTE, daughter and heir of George, Prince Regent, dying in childbirth, to Baron Stockmar, 1817

LAW

Such evidence as survives does agree in depicting [Alfred] as a man who believed in a good deal of personal interference with the world around him. He was indefatigable in revising and adjusting and modifying the natural relationships of men. His interest in the poor, and his anxiety to see justice done them; his assiduity in hearing appeals, all alike hint at a faith in a dispensing and discretionary power which could be exerted in the cause of equity. We can, on the other hand, detect very little sign that he regarded law, as the Romans did, in the light of a power which over-rode all individual discretion. This attitude gave rise, later on, to two distinct streams of tendency – that is to say, to the theory of regal absolutism, and to the habit of statutory legislation. The time had not arrived when such questions could have any practical meaning; but the tradition which we see Alfred expressing unmistakably implies a view that law was intended for the convenience and benefit of man, and should be adjusted to this purpose.

G. P. BAKER, 1931, on King Alfred

He had discretion in the making of laws and the ordering of all his government, and was a clever deviser of decisions in unusual and dark cases.

WALTER MAP, on King Henry II. *De Nugis Curialium*, 1181–1192

Specifically, Barbara Napier was indicted 'for many treasonable conspiracies undertaken by witchcraft to have destroyed the King's person by a picture of wax . . . and for drowning a boat between Leith and Kinghorne, wherein were sixty persons lost'. After hearing these accusations, the jury of the assizes dismissed the case. This action so enraged King James VI that he reassembled the court, and ordered Barbara Napier to be strangled and burned at the stake, her property to be forfeit to him. Those jurymen who had voted for acquittal were then tried for 'willful error on assize, acquitting a witch', provoking the Tolbooth Speech of King James. Mrs Napier pleaded pregnancy, and after a lapse of time, 'nobody insisting in the pursuit of her, she was set at liberty'.

It seems likely that his experience with these North Berwick witch trials encouraged King James to write his *Demonology*, first published in Edinburgh, 1597 – 'to resolve the doubting hearts of many' on the reality of witchcraft.

ROSSELL HOPE ROBBINS, 1959

For witchcraft, which is a thing grown very common amongst us, I know it to be a most abominable sin, and I have been occupied these three quarters of this year for the sifting out of them that are guilty herein. We are taught by the laws both of God and men that this sin is most odious. And by God's law punishable by death. By man's law it is called *malefacium* or *veneficium*, an ill deed or a poisonable deed, and punishable likewise by death.

The thing that moved the jurymen to find as they did, was because they had no testimony but of witches; which they thought not sufficient. By the civil law I know that such infamous persons are not received for witnesses, but in matters of heresy and *lesae majestatis*. For in other matters it is not thought meet, yet in these matters of witchcraft good reason that such be admitted. First, none honest can know these matters. Second, because they will not accuse themselves. Thirdly, because no act which is done by them can be seen.

Further, I call them witches which do renounce God and yield themselves wholly to the Devil; but when they have recanted and repented, as these have done, then I account them not as witches, and so their testimony sufficient.

KING JAMES VI OF SCOTLAND, later King James I of England.
Tolbooth Speech, Edinburgh, 1591

KING CHARLES I, ON TRIAL: But it is not my case alone, it is the freedom and the liberty of the people of England; and do you pretend what you will, I stand more for their liberties. For if power without law may make laws, may alter the fundamental laws of the kingdom, I do not know what subject he is in England, that can be sure of his life, or anything that he calls his own: therefore when that I came here, I did expect particular persons to know by what law, what authority you did proceed against me here. And therefore I am a little [perplexed] to seek what to say to you in this particular, because the affirmative is to be proved, the negative often is very hard to do: but since I cannot persuade you to do it, I shall tell you my reasons as short as I can. My reasons why in conscience and the duty I owe to God first, and my people next, for the preservation of their lives, liberties, and estates, I conceive I cannot answer this, till I be satisfied of the legality of it. All proceedings against any man whatsoever. . . .

JOHN BRADSHAW, LORD PRESIDENT OF THE COURT: Sir, I must interrupt you, which I would not do, but what you do is not agreeable to the proceedings of any court of justice: you are about to enter into argument, dispute concerning the authority of this Court, before whom you appear as a prisoner, and are charged as a high delinquent: if you take upon you to dispute the authority of the Court, we may not do it, nor will any court give way unto it: you are to submit unto it, you are to give a punctual and direct answer, whether you will answer your charge or not, and what your answer is.

KING CHARLES I: Sir, by your favour, I do not know the forms of law; I do know law and reason, though I am no lawyer professed; but I know as much law as any gentleman in England; and therefore (under favour) I do plead for the liberties of the people of England more than you do: and therefore if I should impose a belief upon any man, without reason given for it, it were unreasonable; but I must tell you that the reason that I have, as thus informed, I cannot yield unto it.

LORD PRESIDENT BRADSHAW: Sir, I must interrupt you, you may not be permitted: you speak of law and reason; it is fit there should be law and reason, and there is both against you. Sir, the vote of the Commons of England assembled in Parliament, it is the reason of the kingdom, and they are these that have given to that law, according to which you should have ruled and reigned. Sir, you are not to dispute our authority, you are told it again by the Court. Sir, it will be taken notice of, that you stand in contempt of the Court, and your contempt will be recorded accordingly.

Westminster Hall, 1649

The new government had earlier 'purged' the House of Commons of all but its own supporters. The House of Lords was unrepresented at the trial.

If that is the law, the law must be altered.

QUEEN VICTORIA, following a verdict of 'Not guilty' on grounds of insanity, on Roderick Maclean, who fired a revolver at her, in her carriage, 1882

The law was altered in 1883, allowing verdicts of 'Guilty but Insane', until 1964, when the original verdict which so displeased the Queen was revived.

LEADERSHIP

I am your Queen to whom at my coronation, when I was wedded to the realm and laws of the same – the spousal ring whereof I have on my finger, which never hitherto was, nor hereafter shall be, left off – you promised your allegiance and obedience unto me. . . .

And I say to you, on the word of a Prince, I cannot tell how naturally the mother loveth the child, for I was never the mother of any; but certainly, if a Prince and Governor may as naturally and earnestly love her subjects as the mother doth love the child, then assure yourselves that I, being your lady and mistress, do as earnestly and tenderly love and favour you. And I, thus loving you, cannot but think that ye as heartily and faithfully love me; and then

I doubt not but that we shall give these rebels a short and speedy overthrow.

QUEEN MARY I, to the Lord Mayor and Aldermen of London,
at Guildhall, during Sir Thomas Wyatt's abortive rebellion, 1554

My loving People: we have been persuaded by some that are careful of our safety to take heed how we commit ourselves to armed multitudes, for fear of treachery; but I assure you, I do not desire to live to distrust my faithful, loving people.

Let tyrants fear; I have always so behaved myself that, under God, I have placed my chiefest strength and safeguard in the loyal hearts and goodwill of my subjects, therefore I am among you, as you see, at this time, not for my recreation and disport, but being resolved, in the midst and heat of the battle, to live and die amongst you all, to lay down for my God, and for my Kingdoms and for my People, my honour and my blood, even in the dust.

I know I have the body of a weak and feeble woman, but I have the heart and stomach of a King, and of a King of England too: and I think foul scorn that Parma or Spain, or any Prince of Europe should dare to invade the borders of my realm, to which rather than any dishonour should grow by me, I will myself take up arms, I myself will be your General, Judge and Rewarder of every one of your virtues in the field.

QUEEN ELIZABETH I, to 16,000 men assembled at Tilbury,
on news of the sailing of the Spanish fleet and army to invade England, 1588

The Great Fire, 1666

On King Charles II and his brother, James, Duke of York, afterwards James II.

They rode up and down, giving orders for blowing up of houses with gunpowder, to make void spaces for the fire to die in, and standing still to see those orders executed, exposing their persons not only to the multitude, but to the very flames themselves, and the ruins of the buildings ready to fall upon them, and sometimes labouring with their own hands to give example to others: for which the people now do pay them, as they ought to do, all possible reverences and admiration.

HENRY GRIFFITH, to Lord Conway, 1666

From Sunday morn till Thursday at night
It roared about the Town,
There was no way to quell its might
But to pull houses down;
And so they did
As they were bid
By Charles, His Great Command;
The Duke of York
Some say did work,
With bucket in his hand.

London Gazette, 1666

I'm glad we've been bombed. I can now look the East End in the face.

The children will not leave unless I do. I shall not leave unless their father does, and the King will not leave the country in any circumstances whatever.

QUEEN ELIZABETH, consort of King George VI, after the Nazi bombing of Buckingham Palace, 1940

LEGITIMACY

I am far from being secure that intelligence from London of the Prince's Marriage may not be true. We were apprehensive of it

198

before he went, and spoke freely to him of our opinions of the fatal consequences of it.

> EDWARD HYDE, later Earl of Clarendon, on the exiled Prince of Wales,
> later King Charles II, and his alleged marriage to Lucy Walters, 1649

The King do dote infinitely upon the Duke of Monmouth, apparently as one that he intends to succeed him. God knows what will be the end of it. . . . The Duke of Monmouth hath said that he would be the death of any man that says the King was not married to his mother: though Alsopp says it is well known that she was a common strumpet before the King was acquainted with her.

> SAMUEL PEPYS, 1664

As well as I love the Duke of Monmouth, I would rather see him hanged at Tyburn than own him as my legitimate heir.

> KING CHARLES II, to the Privy Council, 1679

Monmouth's loyalty to his mother's honour, vital indeed to his own, had a controlling and ultimately disastrous effect on his career.

His mother, whose name was Barlow, daughter of some very mean creatures, was a beautiful strumpet, whom I had often seen in Paris; she died miserably without anything to bury her; yet this Perkin had been made to believe that the King had married her, a monstrous and ridiculous forgery! And to satisfy the world of the iniquity of the report, the King his father (if his father he really was, for he most resembled one Sidney who was familiar with his mother) publically and most solemnly renounced it, to be so entered in the Council Book some years since, with all the Privy councillors' attestation.

> JOHN EVELYN, on 'Mrs Barlow', born Lucy Walters,
> mother of James, Duke of Monmouth

Evelyn is ungenerous to her parents, who were of the Welsh gentry, though impoverished. Earlier, he calls her 'a brown, beautiful, bold but insipid creature'.

A few years ago, the late Sir Hew Dalrymple was looking through some of the Buccleuch papers, of which a good many are both scattered and uncatalogued, and came across the following in manuscript, which he copied carefully:

'The Certificate of Marriage was found by Henry, Duke of Buccleuch (3rd Duke, b. 1746) and President Hope (Charles Hope, of Granton, Lord President of the Court of Session and Lord Justice-General) amongst some old papers at Dalkeith; and the Duke thought it best to burn it. It does not seem clear whether it was the original or a copy of one at Liege where they were married by the then Archbishop of Canterbury. I believe it is supposed that the other copy or original, whichever it was, might be found at Liege if looked for.'

LORD GEORGE SCOTT, 1947 on King Charles II's
alleged marriage to Lucy Walters

The Duke, whose direct ancestress, Anna Scott, married the Duke of Monmouth, destroyed the certificate, as likely to cause trouble. The subject is treated more fully by Monmouth's biographer, J. N. P. Watson (1979) in the best assessment of James Scott that I know.

LIBRARIES

We visited the Royal Library: over the door stands a white marble bust of Edward VI. The Library has a good variety of books and also houses a number of choice royal possessions. These include a walking-stick made from a *unicorn's* horn, other sticks containing watches, Henry VIII's skull-cap embroidered with gold wire and of considerable weight, an elk's horn, a horn cup which is said to break in pieces if you put poison in it, cases standing on the floor full of gilt glasses, a horn of pure gold which was used by Henry VIII, a casket in mother of pearl, and a very large marble incense-burner. There is also a most interesting and ingenious musical instrument made in Germany which is decorated with glass of different colours and is studded with jewels . . . also an extraordinary receptacle for combs (a kamfutter) which is shaped like a man, and a pair of gilded spurs which belonged to Henry VIII.

BARON WALDSTEIN, on Hampton Court, 1597

THE LINER

The great liner between the wars, Cunard Liner RMS *Queen Mary*, was originally to have been christened Queen Victoria. George V was told by a Cunard executive that the company wished to name it after 'the greatest of all English Queens'. The delighted King exclaimed, 'Oh, my wife *will* be pleased.'

WILLIAM MANCHESTER, 1983

LITERATURE

On the Sunday, after all the members of the Council had left except the Duke of York, Sir Thomas Percy and Sir Richard [Sturry], I was presented to the King [Richard II], who desired to see the book that I had brought him. I gave it to him in his chamber, and laid it on his bed. He opened it and read it with considerable pleasure, as well he might, for it was beautifully written and illuminated, and bound in crimson velvet with ten silver-gilt studs, and roses embroidered in gold at the centre. The King asked the subject of my poems and I replied that they were concerning love. The King was delighted, and read out several of the poems, for he read and spoke French fluently. He then handed it to one of his knights, Sir Richard Credon, and told him to put it in his private library. The King was most affable to me about the book. FROISSART

It is a great misfortune for Mr Perceval to write in a style that would disgrace a washerwoman.

GEORGE, PRINCE REGENT, on the Prime Minister, Spencer Perceval, 1812

In literature the Queen's taste was said to be deplorable, and although she had little time for reading she never liked the works of the great authors. I remember a discussion taking place once at Balmoral between Queen Victoria and the Empress Frederick on the subject of Marie Corelli. The Queen said she would rank as one of the greatest writers of the time, while the Empress thought that her writings were trash. I was seated at the other end of the large dining-room table and therefore had not, unfortunately, heard the commencement of the discussion. The Empress, suddenly called across the table to me and asked me what I thought of Marie Corelli. Quite unconscious of the fact that the Queen was an admirer of this authoress, I replied that her books undoubtedly had a large sale, but I thought the secret of her popularity was that her writings appealed to the semi-educated. Whereupon the Empress clapped her hands, and the subject dropped with startling suddenness.

SIR FREDERICK PONSONBY, 1951

LONELINESS

There was never a man so alone as I, and therefore very much to be excused for the committing of any error, because I have reason to suspect everything that those advised me, and to distrust my own single opinion, having no single soul to help me.

KING CHARLES I, to Queen Henrietta Maria, 1646

LOVE

King Edward reached Wark Castle on the same day that the Scots left, and he was furious to find them gone, for in his eagerness to fight them, he had come in such haste that both his men and his horses were exhausted. He ordered his army to encamp, for he wished to see the castle and the noble lady who held it, as he had not seen her since before her marriage. Taking ten or twelve knights with him he went to salute the Countess of Salisbury and to examine the damage done by the Scots' attacks.

When the countess heard that the King was coming, she had the gates opened, and went out to meet him so richly dressed that no one could look at her without wonder and admiration at her noble appearance, her great beauty, and her warmth of expression. When she came to the King, she made a deep curtsy, thanking him for coming to her aid, and led him into the castle to entertain him fittingly. Everyone was dazzled by her; the King could not take his eyes off her, and thought he had never seen a lady so noble and beautiful, and at the same time so gay and attractive. A spark of love was kindled in his heart that was to remain burning a long time, for he did not think that anywhere in the world could there be a lady so worthy of love. They entered the castle hand in hand, and first she led him into the great hall, and then to his room, which was as richly furnished as might be expected. All this time the King gazed at her so ardently that she became embarrassed. After looking at her for a long while, he went to a window and leaned on it, reflecting deeply. The countess, thinking no more of it, went to entertain the other knights and to see to the preparation for dinner. She then returned to the King, who was still lost in thought, and cheerfully enquired: 'Sir, what is it that you are pondering so deeply? So much meditation does not suit you, if I may be so bold. You should be feasting, and in high spirits: you have driven off the enemies who dared to attack you.' The King answered: 'Ah, dear lady, since I came here, something has struck me of which I had no notion, and I must reflect on it. I do not know what will be the result, but I cannot take my mind off it.' 'Ah, dear sir,' replied the countess, 'you should always be in good spirits, and feast with your friends and encourage them, and leave off thinking and musing. God has helped you so much in all your enterprises and given you so much grace, that you are the most feared and renowned prince in Christendom. And if the King of Scotland has done harm to your kingdom, you can repay him when you like, as you have done before. So come into the hall to your knights, if you please, for dinner will soon be ready.' 'Ah, dear lady, something else touches my heart – it is not what you think. It is that your sweet nature, your perfect sense, your noble and exceptional beauty have so struck me that I am in love with you. I beg of you to return my love, which nothing can quench.' The countess was taken aback: 'Dear sir,' she said, 'do not mock me, and do not tempt me. I cannot believe that you mean what you have said, nor that so noble and gallant a prince as yourself could think of dishonouring myself and my husband, who is such a valiant knight and has served you so faithfully, and is at this moment in prison for your cause. Certainly, sir, this would not add to your glory, nor benefit you. Such a thought has never entered my mind for any man, nor will it, please God. If I were guilty of such a thing, it is you who ought to blame me and punish my body with death.'

This admirable lady left the King much astonished and went to hasten dinner in the hall. She afterwards returned to the King, with some of his knights, and said: 'Sir, come into the hall. The knights are waiting for you, to wash their hands. They have fasted too long, as you must have too.' The King left his room and went into the hall, and washed, and sat down to dinner with the knights and their hostess. But he ate little, for his mind was on other things, he remained pensive, and cast his eyes in the direction of the countess whenever he could. The others thought it was the Scots who had escaped him that were the object of his anxiety. The King stayed in the castle all day, thoughtful and worried, for he did not know what to do. Sometimes he blamed himself, since honour and duty forbade him to harbour these false thoughts of dishonouring this valiant lady and her loyal husband who had always served him so faithfully. On the other hand, his passion for her was so violent that it overwhelmed all thoughts of honour and duty. His mind was occupied with this all that day and night. In the morning he made his army strike camp and pursue the Scots, to chase them out of his country. He took leave of the countess with the following words: 'Dear lady, God protect you till my return; and I beg you to change your mind.' 'Dear sir,' she replied, 'may God the Father protect you, and drive all wicked and dishonourable thoughts from your heart, for it will always be my wish to serve you in every way that is consistent with my honour and yours.'

The King departed, confused and ashamed.

FROISSART, on King Edward III, 1341

My Mistress and My Friend,

My heart and I surrender ourselves into your hands, and we supplicate to be commended to your good graces, and that by absence your affections may not be diminished by us. For that would be to augment our pain, which would be a great pity, since absence gives enough and more than I ever thought could be felt. This brings to my mind a fact in astronomy, which is, that the further the poles are from the sun, notwithstanding, the more scorching is the heat. Thus it is with our love; absence has placed distance between us, nevertheless fervour increases – at least on my part and hope the same from you, assuring you that in my case the anguish of absence is so great that it would be intolerable were it not for the firm hope I have of your indissoluble affection towards me.

In order to remind you of it, and because I cannot in person be in your presence, I send you the thing which comes nearest that is possible; that is to say, my future, and the whole device, which you already know of, set in bracelets, wishing myself in their place when it pleaseth you. This is from the hand of your servant and friend.

H.R.

KING HENRY VIII, to Anne Boleyn, 1528

You and your sister Mary ought to thank God for escaping that cursed and venomous whore who tried to poison you both.

KING HENRY VIII, to his natural son, the Duke of Richmond,
on Queen Anne Boleyn, on the day of her arrest, 1536

My dear Friend and Mistress,

The bearer of these few lines from thy entirely devoted servant will deliver into thy fair hands a token of my true affections for thee, hoping you will keep it for ever in your sincere love for me. Advertising you that there is a ballad made lately of great derision against us, which if it go abroad and is seen by you, I pray you to pay no manner of regard to it. I am not at present informed who is the setter forth of this malignant writing: but if he is found out, he shall be straitly punished for it.

For the things you lacked, I have minded my lord to supply them to you as soon as he could buy them.

Thus hoping shortly to receive you in these arms, I end for the present.

Your own loving servant and sovereign,
H.R.

KING HENRY VIII, to Jane Seymour, 1536

On April 12th, 1566, a strange event was seen by passers-by in the streets between St Paul's and the river-side. On the morning of that day Lord Leicester, followed by seven hundred footmen, his own and the queen's, came to young Lord Oxford's town house, that stood opposite St Swithin's Church, beside London Stone. When he found no one there to meet him, he departed with his following. Meanwhile the queen, in a boat rowed by one pair of oars, attended by two ladies only, had come up against the tide from Greenwich. A landing could be made only where there were stairs, and the boatman brought her to those on the wharf known as The Three Cranes, from the three great machines that stood there for loading and unloading. Here a blue-painted coach was waiting for her and she drove off to London Stone. Alas, no one was there. Lord

Leicester, though refusing to wait for her at the tryst, had none the less posted himself at a point she must pass on her return to the wharf. When she saw him, she came out of her coach into the high-way and she embraced the Earl and kissed him three times. Then he climbed into the coach with her and they drove across London Bridge and took the road to Greenwich. This vision of the lovers, inconsequent, unaccountable, rose and disappeared again like a happening in a dream.   ELIZABETH JENKINS, 1961

I confess I lived many years by all sorts of debauchery. But since that time I had an affection for the Lady Harriot, and I prayed that if it were pleasing to God, it might continue, otherwise that it might cease. And God heard my prayer. The affection did continue, therefore I doubted not that it was pleasing to God; and that this is a marriage, our choice of one another being guided, not by lust, but by judgement, upon due consideration.

JAMES, DUKE OF MONMOUTH, on Lady Henrietta Wentworth, to Dr Ken, Vicar of St Martin-in-the-Fields, while in the Tower, awaiting execution, 1685

This, emphasizing her virtue, he repeated on the scaffold, avoiding the conventional pieties and protestations.

Good God! Had that poor man nothing to think of but me?

LADY HENRIETTA WENTWORTH, 1685

. . . She died less than a year after her lover, from a broken heart, some said; others, more vindictive, of mercury poisoning from over-painting her face.

ROBIN CLIFTON, 1984 on Lady Henrietta Wentworth

You will be weary of seeing every day a letter from me, it may be; yet being able to flatter myself, I hope you will be as willing to read as I write. And indeed it is the only comfort I have in this world, beside that of trust in God. I have nothing to say to you at present that is worth writing, and I think it unreasonable to trouble you with my grief, which I must continue while you are absent, though I trust every post to hear some good news or other from you; therefore, I shall make this very short, and only tell you that I have got a swell'd face, though not quite so bad yet as it was in Holland some five years ago. I believe it came by standing too much at the window when I took the waters. I cannot enough thank God for you being so well past the dangers of the sea; I beseech him in his mercy still to preserve you so, and send us once more a happy meeting upon earth. I long to hear again from you how the air of Ireland agrees with you, for I must own I am not without fears for that, loving you so entirely as I do, and shall till death.

QUEEN MARY II, in London, 1690, to her husband King William III,
in Ireland to fight her father, the former King James II

Every year his reverence for the concept of kingship grew stronger; nothing illustrates his regard more than his behaviour over Lady Sarah Lennox. This charming girl of fifteen swept him off his feet just before he succeeded to the throne. He longed to marry her. Bute said no, and George III wrote that 'he [Bute] has thoroughly convinced me of the impropriety of marrying a country woman; the interest of my country shall ever be my just care, my own inclinations shall ever submit to it.' And submit he did and married a dull, plain, German Protestant princess who bore him the huge family that was to plague his days.

A sexually timid, if nonetheless passionate man, George may have found it easier to take Bute's advice than many have thought. Lady Sarah attracted lovers as a candle moths, and George, conscious of his faults and of his inadequacies, must have realized that he cut a poor figure amidst her brilliant courtiers. His queen, Charlotte, attracted no one. And yet sacrifice there was, and George paid for it. Shortly after his marriage he experienced his first bout of insanity. Later in life these periods of madness grew longer. It was only during these attacks that his thoughts escaped from his strict concept of marriage, and rioted in adultery. Then, and then only, was it unsafe for a lady of his court to be alone with him.

J. H. PLUMB, 1963

He cried by the hour ... he testified the sincerity and violence of his passion and his despair by the most extravagant expressions and actions, rolling on the floor, striking his forehead, tearing his hair, and swearing that he would abandon the country, forego the crown, sell his jewels and plate and scrape together a competence to fly with the object of his affections to America.

ELIZABETH ARMISTEAD, later Mrs Charles James Fox,
to Lord Holland, *c.* 1785, on George, Prince of Wales,
later King George IV, and Mary Anne Fitzherbert

You reject all my wishes with a haughty disdain that greatly mortifies me. I am open to correction, I avow my errors. I wish you to assume a character which you are most fit to shine in, and which may be of infinite service to me, but I wish and entreat in vain! — unkind Margaritta.

Even the words of an author I passionately admire is quoted against me. Thus you turn me from a book — I might profit from; for when I attempt to read it, it reminds me of the cold, the severe fair one, whose friendship I have most wish'd to cultivate, who attributes to me all the faults of my predecessor Hal, and believes me incapable to finish the character.

Am I to answer all the idle, the unjust things you hear to my disadvantage? Pardon my heat, I am disappointed! Hurt, I acknowledge; but my heart feels now much more so, at the sickly pale of the finest cheek which I beheld this morning! Had I not some merit when I met you on horseback not to join you? I debated it for half a moment; but the reserved air with which you returned my compliments determined me. I was repaid in the look you afterwards gave me, for I thought in that look you approv'd my discretion.

Sickness only, I hope, has chilled that heart formed for more generous sensations. Your restoration to health I earnestly wish, and your return to tender feelings. Judge for yourself if I am not your attentive

Telemachus.

GEORGE, PRINCE OF WALES, to Mrs Fitzherbert

Dearest, best beloved Victoria – Already another dear, dear letter from you which has wholly charmed me, for it once again tells me you love me, and proves that you love me truly and faithfully. You can confer on me no greater happiness. But why do you say you are unworthy? I would allow no one in the world to say such a thing; therefore I may not suffer it from you, for I cannot hear my dear good Victoria disparaged. I hope that in fear of me you will conceive a better opinion of yourself. You say that to you the whole thing seems to be merely a beautiful dream. It is no better with me. I cannot get it into my head that it is all real, though I trust that the moment when we meet again will thoroughly convince me. . . .

You ask after good old Nus, and my faithful but not indisinterested Eos [pet dogs]. She is very well, looks after herself as much as she can, sleeps by the stove, is very friendly if there is plum-cake in the room, very much put out when she has to jump over the stick, keen on hunting, sleepy after it, always proud, and contemptuous of other dogs.

I cannot tell you much, as nothing worth telling occurs to me. Oh yes! there is something; my song of the orange blossoms is finished, and what is more the modest young composer is delighted with it and says it is one of his most successful works, excellent, unsurpassed in melody and harmony! In humblest devotion my insignificance ventures to lay at Your Majesty's feet the said work, the said incomparable work of a moment of youthful inspiration by the trembling undersigned. The composer has taken a great deal of trouble and hopes *que sa composition fera de l'effet et aura un peu de succes.* (This is the modesty of a genius.) . . .

I cannot say how pleased I am that you are walking a lot. In this cold damp weather it is certainly the healthiest thing and will keep your feet warm. Do you remember how I warmed your dear little hands every day in the lovely little blue room? In quiet hours I live on such memories. Good, dear, charming Victoria, in my thoughts I am very much with you.

PRINCE ALBERT OF SAXE-COBURG-GOTHA, later Prince Consort,
to Queen Victoria, 1839

I found these words in an old Diary or Journal of mine. I was in great trouble about the Princess Royal who had lost her child in '66 and dear John said to me, 'I wish to take care of my dear mistress till I die. You'll never have an honester servant.' I took and held his dear kind hand and I said I hoped he might long be spared to comfort me and he answered, 'But we all must die.' Afterwards, my beloved John would say: 'You haven't a more devoted servant than Brown' – and oh! how I felt that!

Afterwards so often I told him no one loved him more than I did or had a better friend than me; and he answered 'Nor you – than me. No one loves you more.'

QUEEN VICTORIA, to Hugh Brown, following John Brown's death, 1883

LOYALTY

I will carry him on my shoulders, one leg on each side, from island to island, from land to land, and I will not fail him, even if he never thanks me for my pains.

WILLIAM MARSHAL, first Earl of Pembroke and guardian of the boy king, Henry III, 1216. *L'Historie de Guillaume Le Marèchal* by Jean, 1225–6

Although rebellion do my body bind
My King alone can captivate my mind.

LORD JOHN SCUDAMORE, royalist, imprisoned by the Roundheads at Hereford. 1643

What then? Thirty thoosan' pounds! Though I had gotten't I could not enjoy it eight and forty hours. Conscience would get up upon me – that money could not keep it down. And though I could get all

Scotland and England for my pains, I would not allow a hair of his body to be touched if I could help it.

DONALD MACLEOD, captured after Culloden, 1746, refusing the reward for the betrayal of Prince Charles Edward

A LUNCHEON

Lift latch, step in, be welcome, Sir,
Albeit to see you I'm unglad
And your face is fraught with a deathly shyness
Bleaching what pink it may have had.
Come in, come in, Your Royal Highness.

Beautiful weather? – Sir, that's true,
Though the farmers are casting rueful looks
At tilth's and pasture's dearth of spryness –
Yes, Sir, I've written several books –
A little more chicken, Your Royal Highness.

Lift latch, step out, your car is there,
To bear you hencefrom this antient vale.
We are both of us aged by our strange brief nighness
But each of us lives to tell the tale.
Farewell, farewell, Your Royal Highness.

MAX BEERBOHM, on the visit for lunch with Thomas Hardy, at the poet's Dorset home, 1923, by Edward, Prince of Wales, later King Edward VIII.

MADNESS

Much has been written by learned scholars to the effect that George III was manic depressive, and suffered from sexual frustration, a difficult wife, and hideous family problems – all acting upon an inherently unstable character which finally gave way under the strain. If this was so why didn't the King 'go mad' far earlier than 1788? . . .

The recurrent toxic and confusional states suffered by the King could have been due to other physical causes such as infectious and metabolic disturbances. The observation of purple urine by itself is not sufficient proof; indeed, medical experience has shown that most cases of modern porphyria are precipitated by barbiturates. . . .

There is no evidence that he was schizophrenic, or depressive, or that he suffered from syphilis of the central nervous system which, when untreated, is steadily progressive. Only in the last ten years of his life when between the ages of seventy and eighty, deaf, blind, deserted by his family, surrounded only by 'mad doctors' and apothecaries who tied him up in straight waistcoats at the slightest sign of opposition to their will and banished him to the north side of Windsor Castle, did he show signs of mental decay associated with natural senility.

I think there can now be little doubt that George III suffered from periodic attacks of a metabolic illness.

CHARLES, PRINCE OF WALES, introducing *King George III* by John Brooke, 1972

MAGNANIMITY

I forgive you, John, and I wish I could as easily forget your offence as you will my pardon.

KING RICHARD I, to his brother John Sans Terre,
later King John, after the latter's treachery. Rouen, 1189

THE MANUFACTURE
OF MONSTERS

Man has always wished to add something to God's work. Man retouches creation, sometimes for better, sometimes for worse. The Court buffoon was nothing but an attempt to lead back man to the monkey. It was a progress the wrong way. A masterpiece in retrogression. At the same time they tried to make a man of the monkey. Barbara, Duchess of Cleveland and Countess of Southampton, had a marmoset for a page. Frances Sutton, Baroness Dudley, eighth peeress in the bench of barons, had tea served by a baboon clad in gold brocade, which her ladyship called My Black. Catherine Sedley, Countess of Dorchester, used to go and take her seat in Parliament in a coach with armorial bearings, behind which stood, their muzzles stuck up in the air, three Cape monkeys in grand livery. A Duchess of Medina-Celi, whose toilet Cardinal Pole witnessed, had her stockings put on by an orang-outang. These monkeys raised in the scale were a counterpoise to men brutalized and bestialized. This promiscuousness of man and beast, desired by the great, was especially prominent in the case of the dwarf and the dog. The dwarf never quitted the dog, which was always bigger than himself. The dog was the pair of the dwarf; it was as if they were coupled with a collar. This juxtaposition is authenticated by a mass of domestic records – notably by the portrait of Jeffrey Hudson, dwarf of Henrietta of France, daughter of Henri IV, and wife of Charles I.

The manufacture of monsters was practised on a large scale, and comprised various branches. . . .

It was the custom, in the palace of the kings of England, to have a sort of watchman, who crowed like a cock. This watcher, awake while all others slept, ranged the palace, and raised from hour to hour the cry of the farmyard, repeating it as often as was necessary, and thus supplying a clock. This man, promoted to be cock, had in childhood undergone the operation of the pharynx, which was part of the art described by Dr Conquest. Under Charles II, the salivation inseparable to the operation having disgusted the Duchess of Portsmouth, the appointment was indeed preserved, so that the splendour of the crown should not be tarnished, but they got an unmutilated man to represent the cock. A retired officer was generally selected for this honourable employment. Under James II, the functionary was named William Sampson, Cock, and received for his crow £9 2s. 6d. annually.

The memoirs of Catherine II inform us that at St Petersburg, scarcely a hundred years since, whenever the czar or czarina was displeased with a Russian prince, he was forced to squat down in the great antechamber of the palace, and to remain in that posture a certain number of days, mewing like a cat, or clucking like a sitting hen, and pecking his food from the floor.   VICTOR HUGO, 1869

MARRIAGE

The passion of John for his queen, though it was sufficiently strong to embroil him in war, was not exclusive enough to secure conjugal fidelity; the king tormented her with jealousy, while on his part he was far from setting her a good example, for he often invaded the honour of the female nobility. The name of the lover of Isabella has never been ascertained, nor is it clear that she was ever guilty of any dereliction from rectitude. But John revenged the wrong that, perhaps, only existed in his malignant imagination, in a manner peculiar to himself. He made his mercenaries assassinate the person whom he suspected of supplanting him in his queen's affections, with two others supposed to be accomplices, and secretly hung their bodies over the bed of Isabella. Her surprise and terror when she discovered them may be imagined, though it is not described by the monkish writer who darkly alludes to this dreadful scene.

> AGNES STRICKLAND, 1840, on King John and Queen Isabella

I see nothing in this woman as men report of her, and I marvel that wise men should have made such report as they have done.

> KING HENRY VIII, to Anthony Browne, having met his future wife, Anne of Cleves

KING HENRY VIII: Do you think the Lady [Anne of Cleves] so fair and of such beauty as report had been made of her?

SIR JOHN RUSSELL: Your Grace, I took her not for fair, but to be of a brown complexion.

KING HENRY VIII: Alas, whom should men trust? I promise you I see no such thing in her as hath been showed unto me of her.

If I had known so much before, she had no coming hither. But what remedy now?

> KING HENRY VIII, on his betrothed, Anne of Cleves, to Thomas Cromwell

KING HENRY VIII: How say you, my Lord, is it not as I told you? Say what they will, she is nothing fair. The personage is well and comely but nothing else.

THOMAS CROMWELL: By my faith, you say truth. [But] me thinketh she had a queenly manner withal.

KING HENRY VIII: That is true. Then there is no remedy but to put my neck in the yoke.   KING HENRY VIII, to Thomas Cromwell

My lord, if it were not to satisfy the world and my realm, I would not do that I must do this day for none earthly thing.

> KING HENRY VIII, to Thomas Cromwell, 'demure and sad'
> on the day of his marriage to Anne of Cleves

THOMAS CROMWELL: Doth your Grace like her better?

KING HENRY VIII: Nay, my lord, much worse, for by her breasts and belly she should be no maid; which, when I felt them, strake me so to the heart that I had neither will nor courage to prove the rest. On the morning after the marriage

As the marriage of Queen Mary was a terrible plague to all England, so now the want of your marriage and issue is like to prove as great a plague. If your parents had been of your mind, where had you been then? Or what had become of us now?

DEAN ALEXANDER NOWELL, to Queen Elizabeth I:
sermon in Westminster Abbey, 1563

I have known her since she was eight years old, better than any man in the world. From that time she has invariably declared she would remain unmarried.

ROBERT DUDLEY, EARL OF LEICESTER, to the French Ambassador, La Foret, 1566

May 21, 1662

I arrived here yesterday about two in the afternoon and as soon as I had shifted myself I went to my wife's chamber, where I found her in bed, by reason of a little cough, and some inclinations to a fever, which was caused, as we physicians say, by having certain things stopped at sea which ought to have carried away those humours. But now all is in their due course, and I believe she will find herself very well in the morning as soon as she awakes.

It was happy for the honour of the nation that I was not put to the consummation of the marriage last night; for I was so sleepy by having slept but two hours in my journey as I was afraid that matters would have gone very sleepily. I can now only give you an account of what I have seen a-bed; which, in short, is that her face is not so exact as to be called a beauty, though her eyes are excellent good, and not anything in her face that in the least degree can shock one. On the contrary, she has as much agreeableness in her looks as ever I saw; and if I have any skill in physiognomy, which I think I have, she must be as good a woman as ever was born. Her conversation, as much as I can perceive, is very good; for she has wit enough and a most agreeable voice. You would much wonder to see how well we are acquainted already. In a word, I think myself very happy.

KING CHARLES II, from Portsmouth, on his bride, Catherine of Braganza,
to the Lord Chancellor, Edward Hyde, Earl of Clarendon

July 6, 1662

To supper with my Lady Sandwich; who tells me, with much trouble, that my Lady Castlemaine is still as great with the King, and that the King comes as often to her as ever he did.

July 16, 1662

This day I was told that my Lady Castlemaine, being quite fallen out with her husband, did yesterday go away with him, with all her plate, jewels, and other best things; and is gone to Richmond to a brother of hers; which I am apt to think was a design to get out of town, that the King might come to her better.

October, 1662

Mr Pierce, the surgeon, tells me how ill things go at Court: that the King do show no countenance to any that belong to the Queen; nor, above all, to such English as she brought over with her, or hath hers since, for fear they should tell her how he carries himself to Mrs Palmer [Lady Castlemaine]; insomuch, that though he has a promise, and is sure of being made her surgeon, he is at a loss what to do in it, whether to take it or no, since the King's mind is so altered and favour all her dependents, whom she is fain to let go back into Portugal (though she brought them from their friends against their wills, with promise of preferment), without doing anything for them. That her own physician did tell me within these three days that the Queen do know how the King orders things, and how he carries himself to my Lady Castlemaine and others, as well as anybody; but though she hath spirit enough, yet seeing that she do no good by taking notice of it, for the present she forbears it in policy; of which I am very glad. But I do pray God help us in peace: for this, with other things, do give great discontent to all people.

SAMUEL PEPYS

One damned German frow is as good as another.

GEORGE, PRINCE OF WALES, on his betrothal
to Princess Caroline of Brunswick, 1795

I observed that marrying a subject was making yourself so much their equal, and brought you so in contact with the whole family. Lord M. quite agreed in this and said, 'I don't think it would be liked; there would be such jealousy.' I said, 'Why need I marry at all for three or four years? Did he see the necessity?' I said I dreaded the thought of marrying; that I was so accustomed to have my own way, that I thought it was 10 to 1 that I shouldn't agree with anybody.   QUEEN VICTORIA. *Diary*, 1834

A civil ceremony, as is the custom on the Continent, preceded the religious service which was held in the château's music room. A handful of newspaper reporters were allowed in to cover the wedding and various French dignitaries and their wives also received invitations. But of their own guests – personal friends of long standing – there were only eight: 'Fruity' Metcalfe, the Duke's former equerry, who was to act as best man; Lady Alexandra Metcalfe; Herman and Katherine Rogers, fellow Americans who had never left Wallis Simpson's side; Randolph Churchill, son of Sir Winston; Walter Monckton (who had borne the news that the Duke's bride was not to share her husband's title of Royal Highness – by order of King George VI); and Eugene and Kitty de Rothschild.

Mrs Simpson, dressed by Mainbocher, in a long, elegant gown of pale blue crêpe satin with a small veiled hat of feathers to match, entered on the arm of Herman Rogers. 'Fruity' Metcalfe slipped the bridegroom the prayer book which Queen Mary had given to him as a boy, and the Rev. R. Anderson Jardine quietly performed what was arguably the most historic and emotionally charged royal wedding of the century. Lady Alexandra Metcalfe noted after the ceremony that: 'It was hard not to cry and in fact I did.' The new Duchess of Windsor put on a brave face even though the Duke, as had been known to happen in the past, gave emotion its head and, according to Lady Alexandra: 'He had tears running down his face when he came into the salon after the ceremony.'

CHRISTOPHER WARWICK, 1980, on the marriage, 1937, of the
Duke and Duchess of Windsor, at the Château de Cande

MARY I

Mary, deep-voiced, short-sighted, courageous, devout and unimaginative, filled herself with distress and the popular imagination with smoke and fury. Disappointed in her father, her husband, her people and herself, disappointed, perhaps, in God, barren Mary Tudor is the saddest failure in Tudor politics. Like Macbeth, though with far more reason and far less poetry, she has become a disgraceful legend, a nursery ogre, which would have astonished her cultured intelligence, outraged her Tudor sensitivity, cut deep into her starved heart. Harold, John, Richard II, Llewellyn the Great, Wallace, Wolsey, More, Aske, Protector Somerset, Charles I, Strafford, the first Earl of Shaftesbury, Monmouth, Charles Edward Stuart, Parnell, Casement, ended in failure or disaster but leaving names often respected and sometimes loved, several finding in death a moral dignity they had not found in life. For Mary, there was an atrocious epithet, popular contempt, and joy that she was dead at last.

PETER VANSITTART, 1969

We have already observed that the characteristics of Mary were bigotry and revenge; we shall only add that she was proud, imperious, froward, avaricious, and wholly destitute of every agreeable qualification.   TOBIAS SMOLLETT, on Queen Mary I, 1757

MARY II

The Princess possessed all that conversed with her with admiration. Her person was majestic, and created respect; she had great knowledge, with a true judgment and a noble expression; a sweetness there was in her deportment that charmed, an exactness in her piety and virtue, a frugality in her expenses, an extensiveness in her charities, and a peculiar grace in bestowing them, so as to make her a pattern to all who saw her. She read much, both in history and divinity, and when the humour in her eyes forced her from that exercise, she set herself to work with such constant diligence, that all the ladies about her were ashamed to be idle. But, above all, she was a singular example of conjugal obedience and affection, insomuch that when it was put to her by me, What she intended the Prince should be if she came to the Crown? her answer was, That the rule and authority should be his; for she only desired that he would obey the command of 'Husbands, love your wives', as she would do that of 'Wives, be obedient to your husbands in all things.'   BISHOP GILBERT BURNET, on the future Queen Mary II, *op. cit.*

MARY QUEEN OF SCOTS

A veil you wore of tissue delicate
With fold on fold in pleating intricate,
A widow's veil, which your fair form embrac'd,

Shrouding you from the forehead to the waist;
And in the wind it billow'd like the sail
Of a swift ship which blows before a gale.
In royal weeds of white you then were dress'd,
The garb of grief, and let it be confess'd,
You grieved for fair France, where of late you reign'd,
As on your breast your crystal tears down rain'd
You trod the garden walks of that château
Which bears a fountain's name – royal Fontainebleau.

PIERRE DE RONSARD. 'Elégie à Marie Stuart', *c.* 1560

With regard to the queen's person, a circumstance not to be omitted
in writing the history of a female reign, all contemporary authors
agree in ascribing to Mary the utmost beauty of countenance and
elegance of shape of which the human form is capable. Her hair was
black, though, according to the fashion of that age, she frequently
wore borrowed locks, and of different colours. Her eyes were a
dark grey, her complexion was exquisitely fine and her hands and
arms remarkably delicate, both as to shape and colour. Her stature
was of a height that rose to the majestic. She danced, she walked,
and rode with equal grace. Her taste for music was just, and she
both sang and played upon the lute with uncommon skill. Towards
the end of her life she began to grow fat; and her long confinement
and the coldness of the houses in which she was imprisoned,
brought on a rheumatism which deprived her of the use of her
limbs. WILLIAM ROBERTSON, 1759

The Daughter of Debate

The doubt of future foes exiles my present joy,
And wit me warns to shun such snares as threaten mine annoy.

For falsehood now doth flow and subject faith doth ebb,
Which would not be, if reason rules or wisdom weaves the web.

But clouds of toys untried do cloak aspiring minds,
Which turn to rain of late repent by course of changed winds.

The top of hope supposed the root of ruth will be,
And fruitless all their graffed guiles, as shortly ye shall see.

The dazzled eyes with pride, which great ambition blinds,
Shall be unseeled by worthy wights, whose foresight falsehood finds.

The daughter of debate, that eke discord doth sow,
Shall reap no gain where former rule hath taught still peace to grow.

No foreign banished wight shall anchor in this port;
Our realm it brooks no stranger's force, let them elsewhere resort.

Our rusty sword with rest shall first his edge employ
To poll their tops that seek such change and gape for joy.

QUEEN ELIZABETH I

*'The Daughter of Debate' was Mary Queen of Scots, on whose
behalf the Catholic Earls of Westmorland and Northumberland
had raised the north in rebellion in 1569, to release Mary from her
English prison and, with Spanish armed help, place her on the
English throne. The Earls found no popular support and the rising
was crushed. Mass executions followed, on a scale unknown since
the Pilgrimage of Grace.*

Royal brother, having by God's will, for my sins I think, thrown
myself into the power of the Queen my cousin, at whose hands I
have suffered much for almost twenty years, I have finally been
condemned to death by her and her Estates. I have asked for my
papers, which they have taken away, in order that I might make my
will, but I have been unable to recover anything of use to me, or
even get leave either to make my will freely or to have my body
conveyed after my death, as I would wish, to your kingdom where I
had the honour to be queen, your sister and old ally.

Tonight, after dinner, I have been advised of my sentence: I am
to be executed like a criminal at eight in the morning. I have not had
time to give you a full account of everything that has happened, but

if you will listen to my doctor and my other unfortunate servants, you will learn the truth, and how, thanks be to God, I scorn death and vow that I meet it innocent of any crime, even if I were their subject. The Catholic faith and the assertion of my God-given right to the English crown are the two issues on which I am condemned, and yet I am not allowed to say that it is for the Catholic religion that I die, but for fear of interference with theirs. The proof of this is that they have taken away my chaplain, and, although he is in the building, I have not been able to get permission for him to come and hear my confession and give me the Last Sacrament, while they have been most insistent that I receive the consolation and instruction of their minister, brought here for that purpose. The bearer of this letter and his companions, most of them your subjects, will testify to my conduct at my last hour. It remains for me to beg Your Most Christian Majesty, my brother-in-law and old ally, who have always protested your love for me, to give proof now of your goodness on all these points: firstly by charity, in paying my unfortunate servants the wages due to them – this is a burden on my conscience that only you can relieve: further, by having prayers offered to God for a queen who has borne the title Most Christian, and who dies a Catholic, stripped of all her possessions. As for my son, I commend him to you in so far as he deserves, for I cannot answer for him. I have taken the liberty of sending you two precious stones, talismans against illness, trusting that you will enjoy good health and a long and happy life. Accept them from your loving sister-in-law, who, as she dies, bears witness of her warm feeling for you. Again I commend my servants to you. Give instructions, if it please you, that for my soul's sake part of what you owe me should be paid, and that for the sake of Jesus Christ, to whom I shall pray for you tomorrow as I die, I be left enough to found a memorial mass and give the customary alms.

Wednesday, at two in the morning.

Your most loving and true sister,

MARY R.

To the Most Christian King, my brother and old ally.

The last letter of MARY QUEEN OF SCOTS. To King Henri III of France, 1587

MEN

You men are far too selfish. You only had the advantages in such a case, whereas we poor women have to bear all the pains and suffering of which you can have no conception.

QUEEN VICTORIA, to her son-in-law, Prince Frederick William of Prussia, afterwards Emperor Frederick III

MISTRESSES

Take her away from hence for she was a whore; and bury her outside the church with the rest, that the religion of Christ may not become contemptible, and that other women, warned by her example, may keep from illicit and adulterous intercourse.

HUGH, BISHOP OF LINCOLN, recorded by Roger de Howden, on Rosamund Clifford, mistress of King Henry II.*Chronica*, c. 1192

I thence walked with him through St James's Park to the garden, where I both say and heard a very familiar discourse between . . . and Mrs Nelly, as they called an impudent comedian, she looking out of her garden on a terrace at the top of the wall, and . . . standing on the green walk under it. I was heartily sorry at this scene. Thence the King walked to the Duchess of Cleveland, another lady of pleasure, and curse of our nation.

JOHN EVELYN, on King Charles II and Nell Gwynn

Had I suffered for my God as I have done for your brother and you, I should not have needed either of your kindness or justice to me.

NELL GWYNN, to King James II, 1686

Pepys first saw the lively little Cockney comedienne standing outside her door in Drury Lane. He admired her 'smock-sleeves and bodice' – something of a fetishist, he once confessed that it had done him good to look upon Lady Castlemaine's 'smocks and linnen petticoats' hanging up to dry – and he decided that Nell was a 'mighty pretty creature'. The King thought so too, and found her not only exciting and lovable as a mistress but enchanting as a companion. The daughter of a woman who had drowned herself when drunk, she had been brought up in a brothel and had been an orange-girl in a theatre before becoming an actress. She was a clever and impudent mimic and a mistress of tart and vulgar repartee. Once when her carriage was stoned by the mob who mistook it for the unpopular Duchess of Portsmouth's, she put out her head and shouted 'Don't hurt me, good people! I'm the Protestant whore'; and once when this rival went into mourning for a French prince to whom she was in no way related, Nell Gwynn dressed herself in even deeper mourning for, so she said, the dear departed Cham of Tartary. In Charles's presence she is said to have called to his son, 'Come here, you little bastard,' and when Charles reproached her for using such a rude word, she replied that she had no other name to give him. Immediately he was made Earl of Burford and afterwards Duke of St Albans.

Such stories delighted a people who detested the King's less honest and far less faithful mistresses. For, claiming no special privileges, Nell Gwynn excited no popular jealousy. She was appointed one of the Queen's Ladies in 1675, some years after the King's munificence had enabled her to leave the stage; but few except the Duchess of Portsmouth, who could tell she had once 'been an orange-girl by her swearing', begrudged her either this honour or her new-found wealth. 'Her joyous laugh, her wild extravagance of speech, her warm-hearted disposition, and imperturbable good-nature' established her not only in the affections of her Charles the Third (as she fondly called him, referring her two previous lovers, Charles, Lord Buckhurst, and Charles Hart, the actor) but also in the affections of her fellow-people.

CHRISTOPHER HIBBERT, 1964

It cannot be my beauty for he must see I have none, and it cannot be my wit for he has not enough to know that I have any.

> CATHARINE SEDLEY, Countess of Dorchester, mistress of James, Duke of York, later King James II, speculating on the reasons for his ardour

God, who would have thought that we three whores should have met here!

> THE COUNTESS OF DORCHESTER, mistress of King James II, on encountering the Duchess of Portsmouth, mistress of King Charles II, and the Countess of Orkney, mistress of King William III, at Queen Caroline's Drawing Room, after the coronation of King George II, 1727

Two fierce black eyes, large and rolling beneath two lofty arched eye-brows; two acres of cheeks spread with crimson; an ocean of neck that overflowed, and was not distinguished from the lower part of her body; and no part restrained by stays.

> HORACE WALPOLE, on Sophia Charlotte, Countess of Darlington, mistress of King George I

She is mighty old!

> TSAR ALEXANDER I OF RUSSIA, when George, Prince Regent, introduced his mistress, Lady Hertford, 1816

MOCKERY

... When someone told K. George III that some eminent soldier had been killed in the war in America (the War of Independence) the K. is said to have ejaculated: 'What? What? What? Shot? Shot? Shot?'

But these tales of the great are usually invented by the Mocker, to divert the Idle, as I so often warn you.

> JOHN MASEFIELD, from a letter to Audrey Napier-Smith, 1958

THE MOTHER

My dear first born is the greatest ass, and the greatest liar, and the greatest *canaille*, and the greatest beast in the whole world and I heartily wish he was out of it.

QUEEN CAROLINE, wife of King George II, on Frederick, Prince of Wales

Her wish was granted, seemingly by a cricket or tennis ball, 1751.

MR MUGGERIDGE AND LORD ALTRINCHAM

According to Muggeridge, the Queen, Prince Philip, their family and doings had come 'to constitute a sort of royal soap-opera'. The Monarchy provided 'a sort of substitute or ersatz religion'. It had become 'a pure show'.

Duchesses, he reported, found the Queen 'dowdy, frumpy and banal'. There were equally those who found 'the ostentation of life at Windsor or Buckingham Palace little to their taste', while 'a more valid criticism of the Monarchy is that it is a generator of snobbishness and a focus of sycophancy'. Like Altrincham, he saw the Queen's entourage as 'exclusively upper-class'.

Apart from the few essentially personal references, both articles were reasoned arguments which if published today, whether one agreed with them or not, would excite much less stir than they did at the time. But at the time of publication Prince Philip's ideas on Monarchy and the Court had not yet taken proper root and the so-called permissive society was not yet upon us. So feelings ran high. Muggeridge was spat upon in the street and had his contract with a Sunday newspaper abruptly terminated. Altrincham was struck in the face, even if lightly. His views, in particular, seemed to bring a rush of blood to certain noble heads. The Duke of Argyll would not have been averse to seeing him 'hanged, drawn and quartered', while the Earl of Strathmore reportedly gave it as his opinion that 'the bounder' should be shot.

GRAHAM AND HEATHER FISHER, 1972, on Malcolm Muggeridge's article, 'Does Britain Really Need a Queen?' published in the *Saturday Evening Post*, 1957. Some weeks earlier, Lord Altrincham, in the *National and English Review*, had judged the Queen's manner of speech 'frankly a pain in the neck' and her personality 'that of a priggish schoolgirl'.

MURDER

Madam,

My ears have been so astounded, my mind so disturbed, my heart so shocked at the news of the abominable murder of your late husband that even yet I can scarcely rally my spirits to write to you; and however I would express my sympathy in your sorrow for his loss, to tell you plainly what I think, my grief is more for you than for him. Oh, Madam, I should ill fulfill the part either of a faithful cousin or of an affectionate friend if I were to content myself with saying pleasant things to you and made no effort to preserve your honour. I cannot but tell you what all the world is thinking. Men say that instead of seizing the murderers, you are looking through your fingers while they escape; that you will not punish those who have done you so great a service, as though the thing would never have taken place had not the doers of it been assured of impunity.

For myself, I beg you to believe that I would not harbour such a thought for all the wealth of the world, nor would I entertain in my heart so ill a guest, or think so badly of any prince that breathes. Far less could I so think of you, to whom I desire all imaginable good, and all blessings which you yourself could wish for. For this very reason I exhort, I advise, I implore you deeply to consider of the matter – at once, if it be the nearest friend you have, to lay hands upon the man who has been guilty of the crime – to let no interest, no persuasion, keep you from proving to every one that you are a noble princess and a loyal wife. I do not write thus earnestly because I doubt you, but for the love I bear towards you. You may have wiser councillors than I am – I can well believe it – but even our Lord, as I remember, had a Judas among the twelve; while I am sure that you have no friend more true than I, and my affection may stand you in as good stead as the subtle wits of others.

Queen Elizabeth I, to Mary Queen of Scots,
following the strangling and blowing up of Henry, Lord Darnley,
her consort, at the house of Kirk o' Field, 1567

Elizabeth Jenkins adds (1961):

The Queen of Scots had left her husband's bedside two hours before the explosion took place; she said she must return to Holyrood to grace the wedding of one of her servants. As she made her way from Kirk o'Field to the palace, she sent back a page to bring away a rich counterpane that covered her bed in the room below her husband's.

Within a few weeks, Queen Mary married James, Earl of Bothwell. They were swiftly defeated by rebels at Carberry Hill, Bothwell fleeing to Denmark, the Queen captured and escorted back to Edinburgh with the population yelling 'Burn the whore!'

MUSIC

Henry's interest in the organ was deeply personal. He was a fine musician who reached very competent professional standards. He was fascinated by the skill needed for difficult keyboard music. He was an excellent performer on the virginals and mastered the organ which in the sixteenth century was a very complex instrument. He was equally adroit with wind or string instruments, and played the recorder as well as the lute. As he possessed a fine singing voice, he liked to accompany himself on the lute while he sang songs of his own composition. In 1509, the year he came to the throne, he wrote both words and music for the charming song, 'Pastime with Good Company'. The next year he is said to have written two five-part masses, as well as songs and ballads, while he was making a progress through the home counties. When deeply in love with Anne Boleyn he wrote what is possibly his best work, the motet *O Lord, Maker of all Kings*, which is still often played. In the same year he wrote *Quam Pulchra Est*, which has survived through the centuries and is still sung. Music, whether a Mass or a bawdy drinking song, was a daily necessity for Henry, and a passion which lasted right through his life. The last portrait of him is in the Psalter that he used. He is there, with his jester, Will Somers, looking old and battered, tired almost to death, yet playing still on his Welsh harp, finding solace in his music.

J. H. PLUMB, 1977, on King Henry VIII

The Lancastrian and Tudor monarchs had serious musical tastes, as performers, patrons and listeners.

But when the Queene of Beautie did inspire
The ayre with perfumes, and our hearts with fire,
Breathing from her celestiall Organ sweet
Harmonious notes, our soules fell at her feet,
And did with humble reverend dutie, more
Her rare perfection, than high state adore.

THOMAS CAREW, 1633, on the singing of Queen Henrietta Maria

George II was invited to attend the first performance of Handel's *Messiah* in London in 1743. The audience was extremely moved by the music, as was the king. When the words, 'And he shall reign for ever and ever' were sung in the 'Hallelujah Chorus', he leapt to his feet, believing, because of his poor command of English, that this was a personal tribute to him from his protégé. The audience, seeing the king on his feet but perhaps not understanding his motive, also rose to their feet. It is still the custom for the audience to stand during this part of the performance, although not everyone knows why.

ALAN ISAACS AND ELIZABETH MARTIN, 1982

The acclaimed musician Johann Peter Salomon gave violin lessons to George III, but found the king neither an apt nor a diligent pupil. Torn between exasperation and the wish to encourage the royal fiddler, Salomon delivered the following pronouncement: 'Your Majesty, fiddlers may be divided into three classes: the first, those who cannot play at all; the second, those who play badly; the third, those who play well. You, sire, have already attained the second class.'   FRANCIS W. GATES, 1898

The King was a devotee of Handel, about whom he insisted on contradicting certain criticisms made by the eminent musicologist, Dr Burney.

To the noble artist who, surrounded by the Baal-worship of corrupted art, has been able by his genius and science to preserve faithfully, like another Elijah, the worship of true art, and once more to accustom our ear – lost in the whirl of an empty play of sounds – to the pure notes of expressive composition and legitimate harmony; to the great master who makes us conscious of the nicety of his conception through the whole maze of his conception – from the soft whispering to the mighty raging of the elements – written in token of grateful remembrance by Albert.

ALBERT, PRINCE CONSORT, inscribing a copy
of Mendelssohn's *Elijah* for the composer, 1847

London was not really musical in the Sixties; it knew very little about music. Probably in all its history London has never known less. And it refused to be informed that music other than which it knew, could ever be music. It dreamed Mendelssohn and blared a Handel chorus, and called such a performance the beginning and end of all music. The fact that Queen Victoria played Mendelssohn, loved him as no British Monarch had ever loved or even deigned to notice a composer – if one excepts the official acknowledgement of

Handel by George II – was a sufficiency that made Mendelssohn – and held him – a fashion. Queen Victoria never played the piano well. Beethoven would have flustered her fingers, and have conveyed to her mind a conglomeration of arithmetic. But she loved a melody – slow and sweet. And were not Mendelssohn's music, his profile and his life alike beautiful? On Sunday evenings at Windsor she played him, gave him the laurel, and conveyed her approval of all he did.   HERBERT SULLIVAN AND NEWMAN FLOWER, 1927

King Edward VII liked French and Viennese light operas, whereas Queen Alexandra preferred grand opera, particularly Wagner. One morning the bandmaster received a message from the King to play Offenbach, and one from the Queen to play Wagner. Finding himself unable to comply with both, he thought he would hit upon the happy medium and selected Gilbert and Sullivan operas, and as always with people who compromise, he got into trouble with both the King and the Queen.   SIR FREDERICK PONSONBY, 1951

When the opera *The Wreckers* was first staged, influential friends of the composer, Dame Ethel Smythe, persuaded Edward VII to grace the opening night. Later, conductor Sir Thomas Beecham asked the king's private secretary, who had accompanied him to the opera, what the king had thought. 'I don't know,' said the private secretary. 'Didn't he say anything?' persisted Beecham. 'Well, yes,' admitted the private secretary, 'he did say something. He suddenly woke up three-quarters of the way through and said, "Fritz, that's the fourth time that infernal noise has raised me."'

HAROLD ATKINS AND ARCHIE NEWMAN, 1979

His Majesty does not know what the band has just played, but it is *never* to be played again.

KING GEORGE V, to the conductor of the Grenadier Guards band,
after extracts from Richard Strauss's *Elektra*

Odd about George and his music, both his parents were quite normal!

THE DUKE OF WINDSOR, on his nephew, now Lord Harewood,
musicologist and opera administrator

What about Tom Jones? He's made a million and he's a bloody awful singer!

PHILIP, DUKE OF EDINBURGH, after a Royal Variety Show, 1969

Tom Jones responded, 'I was singing for charity – not auditioning for Prince Philip.'

NAVAL OCCASIONS

In order to hear how HMS *Eurydice*, a frigate, sunk off Portsmouth, had been salvaged, Queen Victoria invited Admiral Foley to lunch. Having exhausted this melancholy subject, Queen Victoria inquired after her close friend, the Admiral's sister. Hard of hearing, Admiral Foley replied in his stentorian voice, 'Well, Ma'am, I am going to have her turned over, take a good look at her bottom and have it well scraped.' The Queen put down her knife and fork, hid her face in her handkerchief, and laughed until the tears ran down her cheeks.   VIRGINIA COWLES, 1963

THE NONCONFORMIST

I wonder shall History ever pull off her periwig and cease to be Court-ridden? Shall we see something of France and England besides Versailles and Windsor? I saw Queen Anne at the latter place tearing down the Park slopes, after her staghounds, and driving her one-horse chaise – a hot, red-faced woman, not in the least resembling that statue of her which turns its stone back upon St Paul's, and faces the coaches struggling up Ludgate Hill. She was neither better bred nor wiser than you and me, though we knelt to hand her a letter or a washhand-basin. Why shall History go on kneeling to the end of time? I am for having her rise up off her knees, and take a natural posture; not to be for ever performing

cringes and congees like a Court-chamberlain, and shuffling backwards out of doors in the presence of the sovereign.

W. M. THACKERAY, 1852

During the most critical days of the Prince of Wales's illness a friend
of Perch's was present one night amongst a great crowd, when an
unfavourable bulletin came from Sandringham. The crowd had
been patiently waiting some time and when the sad bulletin was
posted and read a groan of dismay ran through the people. One
man exclaimed, 'Serve him right!' Immediately the infuriated
crowd seized him, stripped him naked, knocked him down and
kicked him up and down the street like a football till the police burst
in and rescued him just in time before he was killed.

FRANCIS KILVERT, 1872

OBSERVATIONS

I wish to answer what you said about the bar between high and low. What you say about this is most true but alas! that is the great danger in England now, and one which alarms all right-minded and thinking people.

The higher classes – especially the aristocracy (with of course exceptions and honourable ones) – are so frivolous, pleasure-seeking, heartless, selfish, immoral and gambling that it makes one think (just as the Dean of Windsor said to me the other evening) of the days before the French Revolution. The young men are so ignorant, luxurious and self-indulgent – and the young women so fast, frivolous and imprudent that the danger really is very great, and they ought to be warned. The lower classes are becoming so well-informed, are so intelligent and earn their bread and riches so deservedly – that they cannot and ought not to be kept back – to be abused by the wretched, ignorant, high-born beings who live only to kill time. They must be warned and frightened or some dreadful crash will take place. What I can do, I do and will do – but Bertie ought to set a good example in these respects by not countenancing even any of these horrid people.

QUEEN VICTORIA, to her daughter, Crown Princess Victoria of Prussia, 1867

Mr Disraeli will, I think, make a good minister and certainly a loyal one to me, for he has always behaved extremely well to me, and has all the right feelings for a minister towards the sovereign. . . . He is full of poetry, romance and chivalry. . . .

QUEEN VICTORIA, to Crown Princess Victoria of Prussia, 1868

Her Majesty, by doing nothing except receive her Civil List, is teaching the country that it can get on quite well without a monarch.   *The National Reformer*, on Queen Victoria, 1871

I shall have no more to do with him than what is absolutely necessary.

KING EDWARD VII, to the Prime Minister, H. H. Asquith, on David Lloyd George, 1908

Well, we never did *that* in the olden days.

KING GEORGE V, increasingly often

It is most unfair on Chamberlain to be treated like this after all his good work.   KING GEORGE VI, on the resignation of Neville Chamberlain as Premier during war crisis, 1940

Elizabeth II is well aware of the resentments that her special position and life-style can arouse in the rest of mankind.

'I quite agree with you, Madam,' she once said as her car swept past a woman yelling with fury at the royal vehicle that had spattered her with mud in a lane near Sandringham.

'Hmm?' said the Duke. 'What did she say, darling?'

'She said, "Bastards!" ' replied the Queen.

ROBERT LACEY, 1977

THE OCCULT

Shortly after happened a strange and uncouth wonder, which afterwards was the cause of much trouble in the realm of Scotland, as ye shall after hear. It fortuned as Makbeth and Banquho journeyed towards Fores, where the king then lay, they went sporting by the way together without other company save only themselves, passing through the woods and fields, when suddenly in the middest of a laund, there met them three women in strange and wild apparel, resembling creatures of elder world, whom when they attentively beheld, wondering much at the sight; the first of them spake and said: 'All hail Makbeth, thane of Glammis' (for he had lately entered into that office by the death of his father Sinell). The second of them said: 'Hail Makbeth, thane of Cawdor'. But the third said: 'All hail Makbeth, that hereafter shall be King of Scotland'.

Then Banquho: 'What manner of women (saith he) are you that seem so little favourable unto me, whereas to my fellow here, besides high offices, ye assign also the kingdom, appointing forth nothing to me at all?' 'Yes' (saith the first of them), 'we promise greater benefits unto thee than unto him; for he shall reign indeed, but with an unlucky end; neither shall he leave any issue behind him to succeed in his place, where certainly thou indeed shall not reign at all, but of thee those shall be born which shall govern the Scottish kingdom by long order of continual descent.'

Herewith the foresaid women vanished immediately out of their sight. This was reputed at the first but some vain fantastical illusion by Makbeth and Banquho, insomuch that Banquho would call Makbeth in jest, King of Scotland; and Makbeth again would call him in sport likewise, father of many kings. But afterwards the common opinion was that these women were either the weird sisters, that is (as ye would say) the goddesses of destiny, or else some nymphs or fairies, indued with knowledge of prophecy by their necromatical science, because everything came to pass as they had spoken. RAPHAEL HOLINSHED, 1577

Henry of England was never one to be intimidated by the unreal, the things he could not come to grips with either intellectually or physically. He was a maker of history, a doer, not to be cowed by happenings beyond his control or events instigated by others. A story illustrating this side of his character is told about him when, returning from Ireland, he landed near St David's in Wales. He visited the shrine of David, patron Saint of Wales, which is located in a valley 'called the Vale of Roses; which ought to be named the Vale of Marble, since it abounds with one, and by no means the other. The River Alun, a muddy and unproductive rivulet, bounding the churchyard on the northern side, flows under a marble stone, called Lechlavar, which has been polished by continual treading of passengers' (Giraldus Cambrensis). As Henry and his retinue neared the church a woman approached and asked a favour of him. When he refused she called upon the rock Lechlavar to take vengeance on him.

When Henry's brave superstitious knights turned pale with dread, Henry merely levelled his gaze at her. He knew as well as the warriors surrounding him that Merlin, the magician usually associated with the Arthurian legends, had allegedly predicted that a king of England would die on that rock. He then strode to Lechlavar, his eyes always on the ill-speaking old harridan, mounted the stone and crossed the stream. Henry was cool, amused, a little contemptuous. He sauntered back, 'Who will have my faith in that liar Merlin, now?' he asked of his paralyzed knights.

RICHARD F. CASSADY, 1986, on King Henry II

It may please Your Grace to understand this kind of people, within these last few years, are marvellously increased within your realm. These eyes have seen most evident and manifest marks of their wickedness. Your Grace's subjects pine away even unto death, their colour fadeth, their flesh rotteth, their speech is benumbed, their senses are bereft. Wherefore your poor subjects' most humble petition unto Your Highness is that the laws touching such malefactors may be put into execution. For the shoal of them is great, their doings horrible, their malice intolerable, the examples most miserable.

JOHN JEWEL, BISHOP OF SALISBURY, on witches, to Queen Elizabeth I, 1558

The queen his mother was not forgotten, nor Davison [Elizabeth's State Secretary] either. His Highness told me that her death was visible in Scotland before it did really happen ... spoken of in secret by those whose power of sight presented to them a bloody head dancing in the air.

SIR JOHN HARINGTON, on King James VI,
and his mother, Queen Mary Stuart

King James VI

The King's credulity was confirmed by the trial of the North Berwick Witches, who were made to confess they had gone to sea in sieves and had tried to raise a storm to wreck the King's ship en route to Norway for his bride. James – he was then only twenty-four – accepted this fantastic account because Agnes Sampson, one of the accused, declared unto him the very words which had passed between the King's Majesty in Norway the first night of their marriage, with their answer each to each other. Whereat the King's Majesty wondered greatly, and swore by the living God that he believed that all the devils in hell could not have discovered the same, acknowledging her words to be most true, and therefore gave the most credit to the rest. *News from Scotland*, 1591

The frequency of forged possession wrought such an alteration on the judgment of King James that . . . he grew first diffident of, and then flatly to deny, the workings of witches and devils but as falsehoods and delusions.

DR THOMAS FULLER. *Church History of Britain*, 1655

Following the execution of Charles I in early 1649, commissioners were sent to survey the royal lands and lodgings at Woodstock. They had settled into the king's own rooms on 13 October, but from the 16th began to experience curious manifestations which grew more troublesome day by day. On the 18th someone was heard walking about the bedchamber, making a clatter with the warming-pan. On the 20th the commissioners heard furniture dragging and thumping about, but in the morning nothing was displaced; by the 29th the beds had rearranged themselves, there were noises of breaking glass, stones were thrown and one commissioner nearly skewered another with his sword, mistaking him in the confusion for a Spirit. By 2 November (All Souls' Day) they were subjected to flying warming-pans, glass, stones and horses' bones, had their candles mysteriously snuffed, their firewood tossed around the rooms, bed curtains torn, bed posts pulled away – which brought the canopy down on them – and finally a tub of green 'stinking Ditch-water' was upended on the servants. All the windows were broken with stones to the accompaniment of terrible noises; even the poachers out in the manor grounds ran off in fear. In the flickering candlelight one of the commissioners glimpsed 'the similitude of a Hoof' disappearing through a doorway. Next day they left the manor to return a few days later, but when the rumblings started up again they decamped for good. There were soon reports that the whole thing had been caused by locals unwilling to see the late king's property despoiled by these out-of-town surveyors.   R. C. FINUCANE, 1982

There was something said of the second sight happening to some persons, especially Scotch; upon which his Majesty, and I think Lord Arran, told us that Monsieur ——, a French nobleman, lately here in England, seeing the late Duke of Monmouth come into the playhouse at London, suddenly cried out to somebody sitting in the same box, '*Voilà Monsieur comme il entre sans tête.*' Afterwards his Majesty spoke of some relics that had effected strange cures,

particularly a piece of our Blessed Saviour's cross, that healed a
gentleman's rotten nose by only touching.

JOHN EVELYN, on King James II

OLD AGE

I remember Lord Melbourne using the same arguments many years
ago, but it was not true then and it is not true now.

QUEEN VICTORIA, to Sir Henry Campbell-Bannerman

AN OLD IDIOT

Pedestrian crossings marked by black-and-white poles (called
'Belisha Beacons' for the minister of transport, Leslie Hore-Belisha)
were introduced toward the end of George V's reign. Driving
through London with Queen Mary one day the King, eager to test
one of the new crossings, ordered the chauffeur to stop the car and
let him out. He returned a few minutes later, chuckling with delight.
'One of my devoted subjects,' he declared, 'has just called me a
doddering old idiot.' *The Faber Book of Anecdotes*, 1985

PARLIAMENTARY PRIVILEGE

Freedom of speech is granted, but you must know what privileges you have; not to speak everyone what he listeth, or what cometh into his brain to utter that; but your privilege is *Aye* or *No*.

QUEEN ELIZABETH I, to the Commons, 1593

PATRONAGE

Charles I, greatest collector of the age, had keen rivals in European capitals; notably Philip IV of Spain, who continued the aesthetic tradition of his house, patron of Velasquez; and in France, Richelieu and Mazarin. On Charles's execution the Spanish and French ambassadors moved quickly in, and some of his grandest paintings are to be seen today in the Louvre or in the Prado. . . .

Shortly after the King's execution sales of his goods raised some £30,000 for the new Republic's fleet. Commissions for the sales included the graceless poet Wither, one expert Jan van Belcamp, and Anthony Mildmay, a former gentleman of the Privy Chamber whom Charles disliked – it fell to him to convey the King's body to Windsor. Sales continued through to 1650 and 1651; in 1653 the Council of State permitted the Spanish ambassador to export without licence twenty-four chests of pictures, tapestries and household goods. Think, if only all these things had remained in England, it would have made a treasure-house comparable only to Italy – as Charles I intended.

The King's passion for painting, particularly for Titian, and his superb taste may be gathered from a peep into the first room only of his suite at Whitehall, the Privy Lodgings – and also what was lost from the dispersal. There hung six or seven Titians: *The Pope presenting Jacopo Pesaro to St Peter*, now in Antwerp; *St Margaret* and *The Allocution of the Marquis del Vasto*, now in the Prado; the *Entombment*, the *D'Avalos Allegory*, and *The Supper at Emmaus*, now in the Louvre; *The Woman in a Fur Cloak*, now in Vienna.

A. L. ROWSE, 1986

When Ben Jonson asked his benefactor Charles I for a square foot in hallowed Westminster Abbey after he died, that is exactly what he got. He was buried in an upright position in order that he take up no more space than he had bargained for.   E. LUCAIRE, 1985

I caused Mr Gibbon [sic] to bring to Whitehall his excellent piece of carving. . . . No sooner was [the King] entered and cast his eye on the work, but he was astonished at the curiosity of it; and having considered it a long time, and discoursed with Mr Gibbon, whom I brought to kiss his hand, he commanded it should be immediately carried to the queen's side to show her. It was carried up into her bed-chamber, where she and the King looked on and admired it again; the King, being called away, left us with the queen, believing she would have bought it, it being a crucifix; but, when his Majesty was gone, a French peddling woman, one Madame de Boord, who used to bring petticoats and fans, and baubles, out of France to the ladies, began to find fault with several things in the work, which she understood no more than an ass, or a monkey, so as in a kind of indignation, I caused the person who brought it to carry it back to the chamber, finding the queen so much governed by an ignorant frenchwoman, and this incomparable artist had his labour only for his pains, which not a little displeased me; and he was fain to send it down to his cottage again; he not long after sold it for 80L, though well worth 100L, without the frame, to Sir George Viner.

JOHN EVELYN, on Grinling Gibbons at King Charles II's court, 1671

... in spite of his style and polish, he [George IV] could be quick to take offence; deep down he was an uneasy man, insecure, longing for some great creative success; it never came. Or is that fair? After all, he had the energy to make his dreams a reality at Windsor, as well as Brighton, and so gave Britain two of the most dramatic buildings in Western Europe. And that is not all. He was a splendid patron, personally persuading his reluctant Commissioners of Crown Lands to accept John Nash's vast scheme by which the royal palaces in London were linked by Regent's Street to Regent's Park, which was to be surrounded by imposing terraces of great beauty. To do this required tearing down miles of poor streets and mean buildings. Regent's Park, rightly named, replaced a piece of open country called Marylebone Park; and the Zoo, again, is rightly where it is because George IV helped to bring it into being. The whole concept has a sweep and a grandeur, a sense of scale worthy of a great capital, that appealed to the Prince Regent. He wanted London to be worthy of a triumphant and expanding nation not only visually but also culturally. . . . He wanted its symbols to be worthy of its role. Often, of course, he interpreted this in a very personal way, such as turning the rather small Buckingham House into a great palace – another of his architectural triumphs.

J. H. PLUMB, 1977

As with Jefferson, he [Albert, Prince Consort] merits a volume as architect, designer, farmer, and naturalist. His influence on English music and art appreciation is only now being fully recognized. . . .

Very few men in modern times have made such a lasting and permanent mark in such an astonishing variety of fields, from the popularization of the Christmas Tree to the saving of Cleopatra's Needle and its placing on the Thames Embankment; the spectacular revival of Cambridge University from medieval slumber to a world eminence it has never surrendered; the foundations of Imperial College London were his work, as are the museums in South Kensington, the carved lions at the base of Nelson's Column in Trafalgar Square, the extension to the National Gallery and its glorious Early Renaissance paintings whose purchase he inspired and of which twenty-two are his personal gift, the idea of the Royal Balcony on the façade of Buckingham Palace, the concept of the Model Village, and the inspiration of the Victoria Cross as the highest award for gallantry in battle, to be awarded regardless of rank. It is to him we owe the tragically destroyed Crystal Palace, the great frescoes in the Royal Gallery in the Palace of Westminster, the exact manner in which the Koh-i-Noor diamond was cut, the abolition of duelling and the final defeat of slavery. . . .

Artists and musicians – most notably Mendelssohn – were welcome guests at Buckingham Palace and Windsor. Albert in effect became Master of the Queen's Musick, added strings to the wind instruments of the Queen's private band, transformed its repertoire, and made it give the first performance in England of Schubert's C Major Symphony. Peel's appointment of him as President of the Fine Arts Commission gave him particular pleasure. He greatly increased and extended Victoria's interest in music, and encouraged her painting, for which she had real ability, and installed etching equipment at the Palace.

ROBERT RHODES JAMES, 1983

From the memoirs of Sir Lionel Cust it is clear that although King Edward VII did not set out to be a collector on the scale of Charles I, George III, or George IV, or to direct taste in the manner to which his father had aspired, he did none the less take an active interest in the task, then long overdue, of re-distributing the royal collections. In many particulars these had remained undisturbed since the death of the Prince Consort, and it was Lionel Cust's duty to put them into presentable order and get them into presentable condition, after forty or more years of almost total neglect. In this he could count on the active participation of the king. 'King Edward liked to supervise everything himself', he said later, 'enjoying nothing so

247

much in the intervals of leisure as sitting in a roomful of workmen and giving directions in person. "Offer it up", he would say, "and I will come to see", and when he came he said yes or no at once. He had a quick, trained instinct for what was right and what pleased him.

"I do not know much about Ar-r-r-t", he would say with the characteristic rolling of his Rs, "but I think I know something about Ar-r-r-angement."

JOHN RUSSELL, 1964, in Edwardian England: 1901–14

PEACOCK

During a fit of madness, George III insisted on ending every sentence with the word 'peacock'. This was a grave embarrassment to his ministers until one of them thought of telling him that 'peacock' was a particularly royal word and should therefore only be whispered when the King addressed his subjects. The suggestion helped.

ROBERT HENDRICKSON, 1981

A PERFORMANCE

An Ambassador had arrived from Poland – a magnificent personage, in a long robe of black velvet with jewelled buttons, whom she received in state. Sitting on her throne, with her ladies, her counsellors, and her noblemen about her, she graciously gave ear to the envoy's elaborate harangue. He spoke in Latin; extremely well, it appeared; then, as she listened, amazement seized her. This was not at all what she had expected. Hardly a compliment – instead, protestations, remonstrances, criticisms – was it possible? – threats. She was lectured for presumption, rebuked for destroying the commerce of Poland, and actually informed that his Polish Majesty would put up with her proceedings no longer. Amazement gave way to fury. When the man at last stopped, she instantly leapt to her feet. *'Expectavi orationem'*, she exclaimed, *'mihi vero querelam adduxisti!'* – and proceeded, without a pause, to pour out a rolling flood of vituperative Latin, in which reproof, indignation, and sarcastic pleasantries followed one another with astonishing volubility. Those around her were in ecstasy; with all their knowledge of her accomplishments, this was something quite new – this prodigious power of *ex tempore* eloquence in a learned tongue. The unlucky ambassador was overwhelmed. At last, when she had rounded her last period, she paused for a moment, and then turned to her courtiers. 'By God's death, my lords!' she said with a smile of satisfaction, 'I have been enforced this day, to scour up my old Latin which hath lain long rusting!' Afterwards she sent for Robert Cecil and told him that she wished Essex had been there to hear her Latin.

LYTTON STRACHEY, 1928, on Queen Elizabeth I

PERQUISITES

Evidence has been given before the Court of Claims of some of the perquisites demanded by the principal personages taking part in the Coronation ceremony. There is, in effect, a regular scramble. The Archbishop of Canterbury, for fee, carries off the purple velvet chair, cushion, and footstool set for his occupation during the Coronation. The Dean and Chapter of Westminster, amongst other things, claim the cloth on which the Sovereign walks on entering the west side of the church. The Lord Great Chamberlain not only takes up the King's bed and walks, but claims the bedding and the furniture of the chamber where his Majesty lay the night before the Coronation with his (or her) wearing apparel and nightgown. As recently as the reign of James II the Master of the Horse was permitted to loot the King's table at the Coronation banquet of all the silver dishes and plates served thereat.

SIR HENRY LUCY, 1902

THE PIMP

I hasten to inform your Royal Highness, that chance has thrown me into the company of two most lovely girls, the daughters of an indigent curate, and who, from their apparent simplicity and ignorance, may soon be brought to comply with the wishes of your Royal Highness. I shall immediately devise some plan by which they may be induced to visit the metropolis, and the remainder of my task will then not be difficult of execution. The prize is too valuable to be lost sight of.

COLONEL SIR JOHN MACMAHON, Paymaster of the Widows' Pensions, later
private secretary to George, Prince Regent, later King George IV

The much reviled English class system at least enabled MacMahon, bastard son of an Irish butler and a chambermaid, to be employed at court and paid £2,000 for no work, with extras for such duties as recorded above.

PLATONIC LOVE

The Court affords little news at present, but that there is a love called Platonic Love, which muchsways there of late; it is above abstracted from all corporeal gross impressions and sensual appetite, but consists in the contemplation and ideas of the mind, not in any carnal fruition.

JAMES HOWELL, 1634, to Philip Warwick, on the court of King Charles I

A PLEA

... You have chosen me from a low estate to be your queen and companion, far beyond my desert or desire, if then you found me worthy of such honour, good your grace, let not any light fancy or bad counsel of my enemies, withdraw your princely favour from me, neither let that stain, that unworthy stain of a disloyal heart towards your grace ever cast so foul a blot on your most dutiful wife and the infant princess your daughter; try me, good king, but let me have a lawful trial, and let not my sworn enemies sit as my accusors and judges; yea let me receive an open trial, for my truth shall fear no open shames; then shall you see either my innocence cleared, your suspicions and conscience satisfied, the ignominy and slander of the world stopped, or my guilt openly declared; so that what so ever God or you may determine of me, your grace may be freed from an open censure, and my offence being so lawfully proved, your grace is at liberty both before God and Man, not only to execute worthy punishment on me as an unfaithful wife, but to follow your affection already settled on that party, for whose sake I come now as I am, whose name I could some good while since have pointed unto your grace, being not ignorant of my suspicion therein.

But if you have already determined of me, and that not only my death but an infamous slander must bring you the enjoying your desired happiness, then I desire of God that he will pardon your great sin herein, and likewise my enemies, the investments thereof; and if he will not call you to a straight account for your unprincely and cruel usage of me, at his general Judgement Seat, where both you and myself must shortly appear, and in whose right judgement I doubt not (what so ever the world may think of me), my innocence shall be openly known, and sufficiently cleared; my last and only request shall be, that myself only may bear the burden of your grace's displeasure, and that it may not touch the innocent souls of those poor gentlemen whom I understand are likewise in strait imprisonment for my sake; if ever I have found favour in your sight;

if ever the name of An Bullen have been pleasing to your ears let me obtain this last request. And I will so leave to trouble your grace any further, with my earnest prayers to the Trinity to have your grace in his good keeping, and to direct you in all your actions. From my doleful prison in the Tower this 6 of May,

Your most loyal and faithful wife,
A.B.

QUEEN ANNE BOLEYN, last letter to King Henry VIII, 1536

I your grace's most sorrowful subject and most vile wretch in the world, not worthy to make any recommendations unto your most excellent majesty, do only make my most humble submission and confession of my faults. And where no cause of mercy is given upon my part, yet of your most accustomed mercy extended unto all other men undeserved, most humbly on my hands and knees, [I] do desire one particle thereof to be extended unto me although of all other creatures [I am] most unworthy either to be called your wife or subject. My sorrow I can by no writing express, nevertheless I trust your most benign nature will have some respect unto my youth, my ignorance, my frailness, my humble confession of my faults, and plain declaration of the same referring me wholly unto your grace's pity and mercy. First at the flattering and fair persuasions of Manox, being but a young girl, [I] suffered him at sundry times to handle and touch the secret parts of my body which neither became me with honesty to permit nor him to require. Also Francis Dereham by many persuasions procured me to his vicious purpose and obtained first to lie upon my bed with his doublet and hose and after within the bed and finally he lay with me naked, and used me in such sort as a man doth his wife many and sundry times, but how often I know not, and our company ended almost a year before the Kings Majesty was married to my lady Anne of Cleves and continued not past one quarter of a year or little above. Now the whole truth being declared unto your majesty, I most humbly beseech the same to consider the subtle persuasions of young men and the ignorance and frailness of young women. I was so desirous to be taken unto your grace's favour and so blinded with the desire of worldly glory that I could not, nor had grace, to consider how great a fault it was to conceal my former faults from your majesty, considering that I intended ever during my life to be faithful and true unto your majesty after, and nevertheless the sorrow of my offences was ever before mine eyes, considering the infinite goodness of your majesty towards me from time to time ever increasing and not diminishing. Now I refer the judgement of all mine offences with my life and death wholly unto your most benign and merciful grace to be considered by no justice of your majesty's laws but only by your infinite goodness, pity, compassion, and mercy without the which I knowledge myself worthy of most extreme punishment.

QUEEN CATHERINE HOWARD, last letter to King Henry VIII, 1541

Most Gracious Queen, we thee implore,
To go away and sin no more,
Or if that effort is too great,
To go away at any rate.

Popular song, on Caroline of Brunswick,
wife of King George IV, 1820

PLEASURE

We were pretty merry, but I confess I am wedded from the opinion of Mrs Pierce's beauty upon the discovery of her naked neck to-day, being undressed when we came in. Mr Povy and I to White Hall; he carrying me thither on purpose to carry me into the ball this night before the King. He brought me just to the Duke's chamber, where I saw him and the Duchess at supper; and thence into the room where the ball was to be, crammed with fine ladies, the greatest of the Court. By and by comes the King and Queen, the Duke and Duchess, and all the great ones: and after seating themselves, the King takes out the Duchess of York; and the Duke the Duchess of Buckingham; the Duke of Monmouth my Lady Castlemaine; and so other Lords other Ladies; and they danced the Branle. After that, the King led a lady a single Coranto; and then the rest of the Lords, one after another, other Ladies: very noble it was, and great pleasure to see. Then to country dances, the King leading the first, which he called for; which was, says he, 'Cuckolds all awry', the old dance of England. Of the Ladies that danced, the Duke of Monmouth's mistress, and my Lady Castlemaine, and a daughter of Sir Harry de Vic's, were the best. The manner was, when the King dances all the Ladies in the room, and the Queen herself, stand up; and indeed he dances rarely, and much better than the Duke of York. Having stayed here as long as I thought fit, to my infinite content, it being the greatest pleasure I could wish now to see at Court, I went home, leaving them dancing.   SAMUEL PEPYS, 1662

At George IV's coronation, served to the Lords, watched by the Ladies, was served:

> 160 tureens of soup,
> 160 dishes of fish,
> 160 hot joints,
> 160 dishes of vegetables,
> 480 sauce boats – lobster, mint, butter,
> 80 dishes of braised ham,
> 80 savoury pies,
> 80 dishes of goose,
> 80 dishes of savoury drakes,
> 80 dishes of braised beef,
> 80 dishes of braised capons,
> 1190 side dishes,
> 320 dishes of mounted pastry,

320 dishes of small pastry,
400 dishes of jellies and creams,
160 dishes of lobster and crayfish,
160 dishes of cold roast fowl,
80 dishes of cold lamb.

Though on his deathbed, King George IV consumed for breakfast:

2 pigeons,
3 beefsteaks,
$\frac{3}{4}$ bottle of Moselle,
1 glass of champagne,
2 glasses of port,
1 glass of brandy.

POETRY

As the holly groweth green
    And never changeth hue
So am I, ever hath been
    Unto my lady true;

As the holly groweth green
    With ivy all alone,
When floweres cannot be seen
    And green wood leaves be gone.

Now unto my lady
    Promise to her I make
From all other only
    To her I me betake.

Adieu, mine own lady,
   Adieu, my special,
Who hath my heart truly,
   Be sure, and ever shall.

King Henry VIII

I grieve and dare not show my discontent,
I love and yet am forced to seem to hate,
I do, yet dare not say I ever meant,
I seem stark mute but inwardly do prate.
     I am and not, I freeze and yet am burned,
     Since from myself another self I turned.

My care is like my shadow in the sun,
Follows me flying, flies when I pursue it,
Stands and lies by me, doth what I have done.
His too familiar care doth make me rue it.
     No means I find to rid him from my breast,
     Till by the end of things it be supprest.

Some gentler passion slides into my mind,
For I am soft and made of melting snow;
Or be more cruel, love, and so be kind.
Let me or float or sink, be high or low.
     Or let me live with some more sweet content;
     Or die and so forget what love ere meant.

Queen Elizabeth I, on the departure of her suitor,
Francis, duc d'Alençon, 1582

One thought sustains my hours of solitude,
Yet sweet and bitter grows my mood in turn,
Doubt freezes me and then with hope I burn,
Till sleep and rest my aching heart elude.
Dear Sister, see how I lack quietude;
Desire to meet with you oppresses me,
The torment of delay distresses me;
Let my words end this long incertitude!
I've seen a ship blown wildly from her course,
In sight of port, but ere she came to land,
Driven again into the raging sea.
Likewise I fear to come to grief perforce;
O, do not think I fear it at your hand!
But Fate can mar the fairest destiny.

MARY QUEEN OF SCOTS, to Queen Elizabeth I, following her
flight to England, 1568; trs. Caroline Bingham, 1975

Since thought is free, think what thou will
O troubled heart to ease thy pain
Thought unrevealed can do no ill
But words past out turn not again
Be careful, aye, for to invent
The way to get thine own intent . . .
With patience then see thou attend
And hope to vanquish at the end.

KING JAMES VI AND I, aged fifteen

Osbert Sitwell had rustled up some impressive royal patronage for the 'giant Poets' Reading' that his sister had told Denton Welch they were organizing on 14 April 1943 at the Aeolian Hall – the queen and both the princesses were to attend. . . .

T. S. Eliot recited from *The Waste Land*, Osbert read several of his eclogues from *England Reclaimed*, and Edith was the star of the afternoon, reciting in grand style her new poem, 'Anne Boleyn's Song'. Walter de la Mare, however, was unable to reach the gigantic lectern provided by Osbert (who was considerably taller than de la Mare), and . . . W. J. Turner went on so long that he had to be silenced by the chairman. After the queen had left, Dorothy Wellesley, who had had too much to drink and who was, as Edith told Osbert's friend David Horner, 'beyond any words tiresome', struck Harold Nicolson with her umbrella and had to be restrained by Beatrice Lillie.   MICHAEL DE-LA-NOY, 1984

POLITICS AND POWER

This ground on which you stand was the site of my father's house. This man for whom you pray, while still only Duke of Normandy, took it away from my father by violence, and having refused all compensation, he built this church on it in an abuse of power. That is why I demand this ground and claim it publicly. In God's name, I forbid that the body of the robber should be covered with my earth and buried within my heritage.

> ASCELIN, son of Arthur, at the funeral service at Caen of King William I, when Bishop Gilbert of Evraux invited prayers for the King's soul and forgiveness for his faults, 1087

Look not to find the softness of a down pillow in a crown, but remember that it is a thorny piece of stuff and full of continual cares.   KING JAMES VI AND I, to his son, Henry, Prince of Wales

Certainly never had King more glorious opportunities to have made himself, his people, and all Europe happy, and prevented innumerable mischiefs, had not his too easy nature resigned him to be managed by crafty men, and some abandoned and profane wretches who corrupted his otherwise sufficient parts, disciplined as he had been by many afflictions during his banishment, which gave him much experience and knowledge of men and things; but those wicked creatures took from him all application of becoming so great a King. The history of his reign will certainly be the most wonderful for the variety of matters and accidents, above any extant in former ages: the sad tragical death of his father, his banishment and hardships, his miraculous restoration, conspiracies against him, parliaments, wars, plagues, fires, comets, revolutions abroad, happening in his time, with a thousand other particulars.

JOHN EVELYN, on Charles II

Nowhere does the Constitution demand an indifference on the part of the sovereign to the march of political events, and nowhere would such indifference be more condemned and justly despised than in England. . . .

Why are Princes alone to be denied the credit of having political opinions based upon an anxiety for the national interests and honour of their country and the welfare of mankind? Are they not more independently placed than any other politician in the State? Are their interests not most intimately bound up with those of their country? Is the sovereign not the natural guardian of the honour of his country, is he not *necessarily* a politician? Has he no duties to perform towards his country?

ALBERT, PRINCE CONSORT, 1851, on an article in the *Westminster Gazette* hostile to the alleged influences of the House of Coburg on the Monarchy; anonymous, but clearly written, Mr Rhodes James infers, by Lord Palmerston

King George sent for Mr Ramsay MacDonald. Arthur Henderson, J. H. Thomas and myself accompanied our leader to Buckingham Palace to that fateful interview of which we had dreamed, when a British Sovereign should entrust the affairs of the Empire to the hands of the people's own representatives.

As we stood waiting for his Majesty, amid the gold and crimson magnificence of the Palace, I could not help marvelling at the strange turn of Fortune's wheel, which had brought MacDonald the starveling clerk, Thomas the engine-driver, Henderson the foundry labourer and Clynes the mill-hand, to this pinnacle beside the man whose forebears had been Kings for so many splendid generations. We were making history.

We were, perhaps, somewhat embarrassed, but the little, quiet man whom we addressed as 'Your Majesty' swiftly put us at our ease. He was himself rather anxious; his was a great responsibility, and I have no doubt that he had read the wild statements of some of our extremists, and I think he wondered to what he was committing his people.

The King first created MacDonald a Privy Councillor, and then spoke to us for some time. He gave us invaluable guidance from his deep experience, to help us in the difficult time before us, when we should become his principal Ministers. I had expected to find him unbending; instead he was kindness and sympathy itself. Before he gave us leave to go, he made an appeal to us that I have never forgotten:

'The immediate future of my people, and their whole happiness, is in your hands, gentlemen. They depend on your prudence and sagacity.' J. R. CLYNES, 1937, on King George V

MR POOTER

No one has a higher regard for Attlee as a decent old stick than I have. He and King George VI proved that Britain was a land in which Mr Pooter could get to the top, if only by accident. Here was a heartening democratic development and it will be a happy world when politics are so banal that aspiring young Pooters . . . can safely be put in charge of everything.

PAUL ADDISON, *London Review of Books*, 1986

POPERY

England's faire Hope, (borne, Downe to quell
the rage of Rome; That proud Babell;
Which in its swelling – madde Desires,
to Worlds sole Empire still aspires;)

The Fierie Tryall of God's Saints, 1611, on Henry,
Prince of Wales, elder son of King James VI and I

HEE hated *Poperie* with a perfect hate. . . . All the *world* were sate, to see, and harken, how his Highnesse hopefull, youthfull age should be *employed*, for HIM, a *glimmering light* of the *Golden* times appeared, all lines of expectation meet in this *Center*, all *spirits* of vertue, scattered into others were entracted into him. . . . His *Magnetique* vertue drewe all the *eies* and hearts of the *Protestant* World.

DANIEL PRICE, on Henry, Prince of Wales. Memorial Sermon, 1613

Roy Strong, 1986, comments: The last sentence is crucial, for Henry, had he lived, would have effected in England a successful marriage of all the achievements in the arts of Renaissance Italy with an unshakable and fiercely Protestant ethic.

PORTUGUESE

The Queen arrived with a train of Portuguese ladies in their monstrous fardingales or guard-infantes, their complexions olivader and sufficiently unagreeable. Her Majesty in the same habit, her fore-top long and turned aside very strangely. She was yet of the handsomest countenance of all the rest, and though low of stature, prettily shaped, languishing and excellent eyes, her teeth wronging her mouth by sticking a little too far out; for the rest, lovely enough.

JOHN EVELYN, 1662, on Catherine of Braganza, wife of King Charles II

They have bought me a *bat* instead of a woman.

KING CHARLES II, to Colonel Legge, on his bride, Catherine of Braganza

PRETENDERS

Lambert Simnel

There was a certain subtil priest, Richard Simon, that lived at Oxford and had to his pupil a baker's son named Lambert Simnel, a comely youth and well-favoured, not without some extraordinary dignity and grace of aspect.

FRANCIS BACON. *History of King Henry VII*, 1622

Simon coached Simnel to impersonate Richard, Duke of York, brother of the mysteriously vanished Edward V, later changing the role to that of another Yorkist claimant, Edward Plantagenet. They went to Ireland, a Yorkist stronghold, and in Dublin Simnel was crowned Edward VI. Returning to England he was easily defeated at Stoke, where 'Dead Man's Field' and 'The Red Gutter' can still be seen. King Henry sent Simnel to serve in the royal kitchens. The old story of his giving his name to Simnel cakes seems untrue, and derives from simila *(finest wheat flour).*

As for the priest, he was committed close prisoner, and heard of no more; the King loving to seal up his own dangers.

FRANCIS BACON, *op. cit.*

My masters of Ireland, ye will be crowning apes next.

KING HENRY VII, on Lambert Simnel, 1487

Perkin Warbeck

Warbeck's claim to be Richard, Duke of York, son of Edward IV, and his many years of intrigue and rebellion, gained him recognition as 'King Richard' by France, Scotland, Denmark, Saxony, by Emperors Frederick III and Maximilian; it also gained him a royal Scottish bride.

This little cockatrice of a king.

Francis Bacon. History of the Reign of King Henry VII, 1622

... one of the longest plays of that kind that hath been in memory and might perhaps have had another end, if he had not met with a King both wise, stout and fortunate.   Francis Bacon, op. cit.

Perkin Warbeck, and Mayor Atawater of Cork, his supporter and accomplice, were to be:

... drawn to the place of execution from their prison, as being not worthy any more to tread upon the face of the earth whereof they have been made; also for that they have been retrograde to nature, therefore are they to be drawn backward at a horse-tail. And whereas God hath made the head of man the highest and most supreme part, as being his chief grace and ornament, they must be drawn with their heads declining downward, and lying so near the ground as may be, being unfit to take benefit of the common air.

Lady Jane Grey

LADY JANE GREY (aged fifteen):   The Crown is not my right, and pleaseth me not, the Lady Mary is the rightful heir.

NORTHUMBERLAND: Your Grace doth wrong to yourself and to your House. . . .

LADY JANE GREY: If what hath been given to me is lawfully mine, may thy Divine Majesty grant me such spirit and grace that I may govern to thy Glory and Service, to the advantage of thy realm.

You must put off your royal robes and be content with a private life.   HENRY GREY, DUKE OF SUFFOLK, to his daughter,
Lady Jane Grey, after the triumph of Queen Mary I

I much more willingly put them off than I put them on. Out of obedience to you and my mother I have grievously sinned. Now I willingly relinquish the Crown. May I not go home?

LADY JANE GREY

Good people, I am come hither to die, and by a law I am condemned to the same. My offence against the Queen's Highness was only in consent to the devices of others, which now is deemed treason; but it was never of my seeking, but by counsel of those who should seem to have further understanding of things that I, which knew little of the law, and much less of the titles of the Crown. But touching the procurement and desire thereof by me, or on my behalf, I do wash my hands in innocency thereof before God, and in the face of all you good Christian people this day. I pray you all, good Christian people, to bear me witness that I die a true Christian woman, and that I look to be saved by none other means but only by the mercy of God, in the blood of His only Son, Jesus Christ. And I confess that when I did know the Word of God, I neglected the same, and loved myself and the world, and therefore this Plague and Punishment is justly and worthily happened unto me for my sins; and yet I thank God of His Goodness that He hath given me a time and respite to report. And now, good people, while I am alive, I pray you to assist me with your prayers.

LADY JANE GREY, on the scaffold

James, Duke of Monmouth

Th'admiring crowd are dazzled with surprise
And on his goodly person feed their eyes.
His joy conceal'd, he sets himself to show
On each side bowing popularly low:

His looks, his gestures, and his words he frames
And with familiar ease repeats their names.
Thus form'd by nature, furnish'd out with arts,
He glides unfelt into their secret hearts.

JOHN DRYDEN, on James, Duke of Monmouth.
Absalom and Architophel, 1681

About 11 o'clock at night I saw the Duke of Monmouth ride out, attended by his life Guard of Horse, and tho' then but a boy, observed an alteration in his Look, which I did not like.

JOHN OLDMIXON, on the night of the Battle of Sedgemoor, 1685, the climax of Monmouth's rebellion against King James II. *History of England during the Reign of the House of Stuart*, 1730

The Duke of Monmouth had, from the beginning of this desperate attempt, behaved with the conduct of a great captain, as was allowed by the King, who in my hearing said that he had not made one false step. SIR JOHN RERESBY. *Memoirs*, 1734

It is a pity that so brave a man, as they say he showed himself in the engagement, should deserve the fate that he is to expect very shortly – it is said without the formality of a trial – and that I wish he had rather been knocked on the head in the engagement.

CHALMER CHUTE, on James, Duke of Monmouth, to Lady Rutland, 1685

I, coming from the City by water, unfortunately landed at the same moment, and saw the Duke of Monmouth led up the other stairs on Westminster side, lean and pale, and with a disconsolate physiognomy, with soldiers with pistols in their hands . . . and I wished heartily and often that I had not seen him, for I could never get him out of my mind for years, I so loved him personally.

THOMAS, LORD BRUCE, later Earl of Ailesbury. *Memoirs*

The Duke of Monmouth seemed more concerned and desirous to live, and did behave himself not so well as I expected, nor so as one ought to have expected from one who had taken upon him to be King.   KING JAMES II, to William, Prince of Orange, after interviewing Monmouth, 1685

Claiming the crown at Taunton, Monmouth had unwisely, and unfairly, accused his uncle James II of poisoning his father, Charles II.

Monmouth was this day brought to London and examined before the King, to whom he made great submission, acknowledged his seduction by Ferguson, the Scot, whom he named the bloody villain. He was sent to the Tower, had an interview with his late duchess, whom he received coldly, having lived dishonestly with the Lady Henrietta Wentworth for two years. He obstinately asserted his conversation with that debauched woman to be no sin; whereupon, seeing he could not be persuaded to his last breath, the divines who were sent to assist him thought not fit to administer the Holy Communion to him. For the rest of his faults he professed great sorrow, and so died without any apparent fear. He would not make use of a cap or other circumstance, but lying down, bid the fellow do his office better than to the late Lord Russell, and gave him gold; but the wretch made five chops before he had his head off; which so incensed the people, that had he not been guarded and got away, they would have torn him to pieces. . . .

Thus ended this quondam Duke, darling of his father and the ladies, being extremely handsome and adroit; an excellent soldier and dancer, a favourite of the people, of an easy nature, debauched by lust; seduced by crafty knaves, who would have set him up only to make a property, and taken the opportunity of the King being of another religion, to gather a party of discontented men. He failed, and perished.

He was a lovely person, had a virtuous and excellent lady that brought him great riches, and a second dukedom in Scotland. He was Master of the Horse, General of the King his father's army, gentleman of the Bed-chamber, Knight of the Garter, Chancellor of Cambridge; in a word, had accumulations without end. See what ambition and want of principles brought him to!   JOHN EVELYN

'James III' – The Old Pretender

James had caught the first glimpse of a hope which delighted and elated him. The Queen was with child.

Before the end of October 1687 the great news began to be whispered. It was observed that Her Majesty had absented herself from some public ceremonies, on the plea of indisposition. It was said that many relics, supposed to possess extraordinary virtue, had been hung about her. Soon the story made its way from the palace to the coffeehouses of the capital, and spread fast over the country. By a very small minority, the rumour was welcomed with joy. The great body of the nation listened with mingled derision and fear. There was indeed nothing very extraordinary in what had happened. The King had but just completed his fifty-fourth year. The Queen was in the summer of life. She had already borne four children who had died young; and long afterwards she was delivered of another child whom nobody had any interest in treating as supposititious, and who was therefore never said to be so. As, however, five years had elapsed since her last pregnancy, the people, under the influence of that delusion which leads men to believe what they wish, had ceased to entertain any apprehension that she would give an heir to the throne. On the other hand, nothing seemed more natural than that the Jesuits should have contrived a pious fraud. . . .

The folly of some Roman Catholics confirmed the vulgar prejudice. They spoke of the auspicious event as strange, as miraculous, as an exertion of the same Divine power which had made Sarah proud and happy in Isaac, and had given Samuel to the prayers of Hannah. [Queen] Mary's mother, the Duchess of Modena, had lately died. A short time before her death, she had, it is said, implored the Virgin of Loretto, with fervent vows and rich offerings, to bestow a son on James. The King himself had, in the preceding August, turned aside from his progress to visit the Holy Well, and had there besought Saint Winifred to obtain for him that boon without which his great designs for the propagation of the true faith could be but imperfectly executed. The imprudent zealots who dwelt on these tales foretold with confidence that the unborn infant would be a boy, and offered to back their opinion by laying twenty guineas to one. Heaven, they affirmed, would not have interfered but for a great end. One fanatic announced that the queen would give birth to twins, of whom the older would be King of England, and the younger Pope of Rome. Mary could not conceal the delight with which she heard this prophecy; and her ladies found that they could not gratify her more than by talking of it. The Roman Catholics would have acted more wisely if they had spoken of the pregnancy as of a natural event, and if they had borne with moderation their unexpected good fortune. Their insolent triumph excited the popular indignation. Their predictions strengthened the popular suspicions. From the Prince and Princess of Denmark down to porters and laundresses nobody alluded to the promised birth without a sneer. The wits of London described the new miracle in rhymes which, it may well be supposed, were not the most delicate. . . . Mother East had also her full share of abuse. Into that homely monosyllable our ancestors had degraded the name of Este which reigned at Modena. . . .

In a few hours many public functionaries and women of rank were assembled in the Queen's room. There, on the morning of Sunday, the tenth of June, a day long kept sacred by the too faithful adherents of a bad cause, was born the most unfortunate of princes, destined to seventy-seven years of exile and wandering, of vain projects, of honours more galling than insults, and of hopes such as make the heart sick. . . .

The cry of the whole nation was that an imposture had been practised. Papists had, during some months, been predicting from the pulpit and through the press, in prose and verse, in English and Latin, that a Prince of Wales would be given to the prayers of the Church; and they had now accomplished their own prophecy. Every witness who could not be corrupted or deceived had been studiously excluded. Anne had been tricked into visiting Bath. The Primate had, on the very day preceding that which had been fixed for the villainy, been sent to prison in defiance of the rules of law and of the privileges of peerage. Not a single man or woman who had the smallest interest in detecting the fraud had been suffered to be present. The queen had been removed suddenly and at the dead of night to St James's Palace, because that building, less commodious for honest purposes than Whitehall, had some rooms and passages well suited for the purposes of the Jesuits. There, amidst a circle of zealots who thought nothing a crime that tended to promote the interests of their Church, and of courtiers who thought nothing a crime that tended to enrich and aggrandize themselves, a new born child had been introduced into the royal bed, and then handed round in triumph, as heir of the three kingdoms.

LORD MACAULAY, 1848, on King James II, Queen Mary of Modena, and the alleged 'warming pan' appearance of 'James III', the Old Pretender, 1688

James Francis Edward Stuart, 'James VII and III', during the 1715 rebellion:

His person was tall and thin, seeming to incline to be lean rather than to fill as he grows in years. His countenance was pale, but perhaps looked more so than usual, by reason he had three fits of an ague, which took him two days after his coming on shore. Yet he seems to be sanguine in his constitution; and there is something of a vivacity in his eye, that perhaps would have been more visible, if he had not been under dejected circumstances, and surrounded by discouragement: which, it must be acknowledged, were sufficient to alter the complexion even of his soul, as well as of his body. His speech was grave, and not very clearly expressive of his thoughts, nor overmuch to the purpose; but his words were few, and his behaviour and temper seemed always composed. What he was in his diversions, we know not; here was no room for such things. . . . When we saw the man whom they called our king, we found ourselves not at all animated by his presence; if he was disappointed in us, we were tenfold more in him. We saw nothing in him that looked like spirit. He never appeared with cheerfulness and vigour to animate us. Our men began to despise him; some asked if he could speak. His countenance looked extremely heavy. He cared not to come abroad amongst us soldiers, or to see us handle our arms or do our exercise. Some said the circumstances he found us in dejected him; I am sure the figure he made dejected us; and, had he sent us but five thousand men of good troops, and never himself come among us, we had done other things than we have now done.

A REBEL; true account of the proceedings at Perth, 1716

'Charles III'

I am come home, sir, and will entertain no notion at all of returning to that place whence I came, for I am persuaded that my faithful Highlanders will stand by me.

CHARLES EDWARD STUART, to Alexander Macdonald of Boisdale,
on landing in Scotland to claim the Crown, 1745

PRINCE CHARLES

His prodigious talents in the arts, in sport, in academic life make him perhaps the most accomplished young man in Britain: rich, handsome, intelligent and eligible – the twentieth-century Renaissance man who has done everything, been everywhere, met everyone that matters . . . actor, sportsman, pilot, musician, artist, orator, academic, wit, sailor and future King.   *Woman's Realm*

PRINCE CONSORT

The nation, slow of thought and uneducated, had never given itself the trouble to consider what really is the position of the husband of a Queen Regnant. When I first came over here, I was met by this want of knowledge and unwillingness to give a thought to the position of this luckless personage.

Peel cut down my income, Wellington refused me my rank, the Royal Family cried out against the foreign interloper, the Whigs in office were only inclined to concede to me just as much space as I could stand upon. The Constitution is silent as to the consort of the Queen; – even Blackstone ignores him, and yet there he was, not to be done without. As I kept quiet and caused no scandal, and all went well, no one has troubled himself about me and my doings; and anyone who wished to pay me a compliment at a public dinner or meeting extolled my 'wise abstinence from interfering in political matters'. Now when the present journalistic controversies have brought to light the fact that I have for years taken an active interest in all political matters, the public, instead of feeling surprise at my modesty and my tact in not thrusting myself forward, fancied itself betrayed, because it felt it had been self-deceived. It has also rushed all at once into a belief in secret correspondence with foreign courts, intrigues, etc; for all this is much more probable, than that thirty millions of men in the course of fourteen years should not have discovered, that an important personage had during all that time taken a part in governing them. If *that* could be concealed, then all kinds of secret conspiracy are possible, and the Coburg conspiracy is proved to demonstration.

Beyond this stage of knowledge, whch was certain sooner or later to be reached, we shall, however, soon have passed; and now there is a swarm of letters, and pamphlets to prove that the husband of the Queen, as such, and as Privy Councillor, not only may, but in the general interest must be, an active and responsible adviser of the

Crown; and I hope the debate in Parliament will confirm this view, and settle it once and for ever.

ALBERT, PRINCE CONSORT, to Baron von Stockmar, 1854

Oh! If only I could make you King!   QUEEN VICTORIA, on Prince Albert

With Prince Albert we have buried our Sovereign. This German Prince has governed England for twenty-one years with a wisdom and energy such as none of our Kings have ever shown.

BENJAMIN DISRAELI, 1861

Queen Victoria once paid Disraeli the honour of visiting him at his country house near Beaconsfield. On his deathbed he declined another royal visit. 'No, it is better not. She will only ask me to take a message to Albert.'   PRINCESS MARIE LOUISE, 1956

PRINCE REGENT

You are the *glory of the People* – You are the *Maecanas of the Age* – Wherever you appear you *conquer all hearts*, wipe away tears, excite *desire and love* and win *beauty* towards you – You breathe *eloquence*, you inspire the Graces – You are an *Adonis* in loveliness.

The *Morning Post*, 1812, on George, Prince Regent, later King George IV

'Florizel' and 'Beau' Brummell

Brummell lived in the age of the duel, and drew the danger of his acrobatics from that fact. To balance the effrontery of his perfect dress, he had invented an effrontery of manner and mind which must have kept him constantly on the edge of disaster. He made a point of being as rude to everybody as he could be. He had brought into fashion the 'cut', the untroubled look straight through the *vis-à-vis*, without recognition, which left the latter shattered. He was as famous for this as he was for his bow or for his snuff boxes, and, when one considers the difference between a cut in the duelling age and a cut today, perhaps there was some ground for the half-fascinated horror which had made it famous.

He did not stop at cutting. 'Bedford,' said he, to the shrinking duke of that ilk, fingering his Grace's latest tailor-made, 'do you call this *thing* a coat?' 'Ah,' he remarked to a gentleman called Byng, who was nicknamed Poodle behind his back, on meeting him in a curricle with the French dog, 'Ah, how d'ye do, Byng? A family vehicle, I see.' 'Madam,' he observed to a miserable female who had invited him to take tea with her, 'You take medicine – you take a walk – you take a liberty. But you *drink* tea.' 'Why, sir,' he answered, with superb egoism, to an elderly gentleman who was reproaching him for having ruined his son, 'I did all I could for him. I once gave him my arm all the way from White's to Brooks's.'* 'Some more of that cider,' he ordered from the butler, when dining out and disapproving of the champagne. At another dinner, when the chicken was tough, 'Here, Atons,' to his dog, 'try if you can get your teeth into this, for I'm damned if I can.' 'What could I do, my dear fellar,' he explained to a gentleman who had enquired why he did not marry a certain lady, 'when I actually saw Lady Mary eat cabbage?' He disliked the practice of eating vegetables, though he sometimes confessed to taking 'one pea'. . . .

Florizel [the Prince Regent] and he had quarrelled. Florizel was growing fat and was ashamed. To emphasize the quarrel and show the world that he had dropped the Beau, the unfortunate Prince attempted to administer the *coup de grace* in public – using the Beau's own weapon, the 'cut direct'. They met in St James's Street, according to one version of the story, the Regent walking with an acquaintance (Lord Alvanley) and Brummell with Jack Lee. To

---

* The distance from White's to Brooks's is a matter of a few yards.

make the cut as deadly as possible, Florizel stopped to converse with Lee, while looking straight through Brummell. After some conversation, which the Beau bore patiently, the parties separated and passed on. 'Well, Jack,' said Brummell instantly, when there were a few feet between them, loud enough for all to hear, turning round indeed so that the quaking Florizel might hear it clearly, 'Well, Jack, who's your fat friend?'   T. H. WHITE, 1946

The Prince Regent mounts his horse:

An inclined plane was constructed, rising to about the height of two feet and a half, at the upper end of which was a platform. His Royal Highness was placed in a chair on rollers, and so moved by the ascent, and placed on the platform which was then raised by screws high enough to pass the horse under; and finally, his Royal Highness was let down gently into the saddle.   *The Times*, 1816

The most awesome aspect of the Prince's character was his gargantuan appetite for life, his fantastic gusto. His collections – pictures, statuary, watercolours, prints, furniture, porcelain, armour – are stupendous in size; he built or remodelled four great palaces; he purchased, personally and with attention, prodigious quantities of furs, perfumes, handkerchiefs, walking sticks, jewels, clothes in multicoloured variety; his social life was packed, his love life involved and inordinately preoccupying. He ate and drank to excess from youth to age, and yet managed somehow to be deeply involved in politics and diplomacy. To many – relations, friends and subjects – this compulsive, wanton self-indulgence, this rioting creativity, was extravagant, hateful, thoughtless and selfish at a time when the country was racked with unemployment and poverty, or in the throes of a great war. More Englishmen hated him than loved him throughout his life; fewer still understood him, either during his life or after his death. He has rarely been given his due. He created the setting of monarchy as we know it.

J. H. PLUMB, 1977

PRISON

Prisons are distasteful to men and to be released therefrom is a most delightful refreshment to the spirit.

QUEEN ELEANOR, released by her son, King Richard I, from captivity imposed on her by her late husband, King Henry II

After Hastings had been executed, all those hitherto attendant on the King were forbidden to see him. He and his brother were withdrawn into the inner apartments of the Tower proper, and, with days passing, began to be seen more rarely behind the bars and windows, till at length they ceased to appear at all. A doctor of Strasbourg, the last of his retinue whose offices the King employed, reported that the young monarch, like a victim trussed for sacrifice, sought remission for his sins by daily confessions, because he believed that death lay waiting.

DOMINIC MANCINI, on King Edward V.
De Occupatione Regni Anglie, 1483

To mortals' common fate thy mind resign,
My lot today tomorrow may be thine.

Whilst God assists us, envy bites in vain,
If God forsake us, fruitless all our pain –
I hope for light after the darkness.

LADY JANE GREY, written in Latin on her wall in the Tower, 1554

Oh Fortune, thy wresting wavering state
Hath fraught with cares my troubled wit,
Whose witness this present prison late
Could bear, where once was joy flown quite.
Thou causedst the guilty to be loosed
From lands where innocents were enclosed,
And caused the guiltless to be reserved,
And freed those that death had well deserved.
But all herein can be naught wrought;
So grant to my foes as they have thought.

Much suspected by me, but nothing proved can be.

PRINCESS ELIZABETH, later Queen Elizabeth I, written on the wall
in Latin during her imprisonment at Woodstock, 1555

His Majesty was treated with more rudeness and barbarity than he
had ever been before. No man was suffered to see or speak to him,
but the soldiers who were his guard, some of whom sat up always in
his bedchamber, and drank, and took tobacco, as if they had been
upon the court of guard; nor was he suffered to go into any other
room, either to say his prayers, or to receive the ordinary benefits of
nature, but was obliged to do both in their presence and before
them: and yet they were so jealous of these their janizaries, that they
might be wrought upon by the influence of this innocent prince, or
by the remorse of their own conscience upon the exercise of so
much barbarity, that they caused the guards to be still changed; and
the same men were never suffered twice to perform the same
monstrous duty.

EDWARD HYDE, EARL OF CLARENDON, on King Charles I,
awaiting trial, 1648. *History of the Rebellion*, 1702–4

The Prince and Princess of Wales go through Manchester tomorrow, we're going to see them. What fun if a lot of children sing 'The Prince of Wales in Belle Vue jail/ For robbing a man of a pint of ale.' It's a song that's sung very much here so perhaps they will. Belle Vue is the large jail here.   ELEANOR MARX, to Jenny Marx, 1869

In 1867 three Fenians, the 'Manchester Martyrs', had been executed in Belle Vue following the death of a policeman, provoking considerable pro-Irish sympathy.

PURITANISM

Master Doctor, that loose robe becomes you well, I wonder your notions should be so narrow.

QUEEN ELIZABETH I, to the Puritan, Dr Humphries, visiting Oxford, 1566

A QUARREL

Nerves grew jangled, and tempers dangerously short. Everything, it was clear, was working up towards one of those alarming climaxes with which all at Court had grown so familiar; and, while they waited in dread, sure enough the climax came. But this time it was of a nature undreamt of by the imagination of any courtier: when the incredible story reached them, it was as if the earth had opened at their feet. The question of the Irish appointment had become pressing, and Elizabeth, feeling that something really must be done about it, kept reverting to the subject on every possible occasion, without any result. At last she thought she had decided Sir William Knollys, Essex's uncle, was the man. She was in the Council Chamber, with Essex, the Lord Admiral, Robert Cecil, and Thomas Windebank, Clerk of the Signet, when she mentioned it. As often happened, they were all standing up. Essex, who did not want to lose the support of his uncle at Court, proposed instead Sir George Carew, a follower of the Cecils, whose absence in Ireland would, he thought, inconvenience the Secretary. The Queen would not hear of it, but Essex persisted; each was annoyed; they pressed their candidates; their words grew high and loud; and at last the Queen roundly declared that, say what he would, Knollys should go. Essex, overcome with irritation, contemptuous in look and gesture, turned his back upon her. She instantly boxed his ears. 'Go to the devil,' she cried, flaring with anger. And then the impossible happened. The mad young man completely lost his temper, and, with a resounding oath, clapped his hand to his sword. 'This is an outrage,' he shouted in his sovereign's face, 'that I will not put up with. I would not have borne it from your father's hands.' He was interrupted by Nottingham, who pressed him backwards. Elizabeth did not stir. There was an appalling silence; and he rushed from the room.

Unparalleled as was the conduct of Essex, there was yet another surprise in store for the Court, for the Queen's behaviour was no less extraordinary. She did nothing. The Tower – the block – heaven knows what exemplary punishment – might naturally have been expected. But nothing happened at all. Essex vanished into the country, and the Queen, wrapped in impenetrable mystery, proceeded with her usual routine of work and recreation.

LYTTON STRACHEY, 1928

There is no tempest comparable to the passionate indignation of a Prince; nor yet at any time is it so unreasonable as when it lighteth upon those who might expect a harvest of their careful and painful labours. . . .

When the vilest of all indignities are done unto me, doth religion enforce me to sue? Doth God require it? Is it impiety not to do it? What, cannot Princes err? Cannot subjects receive wrong? Is an earthly power or authority infinite?

ROBERT DEVEREUX, EARL OF ESSEX, after his violent scene with Queen Elizabeth I over the Irish Candidature, 1598

REBELLION

I have never read, heard, nor known that Princes' counsellors and prelates should be appointed by rude and ignorant common people; nor that they were persons meet or of ability to discern and choose meet and sufficient counsellors for a Prince. How presumptuous then are ye, the rude commons of one shire, and that one of the most brute and beastly of the whole realm, and of least experience, to find fault with your Prince, for th'electing of his counsellors and prelates, and to take on you, contrary to God's law and Man's law, to rule your Prince.

KING HENRY VIII, to Lincolnshire rebels, during the Pilgrimage of Grace, 1536

You have got rid of one enemy but a more dangerous one remains behind. LORD DARTMOUTH, to King James II, 1685, on Monmouth and William, Prince of Orange, afterwards King William III

Whatever I did then, I did by express orders; and I have this further to say for myself, that I was not half bloody enough for him who sent me thither.

LORD CHANCELLOR GEORGE JEFFREYS, 1685, on King James II and the 'Bloody Assizes' in the West Country

A REBUKE

Hoots, wumman, canna ye hold your head still!

JOHN BROWN, to Queen Victoria, while pinning up her plaid

REGICIDE

King Edward the Martyr was murdered on Corfe Hill, 978, leaning from his horse to receive a drink:

The thanes, then holding him, one draw him on the right towards him as if he wished to give him a kiss, but another roughly grabbed his left hand and also injured him. And he shouted, with all that he could manage, 'What do you – breaking my right arm?' And suddenly sprang from his horse and perished. . . .

And no worse deed than this for the English was done since they first came to Britain.

Anglo-Saxon Chronicle

One writer, which seemeth to have great knowledge of King Richard's doings, saith that King Henry, sitting on a dais at his table, sore sighing, said: 'Have I no faithful friend which will deliver me of him, whose life will be my death, and whose death will be the preservation of my life?' This saying was much noted of them which were present, and especially of one called Sir Piers of Exton. This knight incontinently departed from the court, with eight strong persons in his company, and came to Pomfret commanding the squire, that was accustomed to do the tasting and serving before King Richard, to do so no more, saying: 'Let him eat now, for he shall not long eat.' King Richard sat down to dinner, and was served without courtesy or attention; whereupon, much marvelling at the sudden change, he demanded of the squire why he did not do his duty: 'Sir,' (said he) 'I am otherwise commanded by Sir Piers of Exton, which is newly come from King Henry.' When King Richard heard that word, he took the carving knife in his hand, and struck the squire on the head, saying: 'The devil take Henry of Lancaster and thee together!' And with that word, Sir Piers entered the chamber, well armed, with eight tall men likewise armed, every one of them having a bill in his hand.

King Richard, perceiving this, put the table from him, and,

stepping to the foremost man, wrung the bill out of his hands, and so valiantly defended himself that he slew four of those that thus came to assail him. Sir Piers, being half dismayed herewith, leapt into the chair where King Richard was wont to sit, while the other four persons fought with him, and chased him about the chamber. And in conclusion, as King Richard traversed his ground, from one side of the chamber to the other, and coming by the chair, where Sir Piers stood, he was felled by a stroke of a pole-axe which Sir Piers gave him upon the head, and therewith rid him out of life; without giving him respite once to call to God for mercy of his past offences. It is said, that Sir Piers of Exton, after he had thus slain him, wept right bitterly, as one stricken with the prick of a guilty conscience, for murdering him whom he had so long time obeyed as king.

RAPHAEL HOLINSHED, 1577, on King Henry IV and King Richard II

Some lingering doubts may remain about the manner of death of Richard II . . . in Pontefract Castle in 1400, since it is possible that he died of neglect or melancholy rather than direct assassination, but it is highly unlikely, in any case, that he would have been allowed to remain alive for long once the supposition that he was still alive made him a focus for rebellion.

CHARLES ROSS, 1981

King Henry VI was a very ignorant and almost simple man and, unless I have been deceived, immediately after the battle the Duke of Gloucester, Edward's brother, who later became King Richard, killed this good man with his own hand or at least had him killed in his presence in some obscure place.

PHILIPPE DE COMMYNES. *Memoirs, c. 1498*

An alternative contemporary account of Henry VI's death, 1453, proposed another possible cause:

A disease and disorder of such a sort overcame the King that he lost his wits and memory for a time, and nearly all his body was so uncoordinated and out of control that he could neither walk, nor hold his head upright, nor easily move from where he sat.

JOHN WHETHAMSTED. *Second Register, c.* 1461

Also, following the defeat of his wife and the death of his son, Prince Edward, at the battle of Tewkesbury, King Henry

took it to so great despite, ire and indignation that, of pure displeasure, and melancholy, he died the twenty-third day of the month of May.

ANON, *The History of the Arrival in England of Edward IV*

Antonia Gransden, 1982, rates this last as official Yorkist propaganda.

The Princes in the Tower

Sir James Tirrel devised, that they should be murdered in their beds. To the execution whereof, he appointed Miles Forrest, one of the four keepers, a fellow fleshed in murder before times. To him he joined one John Dighton, his own horse keeper, a big, broad, square, and strong knave.

Then, all others being removed from them, this Miles Forrest and John Dighton, about midnight (the holy children lying in their beds), came into the chamber, and, suddenly lapping them up among the clothes, so to bewrap them and entangle them, keeping down by force the feather bed and pillows hard onto their mouths, that, within a while, smothered and stifled, their breath failing, they gave up to God their innocent souls into the joys of heaven; leaving to the tormentors their bodies dead in the bed. Which after that the wretches perceived, first by the struggling with the pains of death, and after long lying still, to be thoroughly dead, they laid their bodies naked upon the bed, and fetched Sir James to see them; which, upon the sight of them, caused those murderers to bury them at the stair-foot, meetly deep in the ground under a great heap of stones.

Then rode Sir James in great haste to King Richard, and showed him all the manner of the murder; who gave him great thanks, and (as some say) there made him knight. But he allowed not (as I have heard) the burying in so vile a corner; saying, that he would have them buried in a better place, because they were a king's sons. . . .

Whereupon, they say that a priest of Sir Robert Brackenbury's took up the bodies again, and secretly interred them in such a place, as, by the occasion of his death, he alone knowing it, could never since come to light.

RAPHAEL HOLINSHED, 1577, on King Edward V and Richard, Duke of York

After this abominable deed was done, he never had quiet in his mind, he never thought himself sure. Where he went abroad, his eyes whirled about, his body privily fenced, his hand ever on his dagger, his countenance and manner like one alway ready to strike again, he took ill rest at night, lay long waking and musing, sore worried with care and watch, neither slumbered nor slept, troubled with fearful dreams, suddenly sometimes started up, leapt out of his bed and ran about the chamber, so was his restless heart continually tossed and tumbled with the tedious impression and stormy remembrance of his abominable deed.

SIR THOMAS MORE, on the deaths of young King Edward V and his brother.
The History of Richard III, c. 1513

Here under lie interred the remains of Edward V, King of England, and of Richard Duke of York. Which two brothers their uncle Richard, who usurped the crown, shut up in the Tower of London, smothered them with pillows, and ordered them to be dishonourably and secretly buried. Whose long desired and much sought for bones, after above an hundred and ninety years, were found by most certain tokens, deep interred under the rubbish of the stairs that led up into the chapel of the White Tower, on the 17th of July in the year of our Lord 1674. Charles II, a most merciful prince, having compassion upon their hard fortune, performed the funeral rites of these unhappy princes, among the tombs of their ancestors anno dom. 1678, being the 30th of his reign.

Epitaph in the Tower of London

Whether genuine or spurious, the inurned bones have not yet proved conclusive in identifying a murderer. Those who believe in the guilt of Richard, Buckingham or Henry VII may all continue to believe.

JEREMY POTTER, Chairman of the Richard III Society, 1985

Charles I

Sir, the charge hath called you a Tyrant, a Traitor, a Murderer, and a public enemy to the Commonwealth. Sir, it had been well if that any of all these terms might rightly and justly have been spared.

JOHN BRADSHAW, President of the Court, condemning King Charles I, 1649

It was the Parliament who began the war and not I, but I hope they might be guiltless too, as ill instruments have gone between us. . . . In one respect I suffer justly, and that is because I permitted an unjust sentence to be executed on another. . . . Take heed of the axe, take heed of the axe – take care that they do not put me to pain – I go from a corruptible to an incorruptible crown, where no disturbance can be, no disturbance at all. . . . I shall say but very short prayers, and then thrust out my hands. . . . Remember!

KING CHARLES I, on the scaffold. He has recalled his assent to beheading of his Minister, the Earl of Strafford

The four heavy strokes of the hour struck and boomed in the silence. The hands of the lying figure were stretched out again, this time as a final signal, and right up in the air above them all the axe swung, white against the grey sky, flashed and fell.

In a moment the group upon the scaffold had closed round, a cloth was thrown, the body was raised, and among the hands stretched out to it were the eager and enfeebled hands of the bishop, trembling and still grasping the George.

A long moan or wail, very strange and dreadful, not very loud, rose from the people now that their tension was slackened by the accomplishment of the deed. And at once from the north and from

the south, with such ceremony as is used to the conquered, the
cavalry charged right through, hacking and dispersing these Londoners and driving them every way.

HILAIRE BELLOC, 1908, on the beheading of King Charles I

I followed not my own judgment, I did what I did out of conscience
to the Lord.

MAJOR-GENERAL THOMAS HARRISON, on trial, 1660, for high treason
towards King Charles I, of whom he was one of the judges

I went out to Charing Cross to see Major-General Harrison
hanged, drawn, and quartered; which was done there, he looking
as cheerful as any man could do in that condition. He was presently
cut down, and his head and heart shown to the people, at which
there was great shouts of joy. It is said, that he said that he was sure
to come shortly at the right hand of Christ to judge them that now
had judged him and that his wife do expect his coming again. Thus
it was my chance to see the King beheaded at White Hall, and to see
the first blood shed in revenge for the King at Charing Cross. I went
by water home, where I was angry with my wife for her things lying
about, and in my passion kicked the little fine basket which I
bought her in Holland, and broke it, which troubled me after I had
done it.   SAMUEL PEPYS

RELIGION

You own that Christ gave the keys of the Kingdom of Heaven to
Peter. Has he given any such power to Columba? Then will I
rather obey the gate-keeper of Heaven lest when I reach its gates he
who has the keys turns his back on me and there be none to open.

KING OSWY OF NORTHUMBRIA, presiding at the fateful Synod of Whitby,
664, to decide between the claims of Roman and Celtic Christianity

Happy beast! Never forced to patter prayers, never dragged to the
Sacrament!   KING JOHN, after a stag hunt

PRINCESS MARY: 'I would have hoped that because of the great and
    boundless goodness with which God hath endowed Your
    Majesty, and also because I am Your Majesty's near kindred
    and unworthy sister, that Your Majesty would have allowed me
    to continue in the old religion. There are but two things – soul
    and body. My soul I offer to God, and my body to Your
    Majesty's service. I would rather it pleased Your Majesty to
    take away my life than the old religion, in which I desire to live
    and die.'
KING EDWARD VI: 'I desire no such sacrifice.'

I cannot but marvel at thee and lament thy case, who seemed
sometime to be the lively member of Christ, but now the deformed
imp of the devil; sometime the beautiful temple of God, but now the
stinking and filthy kennel of Satan; sometime the unspotted spouse
of Christ, but now the unshamefaced paramour of anti-Christ. . . .

    When I consider these things I cannot but cry out upon thee,
thou white-livered milksop . . . sink of sin . . . child of perdition . . .
seed of Satan . . . dost thou not quake and tremble?

                              LADY JANE GREY, aged fifteen, to her former tutor,
                          Dr Harding, on his defection to Roman Catholicism, following
                                        the collapse of her brief reign, 1553

How long wilt thou be absent? For ever? Is thy mercy clean gone
. . . and thy Promise come utterly to an end? Why dost thou make
so long tarrying?

                          LADY JANE GREY, from her prayer, facing execution, 1554

I do not seek windows into men's souls.
There is one faith and one Jesus Christ, the rest is a dispute about
trifles.   QUEEN ELIZABETH I

'Twas God the word that spake it,
He took the bread and brake it;
And what the word did make it,
That I believe and take it.

QUEEN ELIZABETH I, on the Sacrament

I am no atheist, but I cannot think God would damn a man for taking a little pleasure out of the way.

KING CHARLES II, to Bishop Burnet

I went to hear the music of the Italians in the new chapel, now first opened publically at Whitehall for the Popish Service. Nothing can be finer than the magnificent marble work and architecture at the end, where are four statues, representing St John, St Peter, St Paul, and the Church, in white marble, the work of Mr Gibbon[s], with all the carving and pillars of exquisite art and great cost. The altar-piece is the Salutation; the volto in *fresco*, the Assumption of the Blessed Virgin, according to their tradition, with our Blessed Saviour, and a world of figures painted by Verrio. The throne where the King and Queen sit is very glorious, in a closet above, just opposite to the altar. Here we saw the Bishop in his mitre and rich copes, with six or seven Jesuits and others in rich copes, sumptuously habited, often taking off and putting on the Bishop's mitre, who sat in a chair with arms pontifically, was adored and censed by three Jesuits in their copes; then he went to the altar and made divers cringes, then censing the images and glorious tabernacles placed on the altar, and now and then changing place; the crosier, which was of silver, was put into his hand with a world of mysterious ceremony, the music playing, with singing. I could not have believed I should ever have seen such things in the King of England's palace, after it had pleased God to enlighten this nation; but our great sin has, for the present, eclipsed the blessing, which I hope He will in mercy and His good time restore to its purity.

JOHN EVELYN, on King James II, 1686

The Rev. Francis Willis was a clergyman who claimed that he had turned to the treatment of the insane from motives of Christian charity and compassion. King George III distrusted him from the start. As Prince Charles has reminded us, the King was no fool when he was in normal health. When he suggested to Willis that it would have been better if he had stuck to his calling as a clergyman, Willis replied that he was only following the example of Christ, who had also gone about healing the sick. 'Yes,' said the King, 'but he did not get £750 a year for it.'

> WYNFORD VAUGHAN-THOMAS, 1982, on a 'self-styled expert in insanity . . .
> it was a marvel that the King ever recovered after the first dose
> of the Willis treatment'

Divine Retribution!

> QUEEN ADELAIDE, on the destruction by fire of the Houses of Parliament, 1824

He gave me great happiness and He took it away leaving me alone to bear the heavy burden in very trying circumstances.

> QUEEN VICTORIA, on God, following the death of
> Albert, Prince Consort. *Journal*, 1861

Too long.

> QUEEN VICTORIA, on the Thanksgiving Service at St Paul's for the
> recovery from typhoid of Albert Edward, Prince of Wales, 1872

Adolphus Frederick, Duke of Cambridge – Queen Victoria's uncle – enjoyed attending the services at Westminster Abbey, where he occupied a seat next that of the Dean. During a period of drought, the Dean asked the congregation to pray for rain, whereupon H.R.H. remarked, 'By all means, Mr Dean; I have no objection in the world to your praying for rain. But it will do no good so long as the wind remains in the east.'   SIXTH DUKE OF PORTLAND, 1937

A fine occasion. Only one thing wrong. Too many damned parsons.

> KING GEORGE V, after the Silver Jubilee service, St Paul's, 1935

Marina even prayed in English. When asked by Queen Olga why she did not do so in Greek, she replied: 'I have arranged it with God. I told Him I liked to talk to Him in English best, and He said: "Please yourself, Marina." '

> DAVID DUFF, 1967, on Marina, Duchess of Kent,
> daughter-in-law of King George V and Queen Mary

REPARTEE

The Duchesses of Cleveland, Portsmouth and Mazarin were all Roman Catholics, the last two by birth, the first by conversion, an event which induced her relations to ask her royal lover to intervene. 'Oh, no!' replied the King [Charles II], he could not, for as to the *souls* of ladies, he never interfered with them *there*.

> CHRISTOPHER HIBBERT, 1964

> Here lies our Sovereign lord the King
> Whose word no man relies on,
> Who never said a foolish thing
> And never did a wise one.
>
> JOHN WILMOT, EARL OF ROCHESTER

This is very true, for my words are my own and my actions are my ministers'. KING CHARLES II

KING CHARLES II: I am the Father of my people.
GEORGE VILLIERS, second Duke of Buckingham: At least, the father of a great many of them, Sir.

Henceforth, you must remember that Christ Himself will be your husband.

RANDALL DAVIDSON, later Archbishop of Canterbury, to Queen Victoria, after the death of the Prince Consort, 1861

That is what I would call twaddle. The man must have known that he was talking nonsense. How can people like that comfort others or teach anybody?

QUEEN VICTORIA

KING GEORGE V: Remember, Mr Gandhi, I won't have any attacks on my Empire.
GANDHI: I must not be drawn into a political argument in Your Majesty's palace, after receiving Your Majesty's hospitality.

PRINCESS VICTORIA (sister to George V): Is that you, you old fool?
TELEPHONE OPERATOR: No, Your Royal Highness. His Majesty is not yet on the line.

During the General Strike, 1926:
LORD DURHAM, wealthy coal owner: The miners . . . a damned lot of revolutionaries.
KING GEORGE V: Try living on their wages before you judge them.

REPUBLICANS

I came one morning into the House well clad, and perceived a Gentleman speaking (whom I knew not) very ordinarily apparelled; for it was a plain cloth-sute which seemed to have bin made by an ill country-taylor; his linen was plain and not very clean; and I remember a speck or two of blood upon his little band, which was not much larger than his collar; his stature was of a good size, his sword stuck close to his side, his countenance swoln and reddish, his voice sharp and untunable, and his eloquence full of fervor. . . .

And yet I lived to see this very gentleman (having a very good taylor and more converse among good company) appeared of a great and majestical deportment and comely presence.

SIR PHILIP WARWICK, on Oliver Cromwell, making his first
speech to the Long Parliament, 1640

I do not believe that God has made the greater part of Mankind with saddles on their backs and bridles in their mouths, and some few booted and spurred to ride the rest.   RICHARD RUMBOLD, 1649

We have seen the pride of kings,
With those much desired things,
Whence their vain ambition springs,
    Scorned, despised, and set at nought.
We their *silk*, their *pearls*, their *gold*
And their precious *gems* behold
Scattered, pawned, bought and sold
    And to shame their glory brought.

GEORGE WITHER, Cromwellian; 'The wretched Withers'
in Alexander Pope's 'The Dunciad'

October 22, 1658

Saw the superb funeral of the Protector. He was carried from Somerset House in a velvet bed of state, drawn by six horses, housed with the same; the pall held by his new Lords; Oliver lying in effigy, in royal robes, and crowned with a crown, sceptre, and globe, like a king. The pendants and guidons were carried by the officers of the army; the Imperial banners, achievements, etc., by the heralds in their coats; a rich caparisoned horse, embroidered all over with gold; a knight of honour, armed cap-a-pie, and, after all, his guards, soldiers, and innumerable mourners. In this equipage, they proceeded to Westminster: but it was the joyfullest funeral I ever saw; for there were none that cried but dogs, which the soldiers hooted away with a barbarous noise, drinking and taking tobacco in the streets as they went.

April 25, 1659

A wonderful and sudden change in the face of the public; the new Protector, Richard, slighted; several pretenders and parties strive for the government: all anarchy and confusion; Lord have mercy on us!

January 30, 1661

This was the first solemn fast and day of humiliation to deplore the sins which had so long provoked God against this afflicted church and people, ordered by Parliament to be annually celebrated to expiate the guilt of the execrable murder of the late King.

This day (O the stupendous and inscrutable judgments of God!) were the carcases of those arch-rebels, Cromwell, Bradshawe (the judge who condemned his Majesty), and Ireton (son-in-law to the Usurper), dragged out of their superb tombs in Westminster among the Kings, to Tyburn, and hanged on the gallows there from nine in the morning till six at night, and then buried under that fatal and ignominious monument in a deep pit; thousands of people who had seen them in all their pride being spectators. Look back at October 22, 1658, and be astonished! and fear God and honour the King; but meddle not with them who are given to change!

JOHN EVELYN

He was not a man of blood, and totally declined Machiavel's method; which prescribes, upon any alteration of government, as a thing absolutely necessary, to cut off all the heads of those, and extirpate their families, who are friends to the old one. It was confidently reported, that, in the council of officers, it was more than once proposed, 'that there might be a general massacre of all the royal party, as the only expedient to secure the government', but that Cromwell would never consent to it; it may be, out of too much contempt of his enemies. In a word, as he had all the wicked-ness against which damnation is pronounced, and for which hell-fire is prepared, so he had some virtues which have caused the memory of some men in all ages to be celebrated; and he will be looked upon by posterity as a brave bad man.

EDWARD HYDE, EARL OF CLARENDON, on Oliver Cromwell, Lord Protector. *History of the Rebellion*, 1702–4

The master fraud that shelters all others.

TOM PAINE, 1776, on the British Monarchy

A horse leech. *Reynold's News*, 1871, on Queen Victoria

The most insensitive and brazen pay claim made in the last two hundred years.

W. W. HAMILTON, MP, in the House of Commons, on a request by Queen Elizabeth II for an increase in the Civil List, 1969

We'll go quietly.

QUEEN ELIZABETH II, on the possibility of a British republic

The Oxford Dictionary does not define the word 'twerp'. Webster's 3rd New International Dictionary defines 'twerp' or 'twirp' as 'an insignificant or contemptible fellow'. Chambers 20th Century Dictionary says it could mean a 'cad'. And the Penguin English Dictionary says it means 'a silly fool; an unimportant person'. . . .

I do not think any of the above descriptions fit. I therefore take this opportunity of publically and unreservedly apologizing for so describing the Prince of Wales in the House of Commons. I believe him to be a sensible, contented, pleasant young man. Who wouldn't be with a guaranteed untaxed annual income of £105,000? W. W. HAMILTON, MP. *The Times*, 1975

REPUTATION

Good God, what a set they are! We talked over the Royal Family, and we agreed that the three kingdoms cannot furnish such a brood, so many and so bad, rogues, blackguards, fools and whores.

CHARLES GREVILLE. Diary, 1829

RESTORATION

May 29, 1660

This day, his Majesty, Charles the Second, came to London, after a long and sad exile and calamitous suffering both of the King and the Church, being seventeen years. This was also his birth-day, and with a triumph of above 20,000 horse and foot, brandishing their swords, and shouting with inexpressible joy; the ways strewed with flowers, the bells ringing, the streets hung with tapestry, fountains running with wine; the Mayor, Aldermen, and all the Companies, in their liveries, chains of gold, and velvet; the windows and balconies all set with ladies; trumpets, music, and myriads of people flocking, even so far as from Rochester, so as they were seven hours in passing the city, even from two in the afternoon till nine at night.

I stood in the Strand and beheld it, and blessed God. And all this was done without one drop of blood shed, and by that very army which rebelled against him; but it was the Lord's doing for such a restoration was never mentioned in any history, ancient or modern, since the return of the Jews from their Babylonish captivity; nor so joyful a day and so bright ever seen in this nation, this happening when to expect or effect it was past all human policy. . . .

The eagerness of men and women, and children, to see his Majesty, and kiss his hands, was so great, that he had scarce leisure to eat for some days, coming as they did from all parts of the nation; and the King being as willing to give them that satisfaction, would have none kept out, but gave free access to all sorts of people.

JOHN EVELYN

The *Naseby*, now no longer England's shame,
But better to be lost in Charles' name
(Like some unequal bride in nobler sheets),
Receives her lord: the joyful *London* meets
The princely York, himself alone a freight;
The *Swiftsure* groans beneath great Gloster's
weight . . .

The winds that never moderation knew,
Afraid to blow too much, too faintly blew;
Or out of breath with joy could not enlarge
Their straiten'd lungs, or conscious of their charge . . .

And welcome now, great monarch, to your own;
Behold th'approaching cliffs of Albion!
It is no longer motion cheats your view,
As you meet it, the land approacheth you.
The land returns, and, in the white it wears,
The marks of penitence and sorrow bears.

JOHN DRYDEN, on the return of the Stuarts from exile, 1660. *Astraea Redux*

Naseby was the site of one of King Charles I's major defeats, and was thus a name now unacceptable for a royal warship.

RETRIBUTION

All, or most of them, were said to have been tainted with the sin of sodomy. Behold the terrible vengeance of God! Suddenly death swallowed them up unshriven, though there was no wind and the sea was calm. HENRY OF HUNTINGDON, on the drowning of William, son of King Henry I, and his courtiers and crew, on the White Ship, 1120. *Historia Anglorum, c.* 1150

RHAPSODY

O eyes that pierce our hearts without remorse,
O hair, of right that wears a royal crown,
O hands, that conquer more than Caesar's force,
O wit, that turns huge kingdoms upside down,
    Then love be judge, what heart may these withstand,
    Such eyes, such hair, such wit and such a hand?

SIR WALTER RALEGH, on Queen Elizabeth I

RICHARD I

This renowned prince was tall, strong, straight, and well-proportioned. His arms were remarkably long, his eyes blue, and full of vivacity: his hair was of a yellowish colour; his countenance fair and comely, and his air majestic. He was endowed with good-natured understanding; his penetration was uncommon; he professed a fund of manly eloquence; his conversation was spirited, and he was admired for his talents of repartee; as for his courage and ability in war, both Europe and Asia resound with his praise. . . .

These are the shining parts of his character, which, however, cannot dazzle the judicious observer so much, but that he may perceive a number of blemishes, which no historian has been able to efface from the memory of this celebrated monarch. His ingratitude and want of filial affection are unpardonable. He was proud, haughty, ambitious, choleric, cruel, vindictive, and debauched; nothing could equal his rapaciousness but his profusion, and, indeed, the one was the effect of the other; he was a tyrant to his wife, as well as to his people, who groaned under his taxation to such a degree, that even the glory of his victories did not exempt him from their execrations; in a word, he has been aptly compared to a lion, a species of animal which he resembled not only in courage, but likewise in ferocity. TOBIAS SMOLLETT, 1757

RICHARD II

O prince, desyre to be honourable,
Cherish thy folk and hate extorcioun!
Suffre no thing, that may be reprevable
To thyn estat, don in thy regioun.
Show forth thy swerd of castigacioun,
Dred God, do law, love trouthe and worthinesse,
And wed thy folk agein to stedfastnesse.

GEOFFREY CHAUCER, to King Richard II. *Lak of Stedfastnesse*, c. 1399

He was seemly of shape and favour and of nature good enough, if the wickedness and naughty demeanour of such as were about him had not altered it.

His chance verily was greatly unfortunate, which fell into such calamity, that he took it for the best way he could devise to renounce his kingdom, for the which mortal men are accustomed to hazard all they have to attain thereunto. But such misfortune (or the like) oftentimes falleth unto those princes which, when they are aloft, cast no doubt for perils that may follow. He was prodigal, ambitious, and much given to the pleasure of the body. . . .

Furthermore, there reigned abundantly the filthy sin of lechery and fornication, with abominable adultery, specially in the king.

RAPHAEL HOLINSHED, 1577

RICHARD III

He was little of stature, deformed in body, the one shoulder being higher than the other, a short and sour countenance, which seemed to savour of mischief, and utter evidently craft and deceit. The while he was thinking of any matter, he did continually bite his nether lip, as though that cruel nature of his did so rage itself in that little carcase. Also he was wont to be ever with his right hand pulling out the sheath to the midst, and putting in again the dagger which he did always wear. Truly he had a sharp wit, provident and subtle, apt both to counterfeit and dissemble.

POLYDORE VERGIL. *Anglica Historia*, 1531

Richard III . . . was in wit and courage equal to either of his brothers, in body and prowess far under them both: little of stature, ill-featured of limbs, crookbacked, his left shoulder much higher than his right, hard-favoured of visage, and such as in states called warly, in other men otherwise. He was malicious, wrathful, envious, and from afore his birth, ever froward. It is for truth reported that his mother the Duchess had so much ado in her travail that she could not be delivered of him uncut, and that he came into the world with the feet forward, as men be born outward, and (as his fame runneth) also not untouched – whether men out of hatred report above the truth, or else that nature changed her course in his beginning. . . .   SIR THOMAS MORE. *History of Richard III, c.* 1513

Jeremy Potter commented, 1985:

This virulent piece of character assassination directed against the last Plantagenet King by someone later put to death by Henry Tudor's son and later still (1935) canonized as a saint, has always been a paradox and a puzzle. The most plausible explanation was put forward in 1975 by Alison Hanham, who drew attention to the fact that More was famous as an intellectual joker and suggested that his account of Richard III is to a great extent ironical, a parody of history, a jest at the expense of Polydore Vergil and the unlikely tales with which he and his like exected to gull the public. More never completed or sought to publish this work, but what was written largely in irony was published after his death and has been read straight ever since.

A surviving letter from Erasmus to Polydore Vergil reveals that the historian believed that he had offended More, and parody may have been More's revenge. . . . More is here setting down, with some relish and in finely turned prose, nonsense which 'men out of hatred report' and some knaves and idiots believe to be true. As we learn from Erasmus, having one shoulder visibly higher than the other was a characteristic joke of More's personal appearance, so that there are private jokes here too. (Of More, Erasmus wrote to Ulrich von Hutten: 'The right shoulder appears slightly more elevated than his left, and this trait most readily apparent in his walk.') Perhaps More also had a reputation for being 'hard-favoured of visage'. Certainly he was short, dark-haired and pale-faced like Richard.

Richard III, of all the English monarchs, bears the greatest contrariety of character. . . . Some few have conferred upon him an almost angelic excellence, have clouded his errors, and blazened every virtue that could adorn a man. Others, as if only extremes would prevail, present him in the blackest dye; his thoughts were evil, and that continually, and his actions diabolical; the most degraded mind inhabited the most deformed body. . . .

But Richard's character, like every man's, had two sides, though most writers display but one.   WILLIAM HUTTON, 1788

As he was a *York*, I am rather inclined to suppose him a very respectable man.

JANE AUSTEN (aged fifteen), on King Richard III. *History of England*, 1790

RIVALRY

After I had heard awhile, seeing her back was toward the door, I ventured within and stood hearing her play [the virginals] excellently well; but she left off immediately, as soon as she turned about and saw me. She appeared to be surprised and came forward, seeming to strike me with her hand. She asked how I came there? I said that as I passed the door, I heard such music as delighted me, whereby I was drawn in ere I knew how. Then she sat down low upon a cushion. She inquired of my queen [Mary Stuart] if she played best? In that I found myself obliged to give her the praise. Then she inquired of me whether she or my queen danced best? I answered that my queen danced not so high or *disposedly* as she did. . . .

She asked me whether my queen's hair or hers was best, and which of them was fairest. I said, she was the fairest queen in England and mine in Scotland. Yet she persisted. I answered, they were both the fairest ladies in their countries; that Her Majesty was whiter but my queen was very lovely. She inquired, which of them was of higher stature. I said, my queen. Then, said Elizabeth, she is too high, for I myself am neither too high nor too low.

SIR JAMES MELVIL, on Queen Elizabeth I and
Mary Queen of Scots. *Memoirs 1549–93*

ROYAL BEHAVIOUR

When Scottish affairs were under discussion and Richard de Humet, constable of Normandy, had spoken up for William the Lion, the new king, Henry, had called Richard a traitor and then behaved like a maniac, hurling his cap to the ground, unfastening his sword-belt and throwing off all his clothes. Finally he had torn the silk coverlet from his bed and, as though 'squatting on a dung-hill' (Job 2:8), had started to chew the straw.

FRANK BARLOW, 1986, on King Henry II

Then the King heaved heavy sighs, began suffering the utmost irritation, started to turn in on himself and tire. He began gnashing his teeth and rolling his staring eyes in passion. Then he would gather sticks and stones, gnawing them like a madman and some-times throwing them away half-eaten. His uncontrolled gesticula-tions showed signs of the melancholy, or rather of the derangement that covered him.

MATTHEW PARIS, on King John. *Chronica Majora*, c. 1250

King James's appearance and manners cannot fail to have distressed so fastidious a boy as [Prince] Charles.

As the King grew older and more infirm this appearance grew increasingly distasteful. 'His skin was as soft as taffeta sarsnet', Anthony Weldon said (1651), 'because he never washed his hands, but only rubbed his fingers' ends slightly with the wet end of a napkin.' He was always scratching himself, and as he was subject to over-heating and sweated profusely he had his clothes cut very loose. He also had them made stiletto-proof with 'breeches in great plaits and full stuffed; he was naturally of a timorous disposition which was the reason of his quilted doublets'. When he got too hot he would throw his outer clothes off, and so he caught cold and was for ever sneezing and blowing his nose. He lost all his teeth and, being unable to chew, bolted his food and so suffered from indigestion and heartburn. He was excessively fond of fruit and when he was brought the first strawberries, grapes or cherries of the season out of the Windsor gardens, he would never wait until the man from the spicery had finished his speech of 'complimental words' and risen from his knees, but plunged his hands impatiently into the basket, so he suffered from intermittent diarrhoea as well. He also had arthritis and gout which he attempted to cure by standing up in the belly of bucks and stags slaughtered in the hunting field.

CHRISTOPHER HIBBERT, 1964, on King James VI and I

This night, his Majesty promised to make my Wife Lady of the Jewels (a very honourable charge) to the future Queen (but which he never performed).   JOHN EVELYN, on King Charles II, 1661

The King [George III] is so rapid in his meals that whoever attends him must be rapid also or follow starving.   FANNY BURNEY

King George would have had a sympathizer not only in Henry II, but in Emperor Franz Josef, who hated formal banquets and contrived to have twelve courses served and eaten in some fifty minutes.

Immediately he himself had finished, all plates were at once removed, however much or little the guests had eaten. Those furthest away from him could thus finish the evening having eaten nothing.

It was easy to talk to him. He was interested in so many things and above all in people and how they lived. He was never pompous or stilted, he enjoyed a joke, and loved to chaff his equerries. He did not think it beneath his dignity to talk with the meanest of his subjects. There are many stories told about King George, the truth of which it is impossible to determine, but all of the same nature. He is said once to have met a boy in Windsor Great Park. 'Who are you?' asked the King. 'I be pig boy,' replied the lad, 'but I don't work. They don't want lads here. All this belongs hereabouts to Georgy.' 'Pray, who is Georgy?' 'He be King and lives at the Castle, but he does no good for me.' The King found him a job on one of his farms. There is another story of his meeting an old woman working alone in a field near Weymouth. When asked where her companions were, she said they had gone to see the King. 'And why did you not go with them?' 'Because I have five children to provide for and cannot afford to lose a day's work.' 'Then,' said the King, slipping her a guinea, 'you may tell your companions that the King came to see you.' There are too many stories of this kind for there not to be a basic truth behind them; that the King could talk freely and easily with any class of his subjects without lowering his dignity. Such stories have never been told about King George II or King George IV.

Horace Walpole has an anecdote about a wealthy American merchant who said: 'They say King George is a very honest fellow; I should like to smoke a pipe with him.'

JOHN BROOKE, 1972, on King George III

The Duke of Wellington told us a good story he heard from Lady Cowper. When she was at Brighton the King talked to her of her mother, Lady Melbourne (by whom the King was supposed to have had a son, Geo: Lamb) and said he used, during her last illness, to walk across the parade to her house every day, to see her constantly and said that at last she died in his arms! Lady Cowper, knowing all the time that for the last ten days of her mother's life she never was out of her room and that, so far from the King calling to see her or having her died in his arms, he never even sent to enquire after her. This is lying with a vengeance!

HARRIET ARBUTHNOT, on King George IV. Journal, 1822

A ROYAL COMMAND

On crossing to Ireland the ship in which Queen Victoria was travelling encountered rough weather. A gigantic wave caused such a violent lurch that the Queen was almost knocked off her feet. Recovering her balance she said to an attendant, 'Go up to the bridge, give the admiral my compliments, and tell him he's not to let that happen again.'

BENNETT CERF, 1956

King speaking. Fetch Garter.

KING EDWARD VIII, on the telephone, 1936

A ROYAL DAY

He sleeps in the same room with the Queen, but in a separate bed; at a quarter before eight every morning his *valet de chambre* knocks at the door, and at ten minutes before eight exactly he gets out of bed, puts on a flannel dressing-gown and trousers, walks into his dressing room and goes at once to the water closet. Let who will be there, he never takes the slightest notice of them till he emerges from the temple. . . . At half-past-nine he breakfasts with the Queen, the Ladies, and any of his family; he eats a couple of fingers and drinks a dish of coffee. After breakfast he reads *The Times* and *Morning*

Post commenting aloud on what he reads in very plain terms, and sometimes they hear 'That's a damned lie' or some such remark, without knowing to what it applies. After breakfast he devotes himself with Sir H. Taylor to business till two, when he lunches (two cutlets and two glasses of sherry); then he goes out and drives till dinner; at dinner drinks a bottle of sherry – no other wine – and eats moderately, and goes to bed soon after eleven.

ADOLPHUS, DUKE OF CAMBRIDGE, on his father, King William IV

ROYALTY, ON ROYALTY

That false Scots urchin!

QUEEN ELIZABETH I, on King James VI of Scotland, 1581

He had too high a notion of the regal power and thought that every opposition to it was rebellion.

GEORGE WILLIAM FREDERICK, Prince of Wales,
afterwards King George III, on King Charles I

Whenever God of his infinite goodness shall call me out of this world, the tongue of malice may not paint my intentions in those colours she admires, nor the sycophant extoll me beyond what I deserve. I do not pretend to any superior abilities, but will give place to no one in meaning to preserve the freedom, happiness and glory of my dominions and all their inhabitants, and to fulfill the duty to my God and my neighbour in the most extended sense.

KING GEORGE III, on himself

ROYAL SLAUGHTERHOUSE

The head and body were placed in a coffin covered with black velvet, and were laid privately under the communion table of St Peter's Chapel in the Tower. Within four years the pavement of the chancel was again disturbed, and hard by the remains of Monmouth were laid the remains of Jeffreys. In truth there is no sadder spot on the earth than that little cemetery. Death is there associated, not, as in Westminster Abbey and St Paul's, with genius and virtue, with public veneration and with imperishable renown; not, as in our humblest churches and churchyards, with everything that is most endearing in social and domestic charities; but with whatever is darkest in human nature and in human destiny, with the savage triumph of implacable enemies, with the inconstancy, the ingratitude, the cowardice of friends, with all the miseries of fallen greatness and of blighted fame. Thither have been carried, through successive ages, by the rude hands of gaolers, without one mourner following, the bleeding relics of men who had been the captains of armies, the leaders of parties, the oracles of senates, and the ornaments of courts. Thither was borne, before the window where Jane Grey was praying, the mangled corpse of Guilford Dudley. Edward Seymour, Duke of Somerset, and Protector of the realm, reposes there by the brother whom he murdered. There has mouldered away the headless trunk of John Fisher, Bishop of Rochester and Cardinal of Saint Vitalis, a man worthy to have lived in a better age, and to have died in a better cause. There are laid John Dudley, Duke of Northumberland, Lord High Admiral, and Thomas Cromwell, Earl of Essex. There, too, is another Essex, on whom nature and fortune had lavished all their bounties in vain, and whom valour, grace, genius, royal favour, popular applause, conducted to an early and ignominious doom. Not far off sleep two chiefs of the great house of Howard, Thomas, fourth Duke of Norfolk, and Philip, eleventh Earl of Arundel. Here and there, among the thick graves of unquiet and aspiring statesmen, lie more delicate sufferers; Margaret of Salisbury, the last of the proud name of Plantagenet, and those two fair queens who perished by the jealous rage of Henry. Such was the dust with which the dust of Monmouth mingled. LORD MACAULAY, 1848

The title for this entry is adapted from a remark of V. S. Pritchett, in a powerful evocation of the Tower, 1962.

ROYAL SONG

When I was fair and young and favour graced me,
Of many was I sought their mistress for to be,
But I did scorn them all and answered them therefore,
Go, go, go, seek some other whore,
     Importune me no more.

How many weeping eyes I made pine with woe,
How many sighing hearts, I have no skill to show,
Yet I the prouder grew, and answered them therefore,
Go, go, go, seek some other whore,
     Importune me no more.

Then spake fair Venus' son, that proud victorious boy,
And said, fine dame since that you been so coy,
I will so pluck your plumes that you shall say no more,
Go, go, go, seek some other whore,
     Importune me no more.

When he had spake these words, such change grew in my breast,
That neither day nor night since that I could take any rest,
Then lo, I did repent of what I said before,
Go, go, go, seek some other whore,
     Importune me no more.

QUEEN ELIZABETH I

ROYAL VISITORS

The queen entertained them generously, paying the expenses of their household, but neither the Princess nor the Margrave understood the manners and customs of the English; they were apt to see slights, and they both, the latter especially, thought it an impertinence on the part of shopkeepers to ask that their purchases should be paid for. The Margrave, making an unostentatious retreat towards the continent, was laid by the heels at Rochester and imprisoned for debt. Finding himself in the Round House, he threatened to shoot his way out, and the Mayor of Rochester sent to the queen, asking either that the Margrave should be told he must keep the laws of the country, or that the town might be relieved of so awkward a prisoner. The queen sent down the money to discharge the Margrave's debt, and he lost no time in getting away. First, however, he sent a servant up to London with a letter to Lord Leicester, demanding a horse.

ELIZABETH JENKINS, 1961, on the visit of the Margrave of Baden and his wife, Princess Cecilia of Sweden, 1565–6, to Queen Elizabeth I

When the Tsar had come to Windsor his first action was to send to the stables for a bundle of straw on which to sleep, and he had spent a large part of the next day making eyes at all the pretty women he saw.

CHRISTOPHER HIBBERT, 1964, on the visit of Tsar Nicholas I of Russia, 1844, to Queen Victoria

The King of Hanover had deliberately arrived late for the christening of Princess Alice [1843], although Queen Victoria had asked him to be one of the baby's sponsors, and had been calculatingly offensive to Albert, and now he was determined to take precedence over him, on the grounds that he was a King, whereas Prince Albert was not. What ensued was described by [George] Anson as 'rather a Bear Garden scene'. When the service ended Hanover hobbled to the Queen and told her that she must walk out with him; she refused; he insisted; Albert shoved him away; he nearly fell over, but was removed by the Lord Chamberlain 'by force, fuming with ire', in Anson's account. There was then a scene at the signing of the register, when Hanover again demanded precedence. The queen seized the register, and he was thwarted again, but, persistent to the end, he now insisted on leading with her to the reception. Victoria resolved this problem brilliantly by giving precedence to the Queen of the Belgians and Albert, she and the furious Hanover walking second. To Prince Albert's immense satisfaction, Hanover, after storming out, slipped and fell badly. Albert wrote to Ernest that 'I was forced to give him a strong punch and drove him down a few steps. . . he left the party in a great wrath. Since then, we let him go, and happily he fell over some stones at Kew and damaged some ribs.'   ROBERT RHODES JAMES, 1983

The Emperor had made himself thoroughly interesting in the Queen's eye: for him an easy process, since practically all women thought him interesting and romantic. He had a short way with them; he fell in love with them all, provided they had a little attraction or could be useful to him. His incessant philandering, begun at an early age, had taught him all the tricks of gallantry and the arts of pleasing women; and rightly seeing that Victoria's prejudice against him could best be overcome by a strong counter-emotion, he had been determined upon a conquest. So out of the Imperial repertoire had come just the right kind and amount of love to meet the rather exceptional occasion. It had, of course, to take the form of a most discreet and respectful homage, for the English sovereign was a modest and virtuous woman very happily married.

At Windsor the Emperor had been the Queen's humble subject, kneeling not before the anointed head of an Empire but paying court to that which he implied was infinitely greater: her own personal charm, beauty and goodness. He managed to make Victoria, so awful and unapproachable in her Majesty, and yet so homely and sensible in her person, feel like a Cleopatra or a Helen of Troy. She was immeasurably flattered.

She was delighted, too, with Louis Napoleon's constant eulogizing of Albert. With Albert the wily Emperor also had the perfect technique; he would quickly metamorphose himself into a typical German professor when he and the Prince had a moment together free from court etiquette; he would be ready to theorize and point morals, and then he would jovially fall to singing German folk songs or to reciting Schiller.

The Queen's love for Albert was deep and sincere; but this little interlude provided an enjoyable change. Albert, although utterly devoted to her, was no gallant knight. At Windsor he was to be seen in their morning walks, striding ahead and not noticing that she had almost to run to keep up with him; and he could speak of his attachment to her as being 'based on reason and duty'. Louis Napoleon suggested to her that there was a world in which love was based upon passion and instinct; contact with such a man who had lived in the great world and taken its knocks in an adventurous career and yet was now her equal, was delightfully thrilling after these many years in which no man had dared address her as an attractive woman, and in which Albert supposed she was too reasonable to require any flattery from him.

EDITH SAUNDERS, 1946, on the state visit to Paris, 1855,
of Victoria and Albert

That he *is* a very extraordinary man with great qualities, there can be *no* doubt. I might almost say a mysterious man. He is evidently possessed of *indomitable courage, unflinching firmness of purpose, self-reliance, perseverance* and *great secrecy*; and to this should be added a great reliance on what he calls his *star*, and a belief in omens and incidents as connected with his future destiny which is almost romantic, and at the same time he is endowed with a wonderful self-control, great *calmness*, even *gentleness*, and with a *power of fascination*, the effect of which upon those who have become more intimately acquainted with him is most *sensibly* felt.

QUEEN VICTORIA, on Napoleon III, 1855

The Emperor is a short person. He has very long moustachios but short hair. The Empress is very pretty.

ALBERT EDWARD, PRINCE OF WALES, aged thirteen,
on Napoleon III and Eugénie

From Lady Longford's biography, we learn that Victoria, on Napoleon's state visit to London, 1855, 'reminded him that they had met in 1848 at a public breakfast in aid of wash-houses in the Fulham Road'.

A report about the Shah's behaviour and entourage that reached Berlin was peculiarly distressing. 'His Majesty generally dines alone, and when so, prefers to have his meals on the carpet. . . '

According to the British ambassador in Berlin, nobody had ever dared venture to tell the Shah that he should not put his arm round the Queen's chair at dinner, 'or put his fingers into dishes, or take food out of his mouth again to look at it after it has been chewed, or fling it under the table if it does not suit his taste', and that he should not make such embarrassing attempts to console himself for the absence of his harem. . . .

Victoria received him in full state at Windsor, wearing her large pearls, and she sat next to him in the middle of the White Drawing Room, surrounded by Persian and English Princes and Princesses, conscious of the absurd figure she must have cut and feeling 'very shy'. But he behaved most decorously and was so impressively attired with huge rubies as buttons in his diamond-studded coat, and epaulettes of diamonds and emeralds. She invested him with the Garter and, having kissed her hand, he gave her two Orders in return and the Grand Vizier helped to save her hat from falling off.

CHRISTOPHER HIBBERT, 1964, on Shah Naser ad Din

A RUSSIAN

Thence to the audience of a Russian Envoy in the Queen's presence-chamber, introduced with much state, the soldiers, pensioners, and guards in their order. His letters of credence brought by his secretary in a scarf of sarsenet, their vests sumptuous, much embroidered with pearls. He delivered his speech in the Russ language, but without the least action, or motion, of his body, which was immediately interpreted aloud by a German that spake good English: half of it consisted in repetition of the Czar's Titles, which were very haughty and oriental: the substance of the rest was, that he was only sent to see the King and Queen, and know how they did, with much compliment and frothy language. Then, they kissed their Majesties' hands, and went as they came; but their real errand was to get money.   JOHN EVELYN, 1667

SATIRE

Of a tall Stature and of Sable Hue;
Much like the son of Kish, that lofty Jew:
Twelve years compleat he suffered in Exile,
And kept his Father's Asses all the while.
At length by wonderful Impulse of Fate,
The People call him home to help the State;
And what is more they send him money too,
And clothe him all, from Head to Foot anew.
Nor did he such small favours then disdain,
Who in his Thirtieth Year began his Reign:
In a slasht Doublet then he came ashore,
And dubb'd poor *Palmer's* Wife his royal Whore.
Bishops and Deans, Peers, Pimps and Knights he
made,
Things highly fitting for a Monarch's Trade;
With Women, Wine and Viands of Delight,
His jolly Vassals feast him Day and Night.

ANON, on King Charles II

Saint Peter sat by the celestial gate,
    And nodded o'er his keys: when, lo! there came
A wondrous noise he had not heard of late –
    A rushing sound of wind, and stream, and flame;
In short, a roar of things extremely great,
    Which would have made aught save a Saint
exclaim;
But he, with first a start and then a wink,
Said, 'There's another star gone out, I think!'

But ere he could return to his repose,
    A Cherub flapped his right wing o'er his eyes –
At which Saint Peter yawned, and rubbed his nose:
    'Saint porter,' said the angel, 'prithee rise!'
Waving a goodly wing, which glowed, as glows
    An earthly peacock's tail, with heavenly dyes:
To which the saint replied, 'Well, what's the matter?
Is Lucifer come back with all this clatter?'

'No,' quoth the Cherub: 'George the Third is dead.'
    'And who *is* George the Third?' replied the apostle:
'*What George? what Third?*' 'The King of England,'
                                    said
    The angel. 'Well! he won't find kings to jostle
Him on his way; but does he wear his head?
    Because the last we saw here had a tustle,
And ne'er would have got into Heaven's good graces,
Had he not flung his head in all our faces.

'He was – if I remember – King of France;
    That head of his, which could not keep a crown
On earth, yet ventured in my face to advance
    A claim to those of martyrs – like my own:
If I had had my sword, as I had once
    When I cut ears off, I had cut him down;
But having but my *keys*, and not my brand,
I only knocked his head from out his hand. . . .'

                LORD BYRON. From *The Vision of Judgement*, 1822

No fatter fish than he
Flounders round the polar sea.
See his bubbles – at his gills
What a world of drink he swills. . . .

Every fish of generous kind
Scuds aside or sinks behind;
But about his presence keep
All the Monsters of the Deep.

By his bulk and by his eye,
By his oily qualities.
This (or else my eyesight fails)
This should be the Prince of Whales.

CHARLES LAMB, on George, Prince Regent. *The Triumph of the Whales*

SCANDAL

It is said that my Lord Robert is fled out of the realm. . . . Say
nothing. It is told me he hath got the Queen with child, and
therefore he is fled. . . .

No words! Say nothing.

ROBERT BROOKE, on Lord Robert Dudley and Queen Elizabeth I,
to Bart Huger, 1563

The Queen of England is going to marry the Master of her Horses,
who has killed his wife to make room for her.

MARY, QUEEN OF SCOTS, on Queen Elizabeth I and Lord Robert Dudley,
later Earl of Leicester, following the 'accidental' death of
Lady Dudley at Cumnor Place, Berkshire, 1560

She had the chaunce to fal from a paire of staires, and so to breake
her necke, but yet wythout hurting of her hoode that stoode upon
her head. . . .

Sir Richard Varney, who by commandment remayned with her
that day alone, with one man onlie . . . can tel how she died, which

man being taken afterward and offering to publish the maner of the said murder, was made awaye privilie in the prison. . . .

Sir Richard, dying about the same time in London . . . cried pitiouslie, and blasphemed God, and said that the divils in hell did teere him in peeces.   ANON. *Leycester's Commonwealth*, 1584

This book was described by Sir Francis Walsingham as 'the most malicious thing that was ever penned sithence the beginning of the world'.

It seems to me very extraordinary that it should be impossible to have esteem and regard for a young man without it being criminal.

KING WILLIAM III

They say, that with Brown and by him she consoles herself for Prince Albert, and they go even further. They add that she is in an interesting condition, and that if she was not present for the Volunteers Review, and at the inauguration of the monument to Prince Albert, it was only in order to hide her pregnancy. I hasten to add that the queen has been morganatically married to her attendant for a long time, which diminishes the gravity of the thing.

Gazette de Lausanne, on John Brown, Queen Victoria's Highland attendant, 1866

Eddy . . . seemed less interested in his heritage than having a good time and this, not surprisingly, gave rise to gossip in the outer world and concern within his family. As with his lessons, he found it impossible to concentrate on one love affair at a time and he fell in and out of love at an alarming rate – often with the most unsuitable types. As James Pope-Hennessy put it in his biography of Queen Mary, 'among the few things Prince Eddy really cared for was every form of dissipation and amusement'. Indeed, the twentieth century was to reveal rather more about this prince than could have been stomached during the reign of his grandmother. There was, for instance, talk of an illegitimate child born to a street-girl in what is now St Stephen's Hospital, Fulham; homosexual liaisons and an ominous link with the Whitechapel murderer who, at various intervals during 1888, mutilated five prostitutes. It would be impossible to identify the Prince himself as Jack the Ripper, but a cloud of mystery shrouds Eddy's rumoured involvement to this day. This is made more tantalizing by the fact that the private papers of both his parents were – at their command – destroyed upon their respective deaths.

CHRISTOPHER WARWICK, 1980, on the elder brother
of the future King George V

SCIENCE

He first used cast iron in building the conservatory of his London home, Carlton House, but later used it in his kitchen at Brighton, where it had to support the full weight of the building, and not merely glass. He realized its importance and wanted both to exploit its possibilities and also to give it the seal of his approval. Not content with cast iron pillars, he also introduced elaborate cast iron staircases. Similarly, he adopted gas-lighting for his palaces as soon, almost, as it was invented. His brother, William IV, had it torn out of all the palaces as too dangerous, but some of George IV's gas standards may still be seen outside Kensington Palace.

He was acutely aware that royal patronage helped to support new technology. He was interested in scientific as well as technological creations; he bought, maybe experimented with, electrical batteries. Most certainly he patronized the Royal Institution, whose president, Humphrey Davy, the greatest chemist of the age, he impulsively knighted. This side of his complex nature needs stressing because it is so easily overlooked in the emotional riot of his life, or in the compulsive, almost manic collecting in which he indulged.   J. H. PLUMB, 1977, on King George IV

Edward was to show himself a characteristic Edwardian in his attitude towards science, which can be charitably described as benevolent impenetrability. One of the last privileges of royalty to be surrendered is the exposure to new inventions, and the opportunity to sample them. One early use of Marconi's development of wireless telegraphy has a delicious flavour of the wonders of science applied to domestic happiness in the royal family. When Albert Edward was recuperating from an injured knee on board the royal yacht at Cowes, he was apparently fascinated by the tapping out of wireless messages. Up to 150 were sent across the water to his Mamma at Osborne, most of them variants on the comfortable theme 'H.R.H. the Prince of Wales has passed another good night and the knee is in good condition.' But apart from such instances of the royal pleasure in the novelties of applied science, the evidence is that social incentives for the development of science came primarily from other directions, not from the ruling classes.

PROFESSOR A. R. UBBELOHDE, 1964, in *Edwardian England 1901–1914*

SEXUAL BEHAVIOUR

She was apter to raise flames than to quench them.

FRANCIS OSBORNE, on Queen Elizabeth I. *Historical memoirs on the Reigns of Queen Elizabeth and King James*, 17th century

SHAKESPEARE

We are amaz'd; and thus long have we stood
To watch the fearful bending of thy knee,
Because we thought ourself thy lawful king:

And if we be, how dare thy joints forget
To pay their awful duty to our presence?
If we be not, show us the hand of God
That hath dismiss'd us from our stewardship;
For well we know, no hand of blood or bone
Can gripe the sacred handle of our sceptre,
Unless he do profane, steal, or usurp.

Richard II

See, see, King Richard doth himself appear,
As doth the blushing, discontented sun
From out the fiery portal of the east,
When he perceives the envious clouds are bent
To dim his glory and to stain the track
Of his bright passage to the occident.

Richard II

RICHARD II: I wasted time, and now doth time waste
me.

Richard II

HENRY VI: Ah, what a life were this. How sweet. How
lovely.
Gives not the hawthorne-bush a sweeter shade
To shepherds looking on their silly sheep,
Than doth a rich-embroidered canopy
To kings that fear their subjects' treachery.

Henry VI, Part III

Off with his head, and set it on York gates;
So York may overlook the town of York.

QUEEN MARGARET OF ANJOU, wife of King Henry VI, on
Richard, Duke of York, father of King Edward IV, executed
after the battle of Wakefield, 1460. *Henry VI, Part III*

Was there ever such stuff as great part of Shakespeare? Only one must not say so! But what think you? What? Is there not sad stuff? What? – What? . . . Oh, I know it is not to be said! But it's true. Only it's Shakespeare and nobody dare abuse him.

KING GEORGE III, to Fanny Burney

'RICHARD THE THIRD. – DUKE OF GLO'STER, 2*l.*; EARL OF RICHMOND, 1*l.*; DUKE OF BUCKINGHAM, 15*s.*; CATESBY, 12*s.*; TRESSEL, 10*s. 6d.*; LORD STANLEY, 5*s.*; LORD MAYOR OF LONDON, 2*s. 6d.*'

Such are the written placards wafered up in the gentlemen's dressing-room, in the green-room (where there is any), at a private theatre; and such are the sums extracted from the shop till, or overcharged in the office expenditure, by the donkeys who are prevailed upon to pay for permission to exhibit their lamentable ignorance and boobyism on the stage of a private theatre. This they do, in proportion to the scope afforded by the character for the display of their imbecility. For instance, the Duke of Glo'ster is well worth two pounds, because he has it all to himself; he must wear a real sword, and what is better still, he must draw it several times in the course of the piece. The soliloquies alone are well worth fifteen shillings; then there is the stabbing King Henry – decidedly cheap at three-and-sixpence, that's eighteen-and-sixpence; bullying the coffin-bearers – say eighteenpence, though it's worth much more – that's a pound. Then the love scene with Lady Anne, and the bustle of the fourth act can't be dear at ten shillings more – that's only one pound ten, including the 'off with his head!' – which is sure to bring down the applause, and it is very easy to do – 'Orf with his ed' (very quick and loud; – then slow and sneeringly) – 'So much for Bu-u-u-uckingham!' Lay the emphasis on the 'uck'; get yourself gradu-ally into a corner, and work with your right hand, while you're saying it, as if you were feeling your way, and it's sure to do. The tent scene is confessedly worth half-a-sovereign, and so you have the fight in, gratis, and everybody knows what an effect may be produced by a good combat. One – two – three – four – over; then, one – two – three – four – under; then thrust; then dodge and slide about; then fall down on one knee; then fight upon it, and then get up again and stagger. You may keep on doing this, as long as it seems to take – say ten minutes – and then fall down (backwards, if you can manage it without hurting yourself), and die game: nothing like it for producing an effect. They always do it at Astley's and Sadler's Wells, and if they don't know how to do this sort of thing, who in the world does? A small child, or a female in white, increases the interest of a combat materially – indeed, we are not aware that a regular legitimate terrific broadsword combat could be done without; but it would be rather difficult, and somewhat unusual, to introduce this effect in the last scene of *Richard the Third*, so the only thing to be done is just to make the best of a bad bargain, and be as long as possible fighting it out.

CHARLES DICKENS. *Sketches by Boz*, 1839

Assassin with the murder-musing smile,
The horrible hunch-back, slim, and garbed in guile
And bulgy-dingy metal, seeks and wins
Unmasked soliloquies, superbly staged.
Slow fades each historical scene; but each begins
In similar pomp. He stabs King Henry caged,
(And wears a scarlet cloak). Next, gets engaged,
Vermilion-clad, black-legged, and sallow with sins.
Another King goes sick. He sneers (in brown).
The King dies, off. Astride his calm white steed
He broods and plots and lours on London town,
And gives two piping nephews all they need.
Then (crafty in a crimson velvet gown)
Limps towards the golden madness of a crown.

No single blood-stained sonnet could have shown
Richard, nor all his registrations told.
Now, shrunk and sable on his tragic throne,
He glowers envenomed (draped in cloth of gold).
. . . Big business with a candle . . . and his Queen
Beautifully poisoned somewhere in the wings
Then doom and gilded armour; and a scene
Of ghosts; dim, husky-voiced Shakespearian things.

The casualties were numerous; and at last
He died (in clashing brass-ware), tired but tense;
Lord of his own undoing, crazed, aghast,
And propertied regardless of expense.
And the whole proud production paled and passed,
Self-conscious, like its brilliant audience.

SIEGFRIED SASSOON. 'First Night: Richard III', 1920

I read in a newspaper that a certain Mrs Winifred Venton, with the help of the Enfield College of Technology computer, has at last cracked the cipher of the *Sonnets*.

The message: Shakespeare was really King Edward VI, who did not die, as the history books say, when he was sixteen, but at the age of 125. In addition to writing 'Shakespeare', he wrote not only all of Ben Jonson and Bacon, but *Don Quixote* as well.

W. H. AUDEN, 1971

SIMPLE FOLK

Any mortal not King,
Not Emperor or Pope, or,
Pitching it at its lowest, Duke . . .
Such a fellow counts for nothing.

GIUSEPPE BELLI, *The Sovereigns of the Old World*

Lunch was a meal unknown to the eighteenth century, and the King ate nothing between breakfast at nine and dinner at four. His dinner was a simple affair: soup, meat and one vegetable, and fruit. He was fond of mutton which he liked with turnips or beetroot, and the traditional English dish of roast beef was reserved for Sundays.

He seems not to have cared for venison, a popular dish with the upper classes. He liked salads and fresh fruit, and if it was made into a tart he would eat the fruit and leave the pastry. He drank sparingly, never more than three or four glasses of wine at a meal and that often mixed with water. He never drank spirits. He was a great tea drinker, and when visiting would prefer a cup of tea to a glass of wine. Often he would go without supper, and if he had the meal it was usually a little fruit or eggs and bread and butter.

JOHN BROOKE, 1972, on King George III

Playing at being 'simple folk' has long been a favourite pastime of Royalty, but it does not entirely explain the alacrity with which Victoria and Albert embraced some of the more primitive Highland customs. It is difficult to explain their patronage of the barbarous 'deer dances' that were held after a good day's stalking. The deer themselves, of course, did not dance but lay stiff and cold on the lawn in front of Balmoral Castle while drunken gillies with lighted torches danced around them. 'Much whisky and inspection of raw meat', was the way Sir Henry Ponsonby described these 'larders', and he avoided them whenever possible. Not so Queen Victoria, who always came out after dinner to join in the festivities. . . .

When Captain Forbes of Strathdon and his clansmen, on their way home from the Braemar Gathering, came to the banks of the Dee, nothing would do but that the Balmoral tenantry should carry them piggy-back to the other side, a bit of horseplay which Queen Victoria found 'very courteous and worthy of chivalrous times'. A spirit stronger than chivalry may have animated the company, for, arrived safe and dry on the south bank of the Dee, Captain Forbes pulled off his boot, filled it with whisky and toasted the Queen. 'Our people in the Highlands are altogether primitive, true-hearted and without guile,' was Prince Albert's comment.

TOM CULLEN, 1960

SLANDER

One word more about the credulity of the public. You will scarcely credit, that my being committed to the Tower was believed all over the country – nay, even 'that the Queen had been arrested'! People surrounded the Tower to see us brought to it! . . . It has been a great worry to me, for the affair was *too serious* not to merit the gravest and closest consideration. It was anything but pleasant to me amidst it all that so many people could look upon me as 'a rogue and a traitor', and I shall not be at ease until I see the debate in Parliament well over. . . . Victoria has taken the whole affair greatly to heart, and was excessively indignant at the attacks. Finally, if our courage and cheerfulness have not suffered, our stomachs and digestions have, as they commonly do when the feelings are kept long on the stretch.

ALBERT, PRINCE CONSORT, to Baron Stockmar, on accusations
of pro-Russian activities on the eve of the Crimean War, 1854

SLEEP

Six hours' sleep is good enough for a man, seven for a woman, and eight for a fool.   KING GEORGE III, to James Wyatt

SNOBS

James I was a Snob, and a Scotch Snob, than which the world contains no more offensive creature. He appears to have had not one of the good qualities of a man – neither courage, nor generosity, nor honesty, nor brains; but read what the great Divines and Doctors of England said about him! Charles II, his grandson, was a rogue, but not a Snob; whilst Louis XIV, squaretoes of a contemporary – the great worshipper of Bigwiggery – has always struck me as a most undoubted and Royal Snob.

W. M. THACKERAY, 1885

THE SOT

Mr Rogers said it was not a thing to be said of any Sovereign Prince, be his weaknesses what they will, to be called a sot, which methinks was very prettily said. SAMUEL PEPYS

SPORT

King Henry the Second of England (or his son Richard: I name both, but shun to distinguish clearly, since my story is in his dishonour), early in his reign, cast his best falcon at a heron, loving that cruel sport. The heron circled higher and higher; but the falcon, the swifter, had almost overtaken him, when the King, feeling sure of triumph cried out, 'By God's eyes or his gorge, that bird shan't escape now, even though God Himself should swear that he should!' (for they had learnt to swear like this in their insolence of youth; and such habits are hard to forswear; even as Henry's grandsire, Henry I, used to swear 'By God's Death'). At these words the heron at once turned to bay; and by a most miraculous transformation from victim to tormentor, thrust his beak into the falcon's head, dashed out his brains and (himself quite whole and unhurt) cast the dying bird to the ground, at the very feet of the King.

GIRALDUS CAMBRENSIS. Opera Omnia, c. 1195

Whereas the people of our realm, rich and poor alike, were accustomed formerly in their games to practise archery – whence by God's help, it is well known that high honour and profit came to our realm, and no small advantage to ourselves in our warlike enterprises – and that now skill in the use of the bow having fallen almost wholly into disrepute, our subjects give themselves up to the throwing of stones and of wood and of iron; and some to handball and football and hockey; and others to coursing and cockfights, and even to other unseemly sports less useful and manly; whereby our realm – which God forbid – will soon, it would appear, be void of archers: we, wishing that a fitting remedy be found in this matter, do hereby ordain, that in all places in your county, liberties or no liberties, wheresoever you shall deem fit, a proclamation be made to this effect: that every man in the same county, if he be able-bodied, shall upon holidays, make use, in his games, of bows and arrows. . . .

Moreover we ordain that you prohibit under penalty of imprisonment all and sundry from such stone, wood and iron throwing; handball, football, or hockey; coursing and cockfighting; or other such idle games.

KING EDWARD III, to the Lord-Lieutenant of Kent

There were certain gentlemen that did strive who should first take away a goose's head, which was hanged alive on two crossposts.

KING EDWARD VI, Diary

Wyatt probably first met his cousin, Anne Boleyn, when she returned from the French court in 1522. Although married he soon became her lover, a dangerous condition once Henry also grew interested in her. Henry warned Wyatt during a bowls match, at which Wyatt measured the distance between the bowls with a locket and Henry pointed with a finger wearing a ring, each of these trophies taken from Anne. Wyatt later told Henry precisely what his connection with Anne had been and warned him against making a queen of such a woman.

THOMAS HINDE, 1986, on Sir Thomas Wyatt, poet,
courtier, Clerk of the King's Jewels

The quarrel had smouldered between the Duke [of Norfolk] and Lord Robert Dudley; between the Duke and the Earl of Leicester it now flared out.

On a day in March 1565 the two men were playing tennis, a fast indoor game for which Henry VIII, who was very fond of it, had put up a building in Hampton Court, with a gallery for spectators. The Queen was watching, and, as it was reported to Randolph, 'My Lord Robert, being very hot and sweating, took the Queen's napkin out of her hand and wiped his face.' The familiarity of the action drove Norfolk into a frenzy; he threatened Leicester's face with his racquet. The spectators were aghast at the commotion, and the Queen's indignation was directed against the Duke of Norfolk. The news of the episode ran the length of the British Isles and was thoroughly exasperating to Randolph, still working to bring about a marriage between Lord Leicester and the Queen of Scots.

ELIZABETH JENKINS, 1961

Thomas Randolph was English ambassador to Scotland.

Like all the Stuarts, James was a fanatic for physical exercise. Perhaps hunting, his favourite sport, freed him from the restrictions of his body; on horseback the ungainly youth became a fleet-footed centaur.

For all the dancing of his childhood, a necessary courtly practice, and possibly golf (there is definite evidence that Mary Queen of Scots played, and James in his turn received presents of 'two golfe clubbes'), the result of this arid concentrated upbringing was to produce what was in effect a little old man. A coin of the period displays the pathetic sight of the slight boy King armed with an enormous sword, a weapon from which the pacific James would have flinched in real life. It illustrates the contrast between his magnificent theoretical position and his tutored practical present.

ANTONIA FRASER, 1974 on King James VI and I

Thence to the Tennis Court, and there saw the King play at tennis, and others: but to see how the King's play was extolled without any cause at all was a loathesome sight, though sometimes, indeed, he did play very well and deserved to be commended; but such open flattery is beastly.

SAMUEL PEPYS, on King Charles II, 1664

James II's passion for hunting was as great as that of his grand-father, James I. The year before he became king, he took part in a famous run which began in Windsor Forest, crossed Middlesex, and ended in Wintry Forest in Essex. He was the first king to hunt fox – never beasts of the forest and previously considered fit quarry only for the lesser gentry. Some fifteen years later, Queen Anne, the last monarch to hunt enthusiastically at Windsor, did so in the most eccentric style of all. When she grew too fat to ride she would pursue her quarry in a single horse carriage with enormously tall wheels, dismaying farmers of the forest by driving across their standing corn. On occasions she would travel 50 miles a day in this contraption. When a deer was killed horns were blown and its head ceremoniously cut off by the senior man present.

THOMAS HINDE, 1985

As he was of wonderful agility, when he had outstripped the swiftest of the racers, he ran again in his boots, and beat them, though running in their shoes.

SIR JOHN DALRYMPLE, on James, Duke of Monmouth. *Memories of Great Britain and Ireland*, 1790

After all the labours of the chase, all the riding, the trotting, the galloping, the leaping; after being wet through overhead and soused through underfoot, and popped into ditches and jerked over gates ... after all this, fagging away like mad from eight in the morning to five or six in the afternoon we come, looking like so many drowned rats, with not a dry thread about us – and then after all this, what do you think follows? 'Here, Goldsworthy,' cries his

Majesty . . . 'Sir,' says I, smiling agreeably with the rheumatism creeping all over me . . . 'Here, Goldsworthy, I say,' he cries, 'will you have a little barley water?' Barley water in such a plight as that! Fine compensation for a wet jacket truly! . . . Barley water after a whole day's hard hunting! And there it was, standing ready in a jug, fit for the sick room.

COLONEL GOLDSWORTHY, to Fanny Burney, on King George III

A vulgar business.

QUEEN CHARLOTTE, consort of King George III, on horseracing

On these occasions [deer-stalking] the Prince wore a grey tartan of his own design, but his appearance in a kilt left something to be desired, if contemporary accounts are to be believed. Emily Crawford speaks of 'the want of whipcord in his thews which proclaims that he is no Highlander'. In general, the kilt was not becoming to 'gentlemen of German physique', she maintained. 'It needs the feline cleanness of build and muscularity of the mountain Celt for the bare knees and legs to look well.'

If the Prince Consort was no hero to his tailor, he likewise lacked valour in the eyes of the gillies with whom he stalked, for quite early he sought to introduce Teutonic efficiency into what had hitherto been a casual sport. Among his 'German tricks', as the gillies called them, the Prince caused to be constructed an elaborate system of trenchworks on a favourite feeding-ground of the deer; this was so that His Royal Highness could approach closer to his quarry before aiming. The Marquis of Huntly overheard two gillies condemn this unsporting practice in no uncertain terms. Also, the Prince was fond of hunting with stag-hounds, and these dogs would often tear the deer to shreds while it was still alive. (The Prince later discontinued this practice; however, it was fairly widespread judging by the prominence which Landseer gives to deer-hounds in his early Highland sketches.) Donald Stewart, the Queen's forester, undoubtedly voiced the disgust of the other gillies when he declared, 'I would rather give a man a week's shooting in the forest than to let loose a hound on a single occasion.'

To make matters worse, Prince Albert was anything but a skilled performer with a gun. He himself was candid enough about his shortcomings. On his very first visit to Balmoral we find him writing to his step-mother, the Dowager Duchess of Coburg, on September 11, 1848, 'I, naughty man, have been creeping stealthily after the harmless stags, and today I shot two red deer – at least, I hope so, for they are not yet found.'   TOM CULLEN, 1960

We went out grouse-shooting every day and the last day M. Poklewski-Koziell, the first Secretary of the Russian Embassy, joined the party. No one knew whether he was safe or not, and as grouse-driving is a particularly dangerous type of shooting, King Edward VII was consulted. He at once hit upon a solution and suggested that Poklewski should be placed on the right of the line and I should go next to him to see whether he was safe. I didn't care much about this as, if he was not a safe shot, I should only find this out by being peppered. It reminded me of a Shah of Persia who on a visit to England was shown the gallows, which interested him very much. He asked whether he could see it in use, but the Governor of the gaol said that unfortunately they had no one who was to be hanged. 'That is all right. Take one of my suite!' exclaimed the Shah.

SIR FREDERICK PONSONBY, 1951, on a visit to Abingdon, 1906

A game of golf:
In the afternoon Queen Alexandra and I played against Princess Victoria and Francis Knollys. The Queen seemed to confuse it with hockey and was under the impression that one had to prevent the opponent putting the ball in the hole. This usually ended by a scrimmage on the green. She also thought that the person who got into the hole first won it, and asked me to hurry up and run between the strokes. It was very good fun, and we all laughed. Francis

Knollys always played in a square billycock hat and a London tailcoat, and hit so hard that his hat almost invariably fell off.

SIR FREDERICK PONSONBY, 1951

At the cottage, our immediate family would be foregathered, together with a lady-in-waiting for Mama and an equerry for Papa, a governess for Mary, and one or two tutors for my brothers and me. The little house would be full almost to bursting, so much so that when someone asked where the servants slept, my father answered that he really didn't know, but supposed it was in the trees. Then for a week the fields and coverts of the estate resounded all day long to the fusillades of my grandfather and his guests, as they proceeded with a methodical decimation of the clouds of pheasants that had been raised the previous summer. . . . Sometimes Bertie and I were allowed to watch the afternoon's shooting. That was an era when monarchs and princes, noblemen and tycoons vied with each other for the honour of bringing down the largest number of birds. When dusk in its slow descent brought an end to the shooting, the day's kill might total nearly 2,000 pheasants.

We were six hours in the field and the show of birds was fantastic. My father was deadly that day and used three guns. He had an individual stylized way of shooting – left arm extended straight along the barrel, both eyes open. An onlooker reported that at one stand he saw my father bring down thirty-nine pheasants before missing one. . . . When in the late afternoon the carnage stopped, almost 4,000 pheasants had been killed. The bright, limp carcases were laid out in rows of 100; the whole place was littered with feathers and spent cartridges. My father had shot over 1,000 birds; I had even passed the 500 mark. He was proud of the way he had shot that day, but I think that the scale of the bag troubled even his conscience; for, as we drove back to London, he remarked, 'Perhaps we went a little too far today, David.'

EDWARD, DUKE OF WINDSOR, on Lord Burnham's shoot
for King George V, 1913

It was so stiff. I would have turned cartwheels for sixpence.

QUEEN MARY, on a shooting party

The English people like riding, and it would make you very unpopular if you couldn't do so. If you can't ride, you know, I am afraid people will call you a duffer.

KING GEORGE V, to Edward, Prince of Wales, later King Edward VIII

STAMPS

SIR ARTHUR DAVIDSON: I know how interested Your Royal Highness is in stamps. Did you happen to see in the newspapers that some damned fool had given as much as £1,400 for one stamp?
PRINCE OF WALES, later King George V: I was the damned fool.

STATE OCCASIONS

In the presence of the bishops, abbots and nobles of the whole realm of Albion, Archbishop Aldred consecrated William, Duke of Normandy, as King of England, and placed the royal crown on his head in the church of St Peter the Apostle, called Westminster Abbey, where the venerable King Edward lies buried. . . . Meanwhile, incited by the Devil, enemy of all good men, an accident filled with evil to both peoples, an omen of future disasters, occurred without warning. For when Aldred was demanding of the English, and Bishop Geoffrey of Coutances of the Normans, whether they consented to William's accession, and the whole assembly loudly proclaimed their willing assent, with one voice but not one tongue, the men-at-arms on guard outside the Abbey, hearing the joyful shouts of acclamation raised by those within, in a language alien to them, suspected treachery and rashly set fire to the houses nearby. Flames rapidly spreading, those in the Abbey were gripped by panic in the very midst of their joys, and hordes of men and women of all classes, fiercely struggled to scape from the church, as if from threats of instant peril. Only the bishops, with some few clerics and monks, stood their ground before the altar, and, trembling with fear, completed their coronation office only with some difficulty, the King himself being greatly alarmed.

ORDERICUS VITALIS, on Christmas Day 1066.
Historiae Ecclesiastica Angliae et Normandie, c. 1136

The King on a large charger suitable for such a person and royally caparisoned, rode after the Marshal, Henry Percy, and the Steward, John, Duke of Lancaster. His sword was borne aloft by Simon Burley (executed 1388), and Sir Nicholas Brode, on foot, led him by the rein. Knights, and those of his own age, and those of his household followed. There was no lack of musical accompaniment with horns and trumpets: the procession itself was preceded by its own trumpeters, and the Londoners had stationed trumpeters on the Water Conduit and on the tower they had erected in the King's honour in the self-same market place, who blew their instruments on the royal arrival: the combined noise was indeed wonderful! In the King's honour the citizens had ordered that wine should flow continually in the Conduit pipes throughout the procession, thus for over three hours. They had also built a castle with four towers at the top of the market called the Cheap, from which wine flowed abundantly in two places. On each of the four towers was a beauteous maiden all in white, of the King's own age and height. When the King approached, the four maidens scattered coins golden and counterfeit before him and his horse. When he reached the castle they took golden cups, filled them with wine from the castle pipes, and handed them to the King and the Lords. Atop the castle, between the four towers, was a dome surmounted by a golden angel holding a crown of gold, so ingeniously fashioned that it appeared to offer the King a bow, as he approached.

THOMAS WALSINGHAM, on the coronation of King Richard II, aged ten, 1377. *Chronica Majora*, 1308–46

The Coronation of Elizabeth I, 1550:

On Sunday the twenty-fifth of January, her Majesty was with great solemnity crowned at Westminster in the abbey church there, by Doctor Oglethorpe, Bishop of Carlisle. She dined in Westminster Hall, which was richly hung, and everything ordered in such royal manner, as to such a regal and most solemn feast appertained. In the meantime, whilst her grace sat at dinner, Sir Edward Dimmocke knight, her champion by office, came riding into the hall in fair complete armour, mounted upon a beautiful courser, richly trapped in cloth of gold, entered the hall, and in the midst thereof cast down his gauntlet: with offer to fight with him in her quarrel, that should deny her to be the righteous and lawful queen of this realm. The queen, taking a cup of gold full of wine, drank to him thereof, and sent it to him for his fee together with the cover.

RAPHAEL HOLINSHED, 1577

The Coronation of George IV, 1821:

The Queen has written to Lord Liverpool to say she means to go to the Coronation, desires to have ladies of high rank appointed to hold her train, and wishes to know *what dress* His Majesty would desire her to wear!! The impudence of this woman is beyond belief. It would have been well to have sent her word to appear in a white sheet. Lord Liverpool wrote her word that it was the King's prerogative to order the ceremonial as he pleased, and that it was not his intention that she should assist at the ceremony. However, she has written another letter to say she is determined to go.

HARRIET ARBUTHNOT, on Caroline of Brunswick, estranged wife of King George IV. *Journal*, 1821

The great sight was truly beautiful both in the Hall and Abbey, perhaps more from the brilliancy of the Spectators than from the sight itself, but the whole thing was indeed very handsome in the Procession and the variety and beauty of the dresses had a very fine effect. Much of the Ceremony in the Abbey was Monkish and twaddling and foolish and spun out, but the music and applause had a grand effect. He [the King] was very well received every-where, and seemed much gratified and had a complete victory over the Queen, who if she could have been lower than she was before, would have made herself so by her miserable attempt of yesterday. Even the Mob and Spectators hooted her away after she had been refused at every door and had walked thro' the mob with only Ly Anne [Hamilton] and jostled by all the lowest rabble. Think what a degradation for a Queen, if Queen she can be called.

LADY PALMERSTON. *Letters*, 1821

The King behaved very indecently; he was continually nodding and winking at Ly Conyngham and sighing and making eyes at her. At one time in the Abbey he took a diamond brooch from his breast and, looking at her, kissed it, on which she took off her glove and kissed a ring she had on!! Anybody who could have seen his disgusting figure, with a wig the curls of which hung down his back, and quite bending beneath the weight of his robes and his 60 years would have been quite sick.　　　HARRIET ARBUTHNOT, 1821

The poor Queen, attended only by a shadow of her former rabble, tried to get into the Abbey by a side door, but was driven away with shouts of 'Shame' and 'Off, off'.　　　SIR ARTHUR BRYANT, 1950

> Yes, my hat, Sirs,
> Think of that, Sirs,
> 　　Vast and plumed and Spain-like,
> See my big
> Grand robes; my wig

Young, yet lion-mane like.
    Glory! Glory!
I'm not hoary,
        Age it can't come o'er me;
Mad caps, grave caps, gazing on the grand man,
    All alike adore me.

LEIGH HUNT. Coronation Soliloquy, 1821

At the Tomb of Napoleon I, Paris, 1855:

There was not a word. All contemplated the coffin in silence. Before me stood Prince Albert, in the red coat of a Field-Marshal; beside the Queen was the Prince of Wales in Highland outfit, with velvet jacket, fur sporran and kilt; to the right was Princess Mathilde, whose fine features were heightened by the torches, and recalled those of her uncle [Napoleon].

After a moment of meditation, of utter silence, the Queen, respectful, calm, severe, turned to the Prince of Wales and put a hand on his shoulder. 'Kneel before the tomb of the great Napoleon.' At that instant a terrible storm, which the torrid heat of the last few days had been preparing, burst forth. Huge claps of thunder shook all the chapel windows, and the clatter echoed through the vaults. Swift, incessant flashes of lightning gave an aspect almost supernatural to the moving and solemn tableau by continually lighting it with unnatural brilliance.

For myself, at first I was absorbed, then profoundly touched, almost breaking down; I began to see nothing. Waterloo, St Helena . . . the English Alliance . . . England, symbolized by her queen and future king now on his knees before Napoleon's remains, all made my senses reel. Giddiness overcame me. I was near the door and had hurriedly to withdraw. No longer able to control myself, I was obliged to weep. GENERAL CANROBERT, Memoirs

There I stood at the arm of Napoleon III, his nephew, before the coffin of England's bitterest foe; I, granddaughter of that king who hated him most, and who most vigorously opposed him, and this

336

very nephew, who bears his name, being my nearest and dearest ally! The organ of the church was playing 'God Save the Queen' at the time, and this solemn scene took place by torch light, and during a thunder-storm. Strange and wonderful indeed. It seems as if in this tribute of respect to a departed foe, old enmities and rivalries were wiped out, and the seal of Heaven placed upon that bond of unity, which is now happily established between two great and powerful nations. May Heaven bless and prosper it.

QUEEN VICTORIA, Diary

Queen Victoria's Diamond Jubilee, 1897:

The great day opened with a touch of haze. But at the very instant that she left the palace the sun, no less punctual and always conscious of its duty to the British Empire, shone out resplendently. It saw the head of the procession winding through the roaring streets – Lord Roberts on his little grey, New South Wales Lancers, Queensland Mounted Rifles, Rhodesian Horse led by the Hon. Maurice Gifford with his empty sleeve, black men in orange caps, brown men in turbans, fezzed Zaptiehs from Cyprus, Hausas from the west coast of Africa, broad-faced Dyaks from Borneo, Chinamen from Hong Kong in the most unlikely hats, the whole variegated spectrum of the British Empire passing through the streets of London in honour of the small imperial emblem seated behind them in an open landau beneath a parasol. That was her rôle, less personal than it had been in former years. For though the crowds acclaimed the little figure in black chiffon and white ostrich feathers, their cheers were less for that miracle of longevity than for their own immense achievement, for the imperial effort which had linked one-fifth of the habitable world in allegiance to the old lady who sat there smiling through her tears and nodding at them with her bonnet.

When she reached St Paul's the vast procession halted. The cathedral steps were packed with clergy, choristers, and bandsmen; and as she sat there in her carriage and the sun blazed down on them, there was a short service of thanksgiving and the waiting crowds caught up the solemn air of the Old Hundredth. That was the crowning moment, when she sat beneath her parasol among the standing horses and the halted men and the Archbishop gave thanks to God for her survival. Then he called for cheers; and as St Paul's Churchyard rang with her subjects' acclamations, the slow drive resumed. The City roared its gratitude; the Lord Mayor took an emotional farewell outside the Mansion House after his perilous feats of equitation; and the royal carriage with the nodding aigrette and the white parasol crossed London Bridge to taste the welcome of her poorer subjects. If they had any grievances, they were forgotten in the uproar. Six miles of roaring Englishmen acclaimed her before she got back to the palace for a quiet lunch; and in the evening she did her best to speak to all the princes and princesses after a state banquet. But she was very tired. For if it was exhausting to be Queen of England, it was a still heavier burden to have become the emblem of an Empire. That was the strange destiny of Albert's widow and Lord Melbourne's pupil and the granddaughter of George III.

PHILIP GUEDALLA, 1936

We stood about in the picture gallery till 11.15 talking to the guests. . . . What rot and a waste of time, money and energy all these State visits are!! This is my only remark on all this unreal show and ceremony!!

EDWARD, PRINCE OF WALES, later King Edward VIII, on the visit of the King and Queen of Denmark. *Diary*, 1913

STRIKES

Strikes are now quite the fashion all over the country.

> ALBERT, PRINCE CONSORT, to Baron Stockmar, 1853, on the strikes
> periodically obstructing the rebuilding of Balmoral Castle

That was a rotten way to run a revolution; I could have done it better myself.　　　KING GEORGE V, on the General Strike, 1926

TACT

When I came down to breakfast at ten I found somewhat better news about the Queen; the Prince of Wales had returned and the German Emperor had arrived. Although the rest of the Royal Family seemed to resent his coming and no-one had asked him to come, he behaved in a most dignified and admirable manner. He said to the Princesses, 'My first wish is not to be in the light, and I will return to London if you wish. I should like to see Grandmamma before she dies, but if that is impossible I shall quite understand.' Nothing could have been better. . . .

At about half past six we were told that the end had come. The Duke of Argyll told me that the last moments were like a great three-decker ship sinking. She kept on rallying and then sinking. The behaviour of the German Emperor was beyond all praise. He kept in the background until they were all summoned. The Prince and Princess of Wales, Princess Christian, Princess Louise, and Princess Beatrice stood around the bed, while the German Emperor knelt down and supported the Queen with his arm, while [Sir James] Reid held her up on the other side. The Emperor never moved for two and a half hours and remained quite still. His devotion to the Queen quite disarmed all the Royal Family.

Sir Frederick Ponsonby, 1951,
on Kaiser Wilhelm II at Osborne House, 1901

TACTLESSNESS

Dinner conversation with ladies was awkward for Kitchener, who had little experience of them and at forty-eight was a solitary, saturnine bachelor. Victoria was not slow to fill the silences, however, as she was eager to tell the liberator of Khartoum how she had upbraided and embarrassed Gladstone after Gordon's death by her telegram *en clair*. Monopolizing the conversation (one did not interrupt the Queen), she went on about what was a favourite subject. At a rare pause, Kitchener seized his opportunity. The capture of Omdurman, he confessed, left him greatly inconvenienced by having two thousand Sudanese women on his hands. Princess Beatrice asked what they were like, which briefly baffled Kitchener. 'Very much like all women,' he said, finally; 'they talked a great deal.'

STANLEY WEINTRAUB, 1987, on Lord Kitchener's Balmoral visit, 1898

THE THIEF

Lord Duncannon was walking with William IV, he said, in Kensington Gardens one day, and when they got to a certain spot the King said to him, 'It was here, my Lord, that my great-grandfather, King George II, was robbed. He was in the habit of walking every morning alone round the garden, and one day a man jumped over the wall, approached the King with great respect, and told him he was in distress, and was compelled to ask him for his money, his watch and the buckles in his shoes. The King gave him what he had about him, and the man knelt down to take off his buckles, all the time with profound respect. When he had got everything, the King told him that there was a seal on the watch-chain of little or no value, but which he wished to have back, and requested he would take it off the chain and restore it. The man said, "Your Majesty must be aware that we have already been here some time, and that it is not safe for me to stay longer, but if you will give me your word not to say anything of what has passed for twenty-four hours, I will place the seal at the same hour to-morrow morning on that stone", pointing to a particular place. The King promised, went the next morning at the appointed hour, the man appeared, brought the seal, and then jumped over the wall and went off.'

CHARLES GREVILLE. *Diary*, 1843

TOBACCO

And for the vanities committed in this filthy custom, is it not both great vanity and uncleanness, that at the table, a place of respect, of cleanliness, of modesty, that men should not be ashamed, to sit tossing of tobacco pipes and puffing of the smoke of tobacco one to another, making the filthy smoke and stink thereof, to exhale across the dishes, and infect the air, when very often men that abhor it are at their repast? Surely smoke becomes a kitchen far better than a dining chamber, and yet it makes a kitchen also oftentimes in the inward parts of men, soiling and infecting them with an unctuous and oily kind of soot, as hath been found in some great tobacco takers, that after their death were opened. And not only meat time, but no other time nor action is exempted from the public use of this uncivil trick. . . .

But herein is not only a great vanity, but a great contempt of God's good gifts, that the sweetness of man's breath, being a good gift of God, should be wilfully corrupted by this stinking smoke. . . .

Have you not reason then to be ashamed, and to forbear this filthy novelty, so basely grounded, so foolishly received, and so grossly mistaken in the right use thereof? In your abuse thereof sinning against God, harming yourselves both in persons and goods, and raking also thereby the marks and notes of vanity upon you; by the custom thereof making yourselves to be wondered at by all foreign civil nations, and by all strangers that come upon you to be scorned and contemned: a custom loathsome to the eye, hateful to the nose, harmful to the brain, dangerous to the lungs, and in the black stinking fume thereof, nearest resembling the horrible Stygian smoke of the pit that is bottomless.

KING JAMES VI AND I. From *A Counterblast to Tobacco*, 1604

Edward's self-permissive conduct as Prince of Wales and King, was partly a reaction to his mother's impossibly virtuous standards of conduct. When Lady Beaconsfield once suggested that her son must be a great comfort to her, Queen Victoria replied, 'Comfort! Why, I caught him smoking a fortnight after his dear father died!'

RICHARD COLLIER, 1984

TRAVEL

A couple of inventories, one made at Lanercost in January 1307 of the royal plate, and a much more detailed list drawn up at Burgh-on-Sands ten days after King Edward I's death, give an idea of what the king usually carried with him. Besides such expected items as gold buckles and fifty-nine gold rings (often given as presents to favoured visitors), a gold cup given him by young Queen Margaret (his second wife) three years before and a pair of table knives with crystal handles, there were two chests with relics of all kinds. These included the usual fragments of bone of a number of saints, especially English saints such as St Richard of Chichester and St William of York, an arm of St David (probably acquired during the conquest of Wales), a reliquary with some milk of the Virgin Mary, a thorn from Christ's crown of thorns and, more unexpectedly, 'a saint's tooth which acts as a protection against thunderstorms'.

MARGARET WADE LABARGE, 1982

He was the first English sovereign of whom it could fairly be said that he knew the world. King Edward had met the Americans in America, the Canadians in Canada, the Indians in India: he had travelled in Spain, Italy, and Russia: he was at home in Denmark and Germany: he especially enjoyed Austria and he loved Paris and the French. He was always loyal to the affections of his youth and he first fell under the charm of Paris when, as a boy, he visited the French emperor with his parents and asked his host whether he could not stay behind, adding that he would not be missed at home because he had so many brothers and sisters. Though this was not an accomplishment of his fellow countrymen or of his generation, he was a remarkable linguist. He spoke German almost inter-changeably with English, and the statesman Haldane was greatly struck by his command of German slang. He had good working knowledge of Italian and Spanish and he spoke French beautifully, showing himself a past master in the idiomatic subtlety of that language. This experience, this capacity through his knowledge of languages to sense something of contemporary feeling abroad, at once gave him authority. The majority of the aristocracy, of cabinet ministers, and of civil servants knew little enough of foreign lands: they travelled to Paris, or to that England by the Mediterranean discovered by Lord Brougham, and too often contented them-selves, as did the Kickleburies on the Rhine, with the intelligence that tea abroad was made from boiled boots.

ROGER FULFORD, 1964, on King Edward VII, in
Edwardian England: 1901–1914

The country, and all of *us*, would like to see you a little more stationary.   QUEEN VICTORIA, to Edward Albert, Prince of Wales

Few sovereigns can have set out for a foreign capital with less illusions than did King Edward when he crossed the Channel in the *Alexandra*, the smaller of the two royal yachts, on 8 February 1909. He had never been eager to go, and his Queen, as he well knew, loathed the prospect. To make matters worse, he was feeling dis-tinctly out of sorts and pining for the early spring sun of Biarritz.

In these circumstances, what was needed, apart from reason-able weather in the German capital, was a programme that went off without a hitch. The King was destined to get neither. Indeed, it was as though an army of mischievous gremlins had boarded the train at Calais alongside the King and his large suite and then had stuck to them throughout the journey.

They first showed their hand, in a very harmless way, at dinner on the train that night. A footman, thrown off his balance by a sudden lurch of the royal dining-car, upset a dish of quails right over the Queen's head, leaving one clinging to her hair. This was taken as a great joke, however, and the Queen set the whole company laughing by declaring that she would arrive in Berlin *coiffée de cailles*. Perhaps offended by this levity, the gremlins gave the carriage another jolt, upsetting the claret all over the table.

The next mishap was much more irritating. It took place, ominously, just as they were entering Brandenburg at the frontier town of Rathenow. A Prussian guard of honour with a Prussian military band were waiting on the platform, and the bandmaster had ordered them to strike up 'God Save the King' as the train stopped and to go on playing it until the King stepped out. Unfortunately, the King's valet had got the times mixed up and had only started dressing him when the train came to a halt. As a result, his suite, and everyone else on the platform, had to endure the British National Anthem played non-stop for ten minutes before the angry Monarch himself appeared, ready at last in the uniform of a German Field-Marshal.

That was not a very auspicious welcome to Prussia, but worse was to follow when they arrived an hour or two later at Berlin's Lehrter railway station. The imperial reception committee was waiting for the King to alight on the precise spot, marked on the platform, where his carriage was supposed to stop. Nobody had apparently informed them that he intended to disembark instead with the Queen from her carriage, which was to the rear of the train. As a result, the Kaiser, with his wife, and all the imperial and royal princes with their wives, had to scuttle more than a hundred yards down the platform in full regalia to bid their guests welcome.

From that point the soldiery took over (in the shape of a massive escort headed by the *Garde du Corps* which clattered ahead of the carriages) and the Kaiser must have thought that, with the army in charge, his troubles were now over. But it was not to be. As the procession got under way, one observer noticed that the carriages were not keeping their proper distances, 'the horses of one being almost in the legs of the footman standing up behind the preceding one so that the poor men kept turning round to see when they would be bitten'. But the sorst thing happened at the worst possible time, just as the cavalcade was approaching the palace, where the dutifully cheering crowd was at its thickest. The ceremonial coach containing Queen Alexandra and the German Empress suddenly stopped altogether and the horses drawing it reared up and then refused to move another yard, despite all the coaxing and whip-cracking of the coachmen. There was nothing for it but for the two royal ladies to dismount and get into an ordinary carriage behind. This vehicle had to be emptied of its occupants and so the process continued right down the line. Whether the last two passengers in the procession had to enter the palace courtyard on foot we are not told. And, as if this was not humiliating enough, two of the caval-rymen of Prince Salm-Salm's escort were thrown off their horses which then galloped around loose causing havoc throughout the squadron. One explanation offered afterwards was that the artil-lery salute had sounded unnaturally loud in the cold air, and had frightened the animals.

The wretched Kaiser, who had reached the courtyard of his *Schloss* with the King, only to find no procession behind him, was, understandably, furious and disinclined to accept any excuses. The Master of the Horse, Baron von Reischbach, was summoned to the presence to receive the stiffest reprimand of his life. Of all people, his Emperor asked him despairingly, why must it be the English, who are so proud about their horsemanship, who have to witness such a shambles? It was rumoured that the one person to be secretly delighted at all this confusion was Queen Alexandra. Presumably, she felt it was some consolation for all the damage that this same legendary Prussian war machine had once (1864) inflicted on her native land.

It is impossible not to feel somewhat sorry for the Kaiser over all this, especially as, inside the palace, he had done his level best to make Queen Alexandra and King Edward feel 'at home'. The Queen's suite of rooms during her stay, the so-called *Konigskam-mer* on the first floor, had been specially equipped with a concert piano for her use, and the Kaiser had personally seen to it that some works in Danish had been included among the books, while pictures of both Copenhagen and Sandringham had been hung on the walls. And in the study of the King's suite (the *Wilhelmsche Wohnung*) his nephew had placed not only a portrait of Queen Victoria, but also, propped up on a large easel, a coloured print of 'British Naval Victories', decorated with the figures of Nelson, St Vincent and Howe. He really could not have tried any harder to please.   GORDON BROOK-SHEPHERD, 1975

I could not help being struck by the way in which all salutations by the Natives were disregarded by the persons to whom they were given. Evidently we are too much inclined to look upon them as a conquered and down-trodden race and the Native, who is becoming more and more educated, realizes this. I could not help noticing that the general bearing of the European towards the Native was to say the least unsympathetic.

GEORGE, PRINCE OF WALES, later King George V, in his notes on India, 1906

Amsterdam, Rotterdam, and all the other dams! I'm damned if I'll do it.   KING GEORGE V, on a proposed state visit to Holland

Abroad is bloody.   (attrib.) KING GEORGE VI

TURKS

George I brought to England with him two Grooms of the Chamber who caused astonishment. They were Mohamet and Mustapha, Turks whom he had captured in Hungary some twenty-eight years earlier when he was fighting for the Emperor against Turkey. At the Hanoverian court during these years they had westernized themselves. Mohamet had married into a well-off Hanoverian family and become a Christian, taking the names of Ludwig Maximilian. He was eventually given by the Emperor the title of Ludwig von Konigstreu. But he retained an exotic imagination, and in England would entertain fellow courtiers with his account of the poisoning of George I's sister, the Queen of Prussia. Diamonds had been used, he claimed, which had made her stomach so thin that he could poke his fingers through it at any point.

Mohamet was also George I's Keeper of the Closet, and in practice joint Keeper of the King's Privy Purse. The privy purse of £30,000 was vital to George I. Because its accounts were secret – he could use it to pay the salaries of the Hanoverians he had brought with him, and so evade the Act of Settlement which prohibited the employment of foreigners – Mohamet used his position at court to enrich himself by selling offices. When he died, a year before George, Mustapha took on his duties and was also well-favoured and rewarded. THOMAS HINDE, 1986

TUTORS

I will tell you, and tell you a truth which perchance you will marvel at. One of the greatest benefits that ever God gave me is that He sent me, with sharp, severe parents, so gentle a schoolmaster. When I am in presence of either father or mother, whether I speak, keep silence, sit, stand or go, eat, drink, be merry or sad, be sewing, playing, dancing or doing anything else, I must do it, as it were, in such weight, measure and number, even as perfectly as God made the world – or else I am so sharply taunted, so cruelly threatened, yea, presented sometimes with punches, nips and bobs and other ways – which I will not name for the honour I bear them – so without measure misordered, *that I think myself in hell* – till the time comes when I must go to Mr Aylmer (her tutor), who teacheth me so gently, so pleasantly, with such allurements, that I think all the time nothing while I am with him.

LADY JANE GREY, to Roger Ascham

One unexpected consequence of our cold war against Mlle Dussau was the decision by my father to call in from semi-retirement another of the former teachers of his naval cadet days – a venerable Anglicized Frenchman with a black beard, a bald head, and the improbable name of Gabriel Hua. Mr Hua could hardly have looked upon my father as one of his most successful pupils, as my father, who no doubt considered French a somewhat effeminate language, would deliberately mispronounce French words whenever they appeared on the menu. Nevertheless, the former pupil held his old tutor in high regard. Mr Hua was an erudite man, a famous and revered Master at Eton with a host of friends. . . .

One day at lunch when we were at Frogmore, Mr Hua digressed from a learned exposition of the subjunctive to praise the excellence of the French cuisine, dwelling at some length on the merit of frogs' legs. As we children had no idea that frogs were in any way edible, our immediate conclusion was that Mr Hua had made up a good story. But, as he talked on, his earnestness impressed us; and we finally realized with amazement that not only did Mr Hua make a practice of eating the legs of frogs but he considered them one of the most succulent delicacies.

I think it was Mary who first had the idea of exploiting Mr Hua's eccentricity, but my mother was in on it, too. Armed with a fine-mesh net and bucket, we sallied forth to the lake in search of frogs. But, as it was the spawning season, we had to content ourselves with a catch of tadpoles. These we carried triumphantly to the kitchen and instructed the cook to broil and serve them on toast that evening as a special savoury dish for the French tutor. Mr Hua was, of course, ignorant of the plot; and when the time came for the savoury and the footman passed the dish to him, I saw out of

349

the corner of my eye that all the conspirators wore an expression of pleasurable anticipation.

Of course, it had not been our intention to carry the joke to the point of allowing the French tutor actually to eat the tadpoles; but, before my mother could utter a warning, he had hungrily attacked the toast with his knife and fork and conveyed a large piece to his mouth. Mama cried, 'No, no! That special savoury is not meant to be eaten at all.' But it was too late.

Horror gripped the whole table. We all expected Mr Hua to be seized at once by a dreadful convulsion. Realizing that something was amiss, he asked in alarm what was wrong. It was Mary, as I remember it, who finally stammered out in a stricken voice the awful truth.

My impression is that Mr Hua gallantly swallowed what was already in his mouth, but wounded pride was in the glance with which he swept the table. With a curt bow to my mother, he strode from the dining-room, his beard bristling with suppressed agitation. Mama's eyes twinkled. 'I am afraid,' she said, smiling, 'that between *grenouilles* and *tetards* a French gourmet draws a fine line.' She directed me to seek out Mr Hua in his room, to make my apology, and to bring him back, mollified, to the dinner-table.

EDWARD, DUKE OF WINDSOR, 1951

VANITY

The great and glorious news from Russia of which I have, under Providence, the heartfelt consolation, without unbecoming vanity, to ascribe in a great degree to my own original and indefatigable endeavours in drawing that Power to those measures which have since been pursued.

GEORGE, PRINCE REGENT, on Napoleon's disasters,
to his mother, Queen Charlotte; 1812

He attributes every wonderful event now passing in the world to his own great talent.   A court lady, on the Prince Regent

VICTORIA

She wore geranium flowers placed here, there, and everywhere. She had plump hands with rings on each finger and even on her thumbs; one of them held a ruby of prodigious size and of a superb blood-red. She found difficulty in using her knife and fork with hands thus loaded like reliquaries, and even more difficult to remove and replace her gloves. On her head was a diamond aigrette, pushed well back; and she wore her hair in long loops which fell over her ears. Her eyes were beautiful; straightforward and intelligent, and she had a sweet expression which gave one confidence. Her complexion was good; but her mouth somewhat spoilt her face which was otherwise pretty . . .

I can still see her – despite the great heat she wore a vast white silk bonnet with streamers behind and a tuft of marbout-feathers on top. . . . Her dress was white and flounced; but she had a mantle and a sunshade of crude green which to me jarred with the rest of her costume. When she put her foot on the steps she lifted her skirt, which (in the English fashion, they inform me), was very short and I saw she had small slippers tied with black ribbons crossed about her ankles. My gaze chiefly fell on a voluminous object carried under her arm, an enormous reticule – like those of our grand-mammas – of white satin or silk on which was embroidered a fat poodle in gold. The Queen I considered very small, but of a most friendly appearance; above all, despite the dreadful toilette, I was struck by her air of dignity.

GENERAL CANROBERT, on Queen Victoria in Paris, 1855. *Memoirs*

Queen Victoria had a beautiful voice and first rate delivery at an age when she could not have played any part on the stage presentably except the nurse in *Romeo and Juliet*.

GEORGE BERNARD SHAW, 1924, to Cecil Lewis

That was a woman! One could do business with her.

PRINCE OTTO VON BISMARCK, on Queen Victoria, 1888

Queen Victoria was like a great paper-weight that for half a century sat upon men's minds, and when she was removed their ideas began to blow about all over the place haphazardly.

H. G. WELLS, in conversation

VICTORY

Thus have we defeated the King of France at Gisors, but it is not we who have done the same, but rather God and our Right.

KING RICHARD I, to the Bishop of Durham

This is the reputed origin of 'Dieu et mon Droit', the British royal motto.

Poitiers, 1356

In the evening the Prince of Wales gave a supper to the French King; for all the vast quantities of provisions that the French had brought with them had fallen into the hands of the English, many of whom had not tasted bread for three days. The Prince also invited the greater part of the counts and barons who had been captured. The King of France and his son Prince Philip were placed at a finely spread table set on a dais. . . .

The Prince himself served the King's table, and all the other tables as well, with every mark of humility, and refused to sit at the King's table, despite many pleadings, declaring that he was still unworthy of so great an honour, and that it would not be seemly for him to sit at the same board as so great a prince, and one who that day had displayed so much valour. He then knelt before the King and continued: 'Sire, do not dine in despair that God has failed your demands: the Lord my father will certainly show to you all honour and amity in his power, and will treat you so reasonably that you will remain the best of friends for ever. . . . To my mind you have all reason for rejoicing, even if the victory was ours; for today you have won a name for valour surpassing all the knights of France. Dear Sir, I do not utter mere flattery, for all in our ranks who saw the contest agree that this is your due and award you the laurels.'

As he said this, murmers of assent and praise arose from English and French alike, that the Prince had spoken nobly, and that the future would hail him as one of the most gallant Lords in all the world, if God allowed him life to pursue his glory.   FROISSART

VIRGINITY

Her intellect and personal magnetism had come to her from King Henry VIII; at his hands also she had received a nervous injury so deep-seated and severe that it had left her with a life-long incapacity to submit herself to a normal sexual relationship.

When she was two years and eight months old her mother Anne Boleyn was beheaded on a five-fold charge of adultery. Just before her arrest, the Queen was seen in the courtyard of Greenwich Palace holding up her little girl in her arms, in a despairing attempt to win a smile from the angry King as he stood frowning in a window above them. Three days later she was committed to the Tower, where her head was cut off on May 19th, three years to the very month after the spectacular triumph of her coronation.

This was the first of a series of domestic events assuring Elizabeth, before her mind could defend itself by reason, that sexual intercourse was the bringer-on of some terrifying form of death. When she was four years old the King's third wife, Jane Seymour, achieved, at the expense of her own life, the feat of bearing him a living son. The association of her brother's birth with the death, after prolonged agonies, of his mother was one but too familiar in many households, but it was followed four years later by a third event, dreadful in itself and to Elizabeth an unspeakable calamity, for it repeated the horror of her mother's death at a time when she herself, no longer protected by infancy, had her faculties wide awake. When she was eight years and five months old the King's fifth wife, Catherine Howard, her mother's cousin, her young, enchanting step-mother, was suddenly brought to book as Anne Boleyn had been. When confined to her rooms in Hampton Court during an investigation, Catherine escaped from her guards and tried to reach the King in the chapel where he was at Mass. She was caught before she had reached the end of the gallery, and dragged back, uttering such screams that the spot is said to be haunted still. Accused, convicted of adultery, the young Queen was brought to the block early in the morning of a day in February. Her head and headless body, wrapped in a sheet, were carried into the chapel on Tower Green and buried under the flags where Elizabeth's mother was already lying. Within this year, while she was still called eight years old, Elizabeth said, 'I will never marry.'

She said it to another child of eight years old, John Dudley's fifth son, Robert Dudley. The boy to whom she said it did not believe her, but she had said it, and time was to show the implacable force of her determination.

When she reached years of discretion she preserved, with very few exceptions, a death-like silence over her mother's name; but she would seem to have thought much about this passionate, reckless woman, whose death lay like a pit in the road of her own young life. She gave signs in her later years that the memory of which she did not speak was living in her; she was strongly drawn to her mother's relatives and the descendants of her mother's friends, and the crowned falcon stamped on the bindings of Queen Elizabeth's books was a cognizance of Anne Boleyn's.

ELIZABETH JENKINS, 1961

WALES

Heart cold in the breast with terror, grieving
    For a king, oak door, of Aberffraw.
        Bright gold was bestowed by his hand,
      A gold chaplet befitted him.
A gold king's gold cups come not to me, mirth
    Of Llywelyn; not for me free raiment.
I grieve for a prince, hawk free of reproach,
    I grieve for the ill that befell him,
I grieve for the loss, I grieve for the lot,
    I grieve to hear how he was wounded.
Cadwaladr's stronghold, sharp-drilling safeguard,
    Lord of the red lance, gold-handed lord,
He showered riches, arrayed each winter
    Around me, the raiment around him.
    Lord rich in herds, he aids us no more,
    Life everlasting is left for him.
    Mine, rage at the Saxon who robbed me,
    Mine, before death, the need to lament.
Mine, with good reason, to rave against God
    Who has left me without him,
Mine to praise him, unstinting, unstilled,
    Mine to be ever mindful of him,
Mine all my lifetime sorrowing for him. . . .

GRUFFUDD AB YR YYNAD COCH (son of the Red Judge).
Lament for Llywelyn ap Gruffud, 1284, trs. Joseph P. Clancy

Llywelyn ap Gruffud, Lord of North Wales, was killed in a minor and almost accidental clash with the English at Builth in 1282. His head was struck off and exhibited on a stake in London. His death was disastrous for Welsh hopes of national independence and called forth many elegies, of which this apocalyptic outburst is the most remarkable.

GWYN JONES, 1983

Thus died that great Achilles the Second, the Lord Llywelyn, whose deeds I am unworthy to recount. For with lance and shield did he tame his foes; he kept peace for the men of religion; to the needy he gave good and raiment. With a wax-like chain he extended his boundaries; he showed justice to all, and by meet bonds of fear or love bound all men to him.

Cistercian chronicler, on Llywelyn the Great, 1240

When Scotland would rebel against him and all England would rid herself of him, the Welsh in a wonderful manner cherished and esteemed him and, as far as they were able, stood by him, grieving over his adversities both in life and in death, composing mournful songs about him in the language of their country, the memory of which lingers to the present time and which neither the dread of punishment nor the passage of time have destroyed.

A Wakefield chronicler, on King Edward II,
earlier the first Prince of Wales. 14th century

And he was beheaded at the Market Place, and his head set upon the highest grise of the market cross: and a mad woman combed his hair and washed away the blood of his face, and she got candles and set about him burning, more than a hundred. This Owen Tudor was father unto the Earl of Pembroke and had wedded Queen Katharine, King Henry VI's mother, weening and trusting all the

357

time that he would not be beheaded, till he saw the axe and the block; and when that he was in his doublet he trusted on pardon and grace till the collar of his red velvet doublet was ripped off. Then he said, 'That head shall lie on the stock that was wont to lie on Queen Katharine's lap'; and put his heart and mind wholly until God, and full meekly took his death.

WILLIAM GREGORY, on the death of Owain ap Maredudd ap Tudor,
after the battle of Mortimer's Cross, 1461.
Gregory's Chronicle, 1189–1469

Then Sir Rhys ap Thomas drawes Wales with him,
A worthy sight it was to see
How the Welshmen rose wholly with him,
And stogged them to Shrewsbury.

'The Rose of England', on the march of the Welsh supporters
of Henry Tudor towards victory at Bosworth, 1485

WARTIME

His brother, Earl Gurth, thus addressed him: 'It is best, dearest brother and lord, that your bravery should be tempered by discretion. You are weary from battle with the Northmen from which you have but now arrived, and you are eager to join the Normans in battle. Permit yourself, I beg you, some time to take rest. Consider, also, in your wisdom, on the oath you took to the Duke of Normandy. Beware of incurring guilt from perjury, lest by so serious a crime you pull down ruin on yourself and the arms of this nation, and stain for all time the honour of your own race. . . .

Harold was very ireful. Disdaining the sensible advice of his friends, he overwhelmed his brother with abuse for his loyal counsel, and even so far forgot himself as to kick his mother when she lingered in his presence in too great anxiety to keep him by her side.

ORDERICUS VITALIS, on King Harold II,
before the battle of Hastings, 1066. *Historia Ecclestiastica*, c. 1136

It is now that your arms must prove your strength and courage. If you fight like men, you will gain victory, honour and wealth. Otherwise you will be covered with eternal ignominy. No road is open for retreat. On one side armed men and a hostile and unknown country bar your passage. On the other the sea and other armed men are opposed to your flight. The carnage of a small number of warriors may easily overcome a greater number of men unskilled in fighting, above all when the cause of justice is protected by Divine aid. Let nothing stand in your way, and soon you will triumph.

DUKE WILLIAM OF NORMANDY, soon King William I of England,
before the Battle of Hastings, 1066

An anonymous chronicler wrote:
Then Duke William sailed from Normandy into Pevensey. When King Harold was informed of this he gathered together a great host and came to oppose him at the grey apple tree, and William came upon him before his army was set in order.

By the God of Heaven by whose grace I stand and in whom I put my trust, I would not have another man if I could. Wottest thou not that the Lord with these few can overthrow the pride of the French?

HENRY V, outnumbered at Agincourt, 1415

The King and Queen had decided to take the rations very seriously and at breakfast those who were late got nothing. . . . Godfrey-Faussett was kept on the telephone one day and came into the dining-room after everyone else had sat down. He found nothing to eat and immediately rang the bell and asked for a boiled egg. If he had ordered a dozen turkeys he could not have made a bigger stir. The King accused him of being a slave to his inside, of unpatriotic behaviour, and even went so far as to hint that we should lose the war on account of his gluttony.

SIR FREDERICK PONSONBY, 1951, on King George V

WATERLOO

A devoted Englishman, named Children, knowing George IV's passion for victory over the French, presented him with a chair made from the elm that Wellington sat under at Waterloo, an odd, rather ugly memento. George IV was also extremely proud of the despatch Wellington wrote after the battle to the government, a copy of which he kept as a most prized possession. For years afterwards he read it repeatedly to his guests. It arrived dramatically. Lord Liverpool, the Prime Minister, and the Regent were at a ball in St James's Square – Mrs Boehme's. Major Percy had ridden post haste from Waterloo in under two days, and was still bloodstained and dusty when he arrived. The ladies withdrew; Lord Liverpool read the despatch announcing victory; the Prince, gracious as ever at a moment of high drama, turned and said, 'I congratulate you, *Colonel* Percy' – giving the major instant promotion. Then he wept – wept at the thought of friends dead or maimed. And for the rest of his life Waterloo haunted him – its glory, its drama, its toll of death. Like any artist, he identified deeply, so deeply indeed that his descriptions of battles he had never fought were as real as if he had been there. There was an occasion when he described, in the Duke of Wellington's presence, a charge down an almost perpendicular hill, and looked to the Duke for confirmation. 'Very steep, Sir, very steep,' said the Duke, never at a loss for a word.

J. H. PLUMB, 1977

Doctor, I know that I am going but I should like to see another anniversary of the battle of Waterloo. Try if you cannot timber me up to last out that day.   KING WILLIAM IV, 1837

WEDDING NIGHT

I look well for one who has been in the midst of Spain.

(attrib.) PRINCE ARTHUR, on his marriage to Princess
Katharine of Aragon, later wife to King Henry VIII, 1501

A most gratifying and bewildering night.

QUEEN VICTORIA, to Lord Melbourne, after her wedding night, 1840

WELLINGTON AND KING GEORGE IV

The King, on account of the feeble state of his health, remained seated; – the company marched past him in a line; each made his bow, was addressed or not, and then either placed himself in the row on the other side of the room, or quitted it. All those who had received any appointment kneeled down before the king and kissed his hand, at which the American Minister, near whom I had accidentally placed myself, made a rather satirical face. The clergymen and lawyers in their black gowns and white, powdered wigs, short and long, had a most whimsical masquerading appearance. One of them was the object of an almost universal ill-suppressed laugh. This personage had kneeled to be 'knighted', as the English call it, and in this posture, with the long fleece on his head, looked exactly like a sheep at the slaughter-block. His Majesty signed to the great Field Marshal to give him his sword. For the first time, perhaps, the great warrior could not draw the sword from the scabbard; he pulled and pulled – all in vain. The King waiting with outstretched arm; the Duke vainly pulling with all his might; the unhappy Martyr prostrate in silent resignation, as if expecting his end, and the whole brilliant Court standing around in anxious expectation: – it was a group worthy of Gillray's pencil. At length the state weapon started like a flash of lightning from its sheath. His Majesty grasped it impatiently, – indeed his arm was probably weary and benumbed with being so long extended – so that the sword, instead of alighting on a new knight, fell on an old wig, which for a moment enveloped King and subject in a cloud of powder.

PRINCE HERMANN PÜCKLER-MUSKAU, 1826

WESTMINSTER HALL

Not half big enough – too large for a room, too small for a hall!

KING WILLIAM II, 1097

It was the great hall of William Rufus, the hall which had resounded with acclamations of thirty kings, the hall which had witnessed the just sentence of Bacon and the just absolution of Somers, the hall where the eloquence of Strafford had for a moment awed and melted a victorious party inflamed with just resentment, the hall where Charles had confronted the High Court of Justice with the placid courage which has half redeemed his fame.

LORD MACAULAY. *Essays*, 1843

WHISKY

She drinks her claret strengthened, I should have thought spoiled, with whisky.

W. E. GLADSTONE, to Mrs Gladstone, on Queen Victoria

WILLIAM I

He was of noble height, very, very fat, and with forehead devoid of all hair.

WILLIAM OF MALMESBURY. *Gesta Regum*, 12th century

He was very harsh and violent, so that none dared oppose him. He enchained earls themselves for contrary behaviour. He drove bishops from their sees, abbots from their houses, and imprisoned thanes, and finally did not spare Odo, his own brother, in Normandy a bishop and in England an earl, standing next to the King himself. The King locked him in prison cells, but amongst all else the excellent security he enforced here is to be remembered, so that any honest wight could traverse the kingdom unharmed with his bosom full of gold; and no one dared practise violence on another, however much wrong he had received. And any rapist was castrated at once.

He ruled England and by his shrewdness it was so thoroughly examined that he knew every hide, each owner, its value; he had all there in the records. Wales he had, and he built castles there; likewise he overcame Scotland, through his personal authority. Normandy was his by inheritance, he was lord of Maine, and with two more years of life he would have subdued Ireland by prudence, not arms. Without any doubt people suffered much oppression, many wrongs.

Anglo-Saxon Chronicle

WILLIAM II

Never was a king so well loved,
Nor honoured by his people . . .
He reigned a long while,
And pacified the realm well,
And kept such justice and right
That none through wrong lost a mite.

GAIMAR. *L'Estoire des Englais*, c. 1139

WILLIAM III

He had a thin and weak body, was brown-haired, and of a clear and delicate constitution. He had a Roman eagle nose, bright and sparkling eyes, a large front, and a countenance composed to gravity and authority. All his senses were critical and exquisite. He was always asthmatical; and the dregs of the small-pox falling on his lungs, he had a constant deep cough. His behaviour was solemn and serious, seldom cheerful, and but with a few. He spoke little, and very slowly, and most commonly with a disgusting dryness, which was his character at all times except in a day of battle; for then he was all fire, though without passion: he was then every-where, and looked to everything. . . .

He was an exact observer of men and things. His strength lay rather in a true discerning and a sound judgement than in imagination or invention. His designs were always great and good; but it was thought he trusted too much to that, and that he did not descend enough to the humours of his people to make himself and his notions more acceptable to them. This, in a government that has so much freedom in it as ours, was more necessary than he was inclined to believe. His reservedness grew on him; so that it disgusted most of those who served him: but he had observed the errors of too much talking, more than those of too cold a silence.

He did not like contradiction, nor to have his actions censured; but he loved to employ and favour those who had the arts of complaisance; yet he did not love flatterers. His genius lay chiefly in war, in which his courage was more admired than his conduct. Great errors were often committed by him; but his heroical courage set things right, as it inflamed those who were about him. He was too lavish of money on some occasions, both in his buildings and to his favourites; but too sparing in rewarding services, or in encouraging those who brought intelligence. He was apt to take ill impressions of people, and these stuck long with him; but he never carried them to indecent revenges. He gave too much way to his own humour, almost in everything, not excepting that which related to his own health. . . .   BISHOP GILBERT BURNET, 1724

Neglected in his education, and perhaps destitute by nature of an elegance of mind, he had no taste for literature, none for the sciences, none for the beautiful arts. He paid no attention to music, he understood no poetry; he disregarded learning; he encouraged no men of letters, no painters, no artists of any kind. In fortification and the mathematics he had a considerable degree of knowledge. Though unsuccessful in the field, he understood military operations by land; but he neither possessed nor pretended to any skill in maritime affairs.   TOBIAS SMOLLETT, 1757

WILLIAM IV

On the throne, as in private life, William IV appears to have been a good-hearted man with frank impulses and kindly feelings; willing to do right but not infrequently doing wrong from want of knowledge and strength of mind. He had little information and strong prejudices. Though sufficiently conceited and self-willed, he was easily imposed upon and led by the designing. . . .

His late Majesty, though at times a jovial and, for a king, an honest man, was a weak, ignorant, commonplace sort of person. . . .

Notwithstanding his feebleness of purpose and littleness of mind, his ignorances and his prejudices, William IV was to the last a popular sovereign, but his very popularity was acquired at the price of something like public contempt.

Obituary. *The Times*, 1837

WISHFUL THINKING

Tell your Master if he will help me, I shall be Queen of England in three months, and Mass shall be said all over the kingdom.

MARY, QUEEN OF SCOTS, imprisoned in England, 1568, to Don Gerald de Spes, Spanish Ambassador in London

WOMEN

He was accustomed . . . to more luxuries and pleasures than any prince of his times on account of his thinking of nothing but women (far more than is reasonable), hunting and looking after himself. During the hunting season he had numerous tents brought along for the ladies.

PHILIPPE DE COMMYNES, on King Edward IV. *Memoirs*, c. 1494

That wicked woman! She never had such delights in her lovers as she shall have torture in her death.

KING HENRY VIII, on his fifth wife, Queen Catherine Howard, 1542

To promote a woman to bear rule, superiority, dominion, or empire above any realm, nation, or city, is repugnant to Nature, contumely to God, a thing most contrarious to His revealed Will and approved ordinance; and finally, it is the subversion of good order, of all equity and justice. . . .

And first, where that I affirm the empire of a woman to be a thing repugnant to Nature, I mean not only that God, by the order of His Creation, hath spoiled woman of authority and dominion, but also that man hath seen, proved, and pronounced just causes why that it should be. Man, I say, in many other cases blind, doth in this behalf see very clearly. For the causes be so manifest, that they cannot be hid. For who can deny but it is repugneth to nature that the blind shall be appointed to lead and conduct such as do see? That the weak, the sick, and impotent persons shall nourish and keep the whole and strong? And finally, that the foolish, mad, and phrenetic shall govern the discreet and give counsel to such as be sober of mind? And such be all women compared unto man in bearing of authority. For their sight in civil regimen is but blindness, their strength weakness, their counsel foolishness, and judgement frenzy, if it be rightly considered.

I except such as God, by singular privilege, and for certain causes, known only to Himself, hath exempted from the common rank of women, and do speak of women as nature and experience do this day declare them. Nature, I say, doth paint them further to be weak, frail, impatient, feeble, and foolish; and experience hath declared them to be unconstant, variable, cruel, and lacking the spirit of counsel and regimen. And these notable faults have men in all ages espied in that kind, for the which not only they have removed women from rule and authority, but also some have thought that men subject to the counsel or empire of their wives were unworthy of all public office. . . .

JOHN KNOX. From The First Blast of the Trumpet
against the Monstrous Regiment of Women, 1558

John Knox did not lack examples to support, or weaken, his case. His contemporaries included several queens and regents, and some notable and formidable female personalities, including Mary of Guise, Margaret of Savoy, Catherine di Medici, Marie di Medici, Louise of Savoy, Margaret of Austria, Mary and Elizabeth Tudor, Mary Stuart, Margaret of Navarre, Isabella of Castille, Juana of Spain, Mary of Hungary, Margaret of Parma, Bess of Hardwick, Countess of Shrewsbury, Vitoria Colona.

Restless he rolls from whore to whore,
A merry monarch, scandalous and poor.
Nor are his high desires above his strength;
His sceptre and his—are of a length.

> JOHN WILMOT, EARL OF ROCHESTER,
> on 'Old Rowley', King Charles II.
> *Complete Poems*, 1731–2

Women as poxed as whores were the reason I am in disgrace.

> PRINCE WILLIAM, later King William IV, to
> the Prince of Wales, later King George IV, 1785

A very nice attention to the rigidities of moral observance can hardly be asked from one who, to the vigour of youth and an eminently handsome person, writes a complete command of fortune, and whose will every man who surrounds him is more anxious to flatter than to regulate. The king at a very early period of his life gave evidence of his fondness for female society; a failing of all others the most excusable, but it not infrequently brings down on its possessor a degree of censure that the colder and darker vices of a disposition inherently evil do not provoke.

> Obituary on King George IV. The *Spectator*, 1830

The Queen is most anxious to enlist everyone who can speak or write to join in checking this mad, wicked folly of 'Women's Rights', with all its attendant horrors, on which her poor feeble sex is bent, forgetting every sense of womanly feeling and propriety. Lady — ought to get a good *whipping*. It is a subject which makes the Queen so furious that she cannot contain herself. God created men and women different—then let them remain each in their own position. Tennyson has some beautiful lines on the difference between men and women in 'The Princess'. Woman would become the most hateful, heartless and disgusting of human beings were she allowed to unsex herself, and where would be the protection which man was intended to give the weaker sex? The Queen is sure that Mrs Martin agrees with her.

QUEEN VICTORIA, 1870, to her biographer, Theodore Martin

THE WORKING CLASSES

Now to the working classes (so called). The improvement of their condition can be aimed at practically only in four ways:

1) Education of the children with industrial training.
2) Improvement of their dwellings.
3) Grant of allotments with the cottages.
4) Savings' Banks and Benefit Societies (if POSSIBLE, managed by themselves), particularly on sound economical principles. I shall never cease to promote these four objects wherever and whenever I can, and you need not be afraid of urging the subject with me.

ALBERT, PRINCE CONSORT, 1849, to Colonel Sir Charles Phipps

YACHTING

In the newspapers this morning we saw the account of the Royal yacht, the *Alberta*, with the Queen on board going from Osborne to Portsmouth running down, cutting in two and sinking Mr Heywood's yacht, the *Mistletoe*, in Stokes Bay with a loss of three lives, the Master, the Mate and Miss Annie Peel, the sister of Mrs Heywood. This is the first accident that has ever happened to the Queen in travelling and she is terribly distressed. It is an awkward thing for the sovereign to destroy her own subjects.

FRANCIS KILVERT. *Diary*, 1875

CHRONOLOGY AND SOURCES

CHRONOLOGY OF
POST-CONQUEST REIGNS

Norman Kings

William I   1066

William II   1087

Henry I   1100

Stephen   1135

House of Plantagenet

Henry II   1154

Richard I   1189

John   1199

Henry III   1216

Edward I   1272

Edward II   1307

Edward III   1327

Richard II   1377

House of Lancaster

Henry IV   1399

Henry V   1413

Henry VI   1422

House of York

Edward IV   1461

Edward V   1483

Richard III   1483

House of Tudor

Henry VII   1485

Henry VIII   1509

Edward VI   1547

Mary I   1553

Elizabeth I   1558

House of Stuart

James I   1603

Charles I   1625

The Commonwealth   1649–60

House of Stuart (restored)

Charles II   1660

James II   1685

William III and Mary II   1689

Anne   1702

House of Hanover

George I   1714

George II   1727

George III   1760

George IV 1820
William IV 1830
Victoria 1837

House of Saxe-Coburg

Edward VII 1901

House of Windsor

George V 1910
Edward VIII 1936
George VI 1936
Elizabeth II 1952

SOURCES AND ACKNOWLEDGEMENTS

The following is a list of those authors, publishers and agents to whom the editor and publishers gratefully acknowledge permission to reproduce copyright material in this book. It also incorporates books that the editor has found useful in preparing this anthology.

ADDISON, Paul: 'Darling Clem' in the *London Review of Books*, Vol. 8 No. 7. Reprinted by permission of the *London Review of Books*.

ARBUTHNOT, Harriet: *Journals of Mrs Arbuthnot, 1820–1832*, London, 1950.

ASHE, Geoffrey: *Kings and Queens of England*, London, 1982. Reprinted by permission of Methuen London Ltd.

ASHLEY, Maurice: *The Life and Times of King John*, London, 1972.

AUDEN, W. H.: *A Certain World*, London, 1971. Reprinted by permission of Faber & Faber Ltd and Random House, Inc., New York.

ATKINS, Harold, and NEWMAN, Archie (eds.): *Beecham Stories*, New York, 1979. Reprinted by permission of St Martin's Press, New York and Robson Books Ltd.

BAKER, G. P.: *The Fighting Kings of Wessex*, London, 1931. Reprinted by permission of Unwin Hyman Ltd.

BEERBOHM, Max: *Max in Verse*, London, 1923. Reprinted by permission of William Heinemann Ltd and the Stephen Greene Press.

BELL, G. K. A.: *Randall Davidson*, Oxford, 1938. Reprinted by permission of Oxford University Press.

BARLOW, Frank: *Edward the Confessor*, London, 1970. Reprinted by permission of Eyre Methuen Ltd.
William Rufus, London, 1983. Reprinted by permission of Methuen London Ltd.

Thomas Becket, London, 1986. Reprinted by permission of Weidenfeld & Nicolson Ltd.

BEHRMAN, S. N.: *Conversations with Max*, London, 1960. Reprinted by permission of A. M. Heath & Co. Ltd.

BELLOC, Hilaire: *The Eye Witness*, London, 1924. Reprinted by permission of J. M. Dent & Sons and A. D. Peters & Co. Ltd.

BEVAN, Bryan: *James, Duke of Monmouth*, London, 1973. Reprinted by permission of A. M. Heath & Co. Ltd.

BINGHAM, Caroline: *The Poems of Mary, Queen of Scots*, London, 1976.

BLAIR, Peter Hunter: *The World of Bede*, London, 1970.

BLAKEMORE, Kenneth: *Snuff Boxes*, London, 1977.

BLUNT, Wilfrid: *Slow on the Feather*, Salisbury, 1986. Reprinted by permission of the author and Michael Russell (Publishers).

BORG, Alan: 'Robert Curthose' in *British History*, Vol. 5, 1978.

BOUMAN, P. J.: *Revolution of the Lonely*, London, 1954. Reprinted by permission of McGraw Hill, Inc., New York.

BROOKE, Christopher: *The Saxon & Norman Kings*, London, 1963.

BROOKE, John: *King George III*, London, 1972. Reprinted by permission of Constable & Co. Ltd.

BROOK-SHEPHERD, Gordon: *Uncle of Europe*, London, 1972. Reprinted by permission of William Collins Ltd.

BRUCE, Marie Louise: *Anne Boleyn*, London, 1972. Reprinted by permission of William Collins Ltd.

BRYANT, Sir Arthur: *The Age of Elegance*, London, 1950. Reprinted by permission of William Collins Ltd.

BYRNE, Muriel St Clare: *Great Tudors*, London, 1925.
The Lisle Letters (ed.), London, 1983.

CARRINGTON, C. E., and JACKSON, J. Hampden: *History of England*, Cambridge, 1932. Reprinted by permission of Cambridge University Press.

CASSADY, Richard F.: *The Norman Achievement*, London, 1986. Reprinted by permission of Sidgwick & Jackson Ltd.

CAUSLEY, Christopher: *Collected Poems*, London, 1975. Reprinted by permission of Macmillan Ltd and David Higham Associates Ltd.

CECIL, Algernon: *Queen Victoria and her Prime Ministers*,
London, 1953.

CERF, Bennett: *Good for a Laugh*, New York, 1956.

CHAMBERLAIN, Russell: *The Idea of England*, London, 1986.
Reprinted by permission of Thames & Hudson Ltd.

CHAPMAN, Hester: *The Last Tudor King*, London, 1961.
Lady Jane Grey, London, 1962.

CHARLES, Prince of Wales: Foreword to *King George III*, by John
Brooke. Reprinted by permission of His Majesty The Prince of
Wales and Constable & Co. Ltd.
'Legend and Reality' in *Books and Bookmen*. Reprinted by
Permission of His Royal Highness The Prince of Wales
and *Books Magazine*.

CHURCHILL, Winston S.: *A History of the English-Speaking
Peoples*, Vol. I, London, 1956. Reprinted by permission of
Cassell Ltd.

CLANCY, Joseph P.: *Medieval Welsh Lyrics*, London, 1965.
'Lament for Llewyn ap Gruffudd' in *The Earliest Welsh Poetry*
(ed. Joseph P. Clancy), 1970. Both reprinted by permission of the
translator.

CLEAR, Celia: *Royal Children*, London, 1965.

CLIFF, Anne: 'All the Dandy O . . .' in *Windmill Magazine*,
Vol. I, 1946.

CLIFTON, Robin: *The Last Popular Rebellion*, London, 1984.
Reprinted by permission of the Gower Publishing Group Ltd.

CLYNES, J. R.: *Memoirs, 1924–1937*, London, 1937.

COLLIER, Richard: *The Rainbow People*, London, 1984. Reprinted
by permission of Curtis Brown.

COPE, Christopher: *Phoenix Frustrated: The Lost Kingdom of
Burgundy*, London, 1986.

CREEVY, Thomas: *Papers* (ed. Herbert Maxwell), London, 1903.

CULLEN, Tom: *The Empress Brown*, London, 1950. Reprinted by
permission of the author.

CURTIS BROWN, Marie (ed.): *The Letters of Queen Anne*,
London, 1968.

DALTON, Hugh: *Call Back Yesterday*, London, 1953. Reprinted by permission of Century Hutchinson Ltd and David Higham Associates Ltd.

DAVIS, I. N.: *The Harlot and the Statesman*, London, 1987.

DE-LA-NOY, Michael: *Denton Welch*, London, 1984.
The Honours System, London, 1985. Reprinted by permission of the author and W. H. Allen Ltd.

DICKENS, Charles: *Sketches by Boz*, London, 1836.
A Child's History of England, London, 1853.

DOUGLAS. David G.: *The Norman Fate*, London, 1976.
William the Conqueror, London, 1977. Both reprinted by permission of Eyre Methuen Ltd.

DUBY, Georges: *William Marshall*, London, 1986. Reprinted by permission of Faber & Faber Ltd.

DUFF, David: *The Shy Princess*, London, 1958.
The Hessian Conspiracy, London, 1967. Both reprinted by permission of the author.

DUTTON, Ralph: *English Court Life*, London, 1963.

ESHER, 2nd Viscount: *Journals and Letters* (4 vols.),
London, 1934–8.

EVANS, H.: *Wales and the War of the Roses*, London, 1963.

FADIMAN, Clifton (ed.): *The Faber Book of Anecdotes*. Reprinted by permission of Faber & Faber Ltd and Little, Brown & Co., Boston.

FAIRLIE, Henry H.: 'On the Monarchy' in *Encounter*, 1961.

FINUCANE, R. C.: *Appearances of the Dead*, New York, 1982.

FISHER, Graham and Heather: *The Crown and the Ring*, London, 1972. Reprinted by permission of Robert Hale.

FRASER, Antonia: *King James I*, London, 1974. Reprinted by permission of Weidenfeld & Nicolson Ltd.

FREEMAN-MITFORD, Algernon Bertram (later first Baron Redesdale): *Tales of Old Japan*, London, 1871.
Memories, London, 1915.

FULFORD, Roger: *Dearest Child*, London, 1964. Reprinted by permission of Unwin Hyman Ltd.
Dearest Mama, London, 1968.
Your Dear Letter, London, 1971.

FULLER, Edmund: *2,500 Anecdotes for all Occasions*, New York, 1943.

FURNEAUX, Roger: *Conquest*, London, 1966.

GATES, Francis W.: *Anecdotes of Great Musicians*, Philadelphia, 1898.

GEORGE, M. Dorothy: *English Political Caricature*, Oxford, 1959.

GIVEN-WILSON, Chris, and CURTEIS, Alice: *The Royal Bastards of Medieval England*, London, 1984.

GRANSDEN, Antonia: *Historical Writing in England I c. 550–1307*, London, 1974.
Historical Writing in England II c. 1307 to the Early Sixteenth Century, London, 1982.

GRAVES, Robert, and HODGE, Alan: *The Long Weekend*, London, 1950. Reprinted by permission of A. P. Watt Ltd on behalf of the Executors of the Estate of Robert Graves and Jane Aiken Hodge.

GREENE, David: *Queen Anne*, London, 1970.

GREVILLE, Charles: *Diary*, London, 1927.

GROOS, G. W. (ed.): *The Diary of Baron Waldstein: 1656*, London, 1981.

GUEDALLA, Philip: 'Long Live the King' in the *Spectator*, 1936. Reprinted by permission of the *Spectator*.
The Hundred Years, London, 1936. Reprinted by permission of David Higham Associates Ltd.

GUINNESS, Jonathan and Catherine: *The House of Mitford*, London, 1984.

GUY, John: 'The Tudor Age' in Morgan, K. O. (ed.), *The Oxford Illustrated History of Britain*, 1984. Reprinted by permission of Oxford University Press.

HACKETT, Francis: *Henry VIII*, London, 1929. Reprinted by permission of Jonathan Cape Ltd and Liveright Publishing Company, New York.

HARVEY, John: *The Plantagenets*, London, 1948.

HASKINS, Charles Homer: *The Normans in European History*, London, 1916.

HATTON, Ragnhild: *George I*, London, 1978.

HAYNES, *The White Bear: The Elizabethan Earl of Leicester*, London, 1987.

HEARSEY, John E. N.: *London and the Great Fire*, London, 1965.

HENDRICKSON, Robert: *The Literary Life and Other Curiosities*, New York, 1981.

HIBBERT, Christopher: *The Court at Windsor*, London, 1964. Reprinted by permission of Penguin Books Ltd. *George IV*, London, 1976.

HINDE, Thomas: *Forests of Britain*, London, 1985. *Hinde's Courtiers*, London, 1986. Both reprinted by permission of the author and Victor Gollancz Ltd.

HOLDEN, Anthony: *Charles, Prince of Wales*, London, 1979. Reprinted by permission of Weidenfeld & Nicolson Ltd and A. P. Watt Ltd.

HOLMES, Richard: *The Little Field-Marshal*, London, 1981.

HOLORENSHAW, Henry: *The Levellers and the English Revolution*, London, 1939.

HOWARD, Michael S.: *Jonathan Cape*, London, 1971. Reprinted by permission of Jonathan Cape Ltd and Sheila Hooper.

HUGO, Victor: *L'homme qui rit*, Paris, 1869.

HUMBLE, Richard: *The Saxon Kings*, London, 1980.

HUME, David: *History of England*, London, 1754–62.

HUTCHISON, Harold F.: *The Hollow Crown*, London, 1961. *Henry V*, London, 1964. Both reprinted by permission of Eyre & Spottiswoode Ltd.

JAGOW, Kurt (ed.): *Letters of the Prince Consort* (trs. E. T. S. Dugdale). Reprinted by permission of John Murray Ltd.

JAMES, Robert Rhodes: *Albert, Prince Consort*, London, 1983. Reprinted by permission of Anthony Sheil Associates Ltd.

JENKINS, Elizabeth: *Elizabeth and Leicester*, London, 1961. Reprinted by permission of the author and Victor Gollancz Ltd.

JESSE, J. H.: *Memories of the Court of England during the reign of the Stuarts*, London, 1901.

JESSE, William: *The Life of Beau Brummell*, London, 1884.

JOLLIFFE, John (ed.): *Froissart's Chronicles*, London, 1967.

JONES, Gwyn (ed.): *The Oxford Book of Welsh Verse in English*, Oxford, 1977. Reprinted by permission of Oxford University Press.

KIGHTLY, Charles: *Folk Heroes of Great Britain*, London, 1982. Reprinted by permission of Thames & Hudson Ltd.

KILVERT, Francis: *Diary* (ed. William Plomer), London, 1976. Reprinted by permission of Jonathan Cape Ltd and Sheila Hooper.

KING-HALL, Magdalen: *The Story of the Nursery*, London, 1958.

KIPLING, Rudyard: 'James I' in *The Definitive Edition of Rudyard Kipling's Verse*, London, 1966. Reprinted by permission of A. P. Watt Ltd.

LABARGE, Margaret Wade: *Medieval Travellers*, London, 1982. Reprinted by permission of Hamish Hamilton Ltd.

LACEY, Robert: *Majesty*, London, 1977. Reprinted by permission of Century Hutchinson Ltd and Harcourt Brace Jovanovich, New York.

LASKI, Harold J.: *Parliamentary Government in England*, London, 1938.

LITTLE, Bryan: *The Monmouth Episode*, London, 1956.

LLOYD, Alan: *The Year of the Conqueror*, London, 1966.

LONGFORD, Elizabeth: *Victoria RI*, London, 1964.
The Royal House of Windsor, London, 1974.

LUCAIRE, E.: *Celebrity Trivia*, New York, 1956.

LUCAS, Angela M.: *Women in the Middle Ages*, London, 1983.

LUCY, Sir Henry: *The Diary of a Journalist*, London, 1924.

MACAULAY, Thomas Babington: *History of England*, London, 1848.

McCLURE, N. E. (ed.): *The Letters and Epigrams of Sir John Harington*, London, 1930.

MANCHESTER, William: *The Last Lion*, London, 1983. Reprinted by permission of Little, Brown and Co., Boston.

MANSEL, Philip: *Pillars of Monarchy*, London, 1984.

MARIE LOUISE, Princess: *My Memories of Six Reigns*, London, 1956. Reprinted by permission of Evans Brothers Ltd.

MASEFIELD, John: *Collected Poems*, London, 1941.
Letters to Reyna (ed. William Buchan), London, 1983. Both reprinted by permission of Buchan & Enright Ltd and the Society of Authors as the Literary Representatives of the Estate of John Masefield.

MEIER, Olga (ed.): *The Daughters of Karl Marx*, London, 1982.

MELVILLE, Lewis: *Beau Brummell*, London, 1924.

MILLER, John: *The Life and Times of William and Mary*, London, 1974.

MITFORD, Nancy: *Madame de Pompadour*, London, 1953.
The Sun King, London, 1966.

MOORE, Charles and HAWTREE, Christopher: *1936*, London, 1986.

NEWBY, Eric: *A Book of Travellers' Tales*, London, 1985.

NICOLAS, N. Harris: *Memoires and Literary Remains of Lady Jane Grey*, London, no date.

NICOLSON, Harold: *King George V*, London, 1952.

NOWELL-SMITH, Simon (ed.): *Edwardian England 1901–1914*, Oxford, 1964. Reprinted by permission of Oxford University Press.

NUSSEY, Helen: *London Gardens of the Past*, London, 1939. Reprinted by permission of the author and The Bodley Head.

PACKE, Michael: *King Edward III*, London, 1983.

PAIN, Nesta: *George III at Home*, London, 1975.

PAKULA, Hannah: *The Last Romantic*, London, 1985.

PALMER, Tony: *Charles II*, London, 1979. Reprinted by permission of Macmillan Publishing Co., New York.

PALMERSTON, Lady: *Letters*, London, 1957.

PERNOUD, Regine: *Eleanor of Aquitaine*, London, 1967.

PETRIE, Sir Charles (ed.): *The Letters of King Charles II*, London, 1968.

PLAT, Sir Hugh: *Delights for Ladies*, London, 1948.

PLUMB, J. H.: *Men and Places*, London, 1963. Reprinted by permission of the author and Curtis Brown Ltd.

PLUMB, J. H. and WELDON, Huw: *Royal Heritage*, London, 1977. Reprinted by permission of BBC Enterprises Ltd.

PONSONBY, Sir Frederick: *Recollections of Three Reigns*, London, 1951. Reprinted by permission of Eyre Methuen Ltd.

POPE-HENNESSEY, James: *Queen Mary*, London, 1959.

PORTLAND, Duke of: *Men, Women and Things*, London, 1937. Reprinted by permission of the Estate of the Sixth Duke of Portland.

POTTER, Jeremy: *Good King Richard?*, London, 1983. *Pretenders*, London, 1986. Both reprinted by permission of Constable & Co. Ltd.

PRICE, R. G.: *A History of Punch*, London, 1957.

PRIESTLEY, J. B.: *The Prince of Pleasure*, London, 1969.

PRITCHETT, V. S.: *London Perceived*, London, 1962.

REES, David: *The Son of Prophecy*, London, 1985.

REEVES, Marjorie: *The Elizabethan Court*, London, 1956. Reprinted by permission of the Longman Group Ltd.

ROBBINS, Rossell Hope (ed.): *The Encyclopaedia of Witchcraft and Demonology*, London, 1959.

ROBERTSON, William: *History of Scotland*, London, 1759.

ROCHE, T. W. E.: *A Pineapple for a King*, London, 1971.

ROOSEVELT, Eleanor: *On My Own*, New York, 1959. Reprinted by permission of Laurence Pollinger Ltd., Hutchinson Ltd, Harper & Row, New York and the Estate of Eleanor Roosevelt.

ROSE, Kenneth: *King George V*, London, 1983. Reprinted by permission of Weidenfeld & Nicolson Ltd.

ROSS, Charles: *Richard III*, London, 1981.

ROWSE, A. L.: *The England of Elizabeth*, London, 1953. *Bosworth Field*, London, 1966. *Eminent Elizabethans*, London, 1983. *Reflections on the Puritan Revolution*, London, 1986.

SAINT-SIMON, Duc de: *Memoirs*, Paris, 1829 edition.

SASSOON, Siegfried: *Collected Poems*, London 1947. Reprinted by permission of George Sassoon as Executor of the Estate of Siegfried Sassoon.

SAUNDERS, Edith: *A Distant Summer*, London, 1946. Reprinted by permission of Macdonald & Co. Ltd.

SCOTT, Lord George: *Lucy Walters, Wife or Mistress*,
London, 1947.

SENIOR, Michael: *The Life and Times of Richard III*, London, 1981.

SERPELL, James: *In the Company of Animals*, London, 1986.
Reprinted by permission of Basil Backwell Ltd.

SITWELL, Edith: *Green Song*, London, 1944.
The Queen and the Hive, London, 1963. Reprinted by
permission of Macmillan Ltd and David Higham Associates Ltd.

SITWELL, Sacheverell: *Gothic Europe*, London, 1969. Reprinted by
permission of Weidenfeld & Nicolson Ltd.

SLOCOMBE, George: *William the Conquerer*, London, 1959.
Sons of the Conquerers, London, 1960.

SMALLEY, Beryl: *Historians of the Middle Ages*, London, 1974.

SMOLLETT, Tobias: *History of England*, London, 1757.

SPENCE, Joseph: *Anecdotes, Observations and Characters of Books
and Men,* London, 1820.

STAFFORD, Pauline: *Queens, Concubines and Dowagers*,
London, 1983.

STONE, Brian (ed.):*Medieval English Verse*, London, 1964.

STRACHEY, Lytton: *Elizabeth and Essex*, London, 1928.

STRICKLAND, Agnes: *Lives of the Queens of England*,
London, 1840.

STRONG, Sir Roy: *Henry, Prince of Wales*, London, 1986. Reprinted
by permission of Thames & Hudson Ltd.

SULLIVAN, Herbert and FLOWER, Newman: *Sir Arthur Sullivan*,
London, 1927. Repringed by permission of Macmillan
Publishing Co., New York.

THACKERAY, W. M.: *The History of Henry Esmond*, London, 1852.
The Four Georges, London, 1857.
Book of Snobs London, 1885.

THORNE, A. G. (ed.): *The History of Parliament*, Vol. I,
London, 1986.

TISDALL, E. E. P.: *Queen Victoria's John Brown*, London, 1938.

TOYNBEE, Arnold: *Acquaintances*, Oxford, 1986. Reprinted by
permission of Oxford University Press.

TURNER, James (ed.): *Love Letters*, London, 1970.

UBBELOHDE, A. R.: 'Science' in Simon Nowell-Smith (ed.), *Edwardian England 1901–1914*, Oxford, 1964. Reprinted by permission of the Oxford University Press.

VANSITTART, Peter: *Green Knights, Black Angels*, London, 1969. Reprinted by permission of the author.

VAUGHAN-THOMAS, W.: *The Prince of Wales*, London, 1982. Reprinted by permission David Higham Associates and Kaye & Ward Ltd.

QUEEN VICTORIA: *Leaves from the Journal of Our Life in the Highlands*, London, 1868.

WARWICK, Christopher: *Two Centuries of Royal Weddings*, London, 1980. Reprinted by permission of Arthur Barker and Weidenfeld & Nicolson Ltd.

WATSON, D. R.: *The Life and Times of Charles I*, London, 1972.

WEINTRAUB, Stanley: *Victoria*, London, 1987. Reprinted by permission of Unwin Hyman Ltd.

WELCH, Denton: *Journals* (ed. Jocelyn Brooke), London, 1952.

WHEELER BENNETT, Sir John: *King George VI: His Life and Reign*, London, 1958. Reprinted by permission of the Trustees of the Estate of Sir John Wheeler Bennett.

WILLIAMS, Charles: *Taliessen Through Logres*, Oxford, 1939. Reprinted by permission of David Higham Associates and the Oxford University Press.

WILSON, John Dover: *Life in Shakespeare's England*, Cambridge, 1911.

WILSON, Peter: *The Man They Couldn't Gag*, London, 1977.

WINDSOR, Duke of: 'Duke' in the *New York Daily News* 1966. *A King's Story*, London, 1951. Reproduced by permission of Cassell Ltd.

WOODRUFF, Douglas: *The Life and Times of Alfred the Great*, London, 1974.

ZIEGLER, Philip: *King William IV*, London, 1971.

INDEX

Entries in capitals refer to authors or sources; the remainder refer to mentions in the text.